Finding Your
Financial
★★★★★★★★★★★★
Freedom

JOYCE WARD

EVERY WOMAN'S
GUIDE TO SUCCESS

Dearborn
Financial Publishing, Inc.®

This publication is designed to provide accurate and authoritative information in regard to the subject matter covered. It is sold with the understanding that the publisher is not engaged in rendering legal, accounting, or other professional service. If legal advice or other expert assistance is required, the services of a competent professional person should be sought.

Executive Editor: Cynthia A. Zigmund
Managing Editor: Jack Kiburz
Interior Design: Lucy Jenkins
Cover Design: S. Laird Jenkins Corp.
Typesetting: Elizabeth Pitts

©1997 by Joyce Ward

Published by Dearborn Financial Publishing, Inc.®

Printed in the United States of America

97 98 99 10 9 8 7 6 5 4 3 2 1

Library of Congress Cataloging-in-Publication Data

Ward, Joyce, 1932–
    Finding your financial freedom : every woman's guide to success / by Joyce Ward.
        p.   cm.
    Includes index.
    ISBN 0-7931-2346-1 (pbk.)
    1. Women—Finance, Personal.   I. Title.
HG179.W318   1997   96-46564
332.024′042—dc20   CIP

Dearborn books are available at special quantity discounts to use as premiums and sales promotions, or for use in corporate training programs. For more information, please call the Special Sales Manager at 800-621-9621, ext. 4384, or write to Dearborn Financial Publishing, Inc., 155 N. Wacker Drive, Chicago, IL 60606-1719.

Dedication

For Jill, Bob, Beth, and Doug

Contents

Part Four   Savoring the Savvy

Part Five   Playing Catch-Up

*P*reface

7o my readers: Sometimes even the most daunting goals can be reached by a few simple steps. Achieving financial freedom is an example.

The numbers are boggling: During her lifetime, the average American woman has a 70 percent chance of becoming solely responsible for her own financial well-being, and an 80 percent chance of being responsible for another's financial well-being. In fact, female-headed households are up 125 percent since 1960.

Yet, ask us to make a financial decision and a four-letter word pops into our minds: *fear.* Ask us to pick up a book on money and our eyes glaze over. Why is that? It's because we've heard the fast-lane explanations and the mind-numbing buzzwords often enough to know we're in over our heads. So, we seek expert help.

Is reliance on experts the answer to our needs? Emphatically, no. Instead of gaining control over our financial lives, we give it away. And all because we grew up and grew older believing that our partners would take care of things or our advisers would take care of things, and that financial expertise required mathematical wizardry beyond our reach.

Despite these beliefs, in the 20 years I've worked with people making financial decisions, I have seen how smart women really are. Yet, the "everyday" puts obstacles in our paths. The common-place of our lives is not simple, understood, or under control. And the resulting confusion makes us doubt ourselves and undermines our growth.

This book seeks to erase that confusion. Together, we can take what you already know and use at-home tools and your own un-tapped abilities to transform what seems like commonplace infor-mation into a "power base."

Although this power base can influence everything from house-hold bills to Wall Street investments, no high-flown treatises on products, marketplaces, or economic theories will be thrown at you in this book. Think down-to-earth. We start at the beginning and take one step to the next. So whether you are lost in a maze of statements, confronted with shouldering sizable assets for the first time, or just awakening to the challenge of saving for your future, you are in the right place.

A serious subject does not require a somber tone. This book will help you without intimidation. Keep it next to your dictionary. Over the years, it will reinforce your confidence and control as it guides you to the fulfillment of your financial dreams. And therein lies financial freedom.

*A*cknowledgments

*M*y thanks go first to the many wonderful clients, both women and men, who, over the years, have taught me to see the similarities in their financial roadblocks by sharing with me their dissimilar experiences and solutions. They need not fear for their privacy. I have avoided using any specific situation or individual in my examples.

Thanks go to Lois McConnell for triggering the format of the book. Before preparing a talk for a group of women leaders, I asked her what they wanted to know. She told me their unanimous answer was, "Give us the confidence to do it ourselves." I hope this book fulfills that request for every woman.

It took many people to bring this book into existence. Friends, writers, and other professionals were kind enough to take time out of their busy lives to read various drafts of the manuscript and comment on it. Without their remarks and encouragement, I would not have been able to complete it. My sincerest thanks go to Valerie J. Dean, Dick Davidson, Jerry Krueger, Jeanette Simonini, MarJean Standish, Natalie Tenney, and Olga Streb and her friend Mary. Thanks, too, for the generous support and input from writers Pat Gibson, Robert Irvine, Vella Munn, Mary Lou Rich, Talley Thompson, Darlene Turner, Patricia White, and, from the Santa Barbara Writers' Conference, Sid Stebel.

I also want to thank my agents, Elizabeth and Jim Trupin, for believing in the book's importance and finding it a home. Thanks also go to my editor, Christine Litavsky, for her enthusiasm and attention to detail in making it a better book, and to editor Sue Telingator for having a sharp eye for structure.

I owe a very special thank you to writer Robert Campbell, for his faith in my abilities, his guidance, and his unwavering moral support throughout the years. And last, thanks go to my family for their unrestricted encouragement: my parents Gene and Lee Lynch, my dear husband Doug for taking over the household chores so I could closet myself with my computer, and our children and their spouses for their faith in my success. Thank you Jill and Scott, Bob and Jenilee, and Beth and Casey.

Chapter *1*

*W*hat You Don't Know *Can* Hurt You

*N*ot long ago, I listened to my mother on the phone with some-one from the bank. It was a call about a certificate of deposit that had matured. (A certificate of deposit, or CD, is an interest-earning time deposit.) "Yes," my mother said, nodding at the wall, "I guess it should be renewed, but . . . "

She chewed on her lip, her eyes rolling to the ceiling as she lis-tened. I could hear the voice chirping at her on the line but couldn't make out the words. I sipped my tea and eavesdropped on her end of the conversation.

"Oh, yes, I'm sure it is, but . . . I just think we'll wait . . . until my husband comes—" Her head bobbed. "Oh, I'm certain, but . . . two years? Yes, uh, we'll have to call back." She clacked the phone down and let go a heavy sigh. "I don't know why they press so," she said dropping onto the couch. "Your father knows whether we want to renew or not. I don't know what to tell them."

"Did you get enough information to discuss it with Dad?" I asked.

"No, dear," she waved me away. "He'll take care of it."

Mother avoids decisions. Why does she do that? Is she afraid to make a mistake? Or is it easier to rely on Dad?

Then there's my friend Hillie. For several weeks, she and I have talked about going to a movie on a Monday night. That's the night my husband watches football and her husband catches up on the bills. So Sunday night she calls me up, and we make our plan. We choose a film, set the time, and Hillie offers to drive. The thing is, I know by now that even though her intentions are the best, she won't show up.

The phone rings and she'll say, "God, I'm so sorry, but Gil's hunting for a lost paper."

"What is it this time?" I ask.

"Mortgage coupons. He thinks he paid twice last month."

"Shall we go later?" I already know the answer.

"Guess not. You know what happened last week. Sorry."

Hillie's husband takes care of their money. That means he's the caretaker of their papers. He has a system of three expandable files: TO BE DONE, BEING DONE, and DONE. I think Hillie is secretly relieved she's not allowed to touch them.

Last time, he was looking for a tax receipt. She had called me at 7 PM. "I have to stick around until he finds it. He gets upset if I leave him like this."

"Will it take long?" I ask.

"Shouldn't," she giggles. "He's hunched over TO BE DONE, fingering his way through."

At 8:00 (the last show starts at 8:30) she calls again, "He's halfway through BEING DONE. He says the damn thing's in there someplace."

He gets testy when Hillie nags. At 8:30 she calls again.

"Any hope?" I ask.

"He's back in TO BE DONE. I'd better cancel."

It's as Old as Time

These are two classic cases of financial phobia. My mother has suffered from it for years. She turns a deaf ear and pretends Dad's smarter. I don't know when Hillie and her husband came down with it. Hillie hides behind humor, and her husband's systems provide a lot of it. I once had a bad case of the phobia myself. The condition is kept out of the news, but between you and me, I think it's epidemic.

In the typical couple, symptoms are masked. Papers and decisions are shuffled back and forth behind closed doors. There's consolation in having someone at your side saying "Sure, that's okay. That's right. Yes." But let divorce or death or illness split up the team and dump the responsibilities onto one person's shoulders, and bang!, symptoms flare up over night. Imagine my mother all alone. She'd be in a panic if she had to give instructions to the bank on that certificate of deposit. Or picture Hillie, frantically rummaging through her husband's files.

Watch For the Signs

Interviews with those stricken with the phobia show a surprisingly common set of symptoms. Women on their own may put up a brave front, but too many widows suffer from sleeplessness haunted by vague worry, confusion, and an indefinable fear that life is out of control. Deep sighing is common. Nail biting and swollen eyes may develop. Many victims experience a shocking inability to make decisions. They may even confess to wishing someone else would make their decisions for them! In the final stages, anxiety sets in, and the patient can actually be seen running for expert help.

Beware the Rescuer

Unfortunately, experts welcome these patients with open arms. By now distraught and crying for reassurance, the sufferer blurts, "Please, tell me what to do." The expert, imbued with an aura of the divine, smiles with just the right touch of warmth, accepts all of the lady's private and personal papers, and purrs, "I'd be happy to." And, without so much as a clap of thunder or flash of lightning, control passes forever into the hands of a stranger. The patient has succumbed.

Are You a Phobia Victim?

Maybe that's not you. But if it is, it's okay to admit to it. In fact if you don't admit it, you can't be cured. And many of us can't. That's part of the phobia, too. Do you suspect that this book will hand you a demeaning experience or that you'll be proved financially inept? Not a chance. Besides, the cure for this phobia is simpler than you think.

Let's take a situation that has nothing to do with money or personal business, but an ordinary one you take for granted, one in which you *are* confident. I'm going to show you how, with only a slight change, I can shake your confidence. Then I'll infect you with phobia symptoms: confusion, doubt, and frustration. You'll *want* to ask for help.

Situation #1: Lost in the Library

Here's the assignment: We're at the public library. You have ten minutes to find two Agatha Christie mysteries. Piece of cake, you say? Good. That's the normal reflex reaction of someone with confidence. But this is *my* library situation.

The library staff is off today, but not to worry. Following the earthquake, the staff reshelved the library's 50,000 volumes in alphabetical order according to title. Of course that means the card catalog and computers are useless. And, sadly, those crucial subsections—such as Mystery, Fiction, Large Print, Nonfiction, and Research—have been disbanded. Every book is now mixed in with all others, shelved in one simplistic, mega-alphabetical arrangement.

Okay, time is ticking. Want to take a moment to visualize your strategy? Perhaps you'll look under *C* for *C*hristie? Maybe *M* for The *M*ystery of . . . ? Or *T* for *T*he Mystery of . . . ? About now you should be chewing a thumbnail, trying to recall a specific title.

Time's up. What a time-waster, huh? No wonder the real-world library uses subcategories and numbers. Alphabetical arrangement alone doesn't cut it.

Situation #2: A Bird in the Hand?

Now, try this one: You're in Pittsburgh, Pennsylvania. You and your husband, "Harry," must drive to Bird-in-Hand. You have a vague idea that the town is near Philadelphia, at the opposite end of the state. How do you find it? (Harry is a sweet guy, but he does not ask directions.)

Maybe you decide to buy a map and take the turnpike. Did I mention that your map doesn't show those handy little mileage indicators—the numbers that tell how far it is between towns?

No problem, you say. Being resourceful as always, you offer to thumb-measure city-to-city distances on the map, and estimate the miles. Will that suffice?

Sorry. Your map has an alphabetical listing of every city and town in the state, but it seems to be missing the correlating codes or grids for locating them. You can't even find Harrisburg, let alone Bird-in-Hand.

Not being one who gives up, you decide to follow road signs.

Sadly, a recent hurricane knocked those signs down. What's left? Without road signs, how does anyone know which exit to take? Or which direction to go at the intersection?

Yes, I set you up for failure. Without a good map or road signs, it's hardly worth starting out. Will Harry stop at a gas station and ask directions?

Maybe we're being too hard on Harry.

Information Retrieval Is Everything

If you were actually stuck with either of those situations, you'd be just a bit frustrated. Maybe a little crazed. Maybe divorced. Your hands were tied. And I should be ashamed of myself. But, I did give you the phobia.

I know you succumbed only because I threw you into impossible situations, but it was to prove my point. There was no missing library book and no lost town. Agatha Christie was right there on the shelf. Bird-in-Hand was bustling away in eastern Pennsylvania. Everything was where it should have been. Yet, you failed to find the books in the library and you failed to find the town.

So, the glitch in each situation—and it caused no small frustration—was your not being able to get at the information you needed to solve the problem. There was *never* anything wrong with you. Your retrieval system was flawed. That's all.

Sounds like old news, doesn't it? But, let me ask: Where do you keep your business and financial information? At home? Most everyone does, but where at home?

My mother used to tell me, "It's filed. Don't worry, I save everything."

So I presented her with two situations, and then asked, "How do you save your papers?"

"How? In alphabetical order!" Suddenly her eyes widened, "But that's different, because I—"

"Maybe," I said. I can't push my mother, she's had too many life experiences. She has to be convinced something's right before she'll try it. You're probably waiting for the same proof. Does this book have anything to offer you that will *work?* Do you even need this information? Let's find out.

A Moment of Truth

Ask yourself these 11 questions, and judge for yourself whether your own retrieval system works.

1. There is an emergency. Where will you find $2,000?
2. Your accountant called. What have you spent so far this year?
3. When are estimated taxes due? Find a copy of your last return.
4. When is your mortgage paid? Are taxes or insurance included?
5. Your husband is seriously ill. What happens to his pension if he dies? Does it end? Is it reduced? If so, by how much?
6. At death, what happens to his Social Security income?
7. What would your total income be if you are widowed? Would it be *enough?*
8. A municipal bond matures. Can you choose a proper replacement?
9. Friends urge you to invest in mutual funds. Should you?
10. Do you have a will? Can it protect you?
11. What should you be doing with your money right now?

Could you answer every question? No? Could you find the answers in five minutes? No? A half hour? Yikes, five days? Were you about to throw your hands up and run for help? If you were alone today and had to deal with matters like these, would you be in control—or in tears?

By answering—or not answering—these questions, you just found out whether you could handle your financial life all by yourself. You didn't need me or any other outsider to make that judgment for you. Now let's get your doubts and fears out in the open so we can disarm them with practical know-how.

You are about to experience a new self-confidence and a wonderful sense of security. Soon, answering those 11 questions will be a breeze. Others just as crucial will take less than a minute to answer. Review them again. We'll find the answers as we go along. And you have a surprise coming, because getting there is much easier than you think.

And relax, because this book is different. I'm not out to prove that I'm the expert. I won't pretend to know what's good or right for you. There is no way I (or any expert) can guess your situation, your emotional makeup, or your attitudes, and then hand you packaged life answers that work. Still, if our time together is to be successful, it's crucial to integrate these ingredients. So we'll team up. Sharing our expertise will put you in the center of the picture where you belong. What will emerge is a unique framework to guide you to financial freedom. We might even have fun along the way. After all, who ruled that *important* had to mean *humorless?*

Five Keys to Financial Power

You may think that you don't know anything, but don't sell yourself short. You have a built-in expertise on your situation, your emotional makeup, and your attitudes, that no one else in the world can match. Contrary to what you may believe, this untapped knowledge that you have is powerful and dynamic.

If what you know seems mundane and ordinary to you, that's because something is missing—some link, a catalyst—that can unleash its potential. That's where I come in.

Here's the deal. I'm going to provide five keys that will transform what you already know into an exciting power base. From that power base you will extract precise and insightful information that will amaze you. Expertise doesn't happen, it's *produced.*

Tapping into a mine of rich information may help you clear the path to expertise, but it's just the first step. We're going beyond that encyclopedic stage by using five keys that will bring your expertise to life. You will understand crucial financial information. And you will be able to count on your keys to guide you simply, accurately, and specifically to confident decisions, smart choices, and delicious peace of mind. Best of all, it is a simple once-and-done process.

You'll know the papers you must have, where to find them, questions you absolutely must ask, whose brains you can pick, how to know whether to take notes or hold your nose, and why a minute's use of these keys will make you a dynamite expert—forever. And if you've ever been intimidated by money advice and money advisers, that's past history. Get ready to be wowed.

Chapter 2

*7*here's Danger in Saving Too Much

Retooling the Brain

John D. Rockefeller once said, "If you take care of the pennies, the dollars will take care of themselves." For many of us, this translates into a string of familiar cautionary maxims—"Waste not, want not," "For want of the nail, the shoe was lost."

Does that mean, in Rockefeller's day, our mothers deduced that, if saving pennies started us on a pathway to wealth, then saving *everything* guaranteed our arrival? Help me out here, I'm groping for a genetic defect to blame for our flawed belief that saving equals security.

Our unquestioned acceptance of this belief reminds me of the story of the man who, for years, trekked the world over, searching for the meaning of life. Finally, on the highest mountaintop, he found the wisest guru. At once, the seeker asked the question that burned within him. "Tell me, oh Great One, what is the meaning of life?"

"Life," the ancient man whispered, stroking his long beard. "Life is like a river."

After taking a moment to ponder this answer, the puzzled traveler asked, "It is?"

Whereupon the guru blinked, "Isn't it?"

Is Saving Always Good?

Here we are saving everything—old clothing, leftover spices, empty flower pots, worn out bras, and all the mail, just in case. I can't speak for the other stuff that fills up closets and drawers and garages, but saving the mail? I know that's trouble.

The save-the-mail habit begins in innocence, couched in good intentions. Why would expensive-looking forms and ads and reminders be sent to us if they weren't important? We know what a postage stamp costs. Maybe that paper will be needed later, for some purpose not discernible at the moment. So we set it aside, move it, add to it, move it, file it, add to it—and the mail keeps coming.

Let me tell you about poor Widow M. The woman was almost carted away. It was a clear case of mail flood hysteria. In desperation, she taped her mailbox shut. The authorities said that was against the law, and her mail was piling up on the curb. They cut the tape. She applied more. The letter carrier knocked at her door. She shut the blinds. He rang the bell. It went on like that until one day, she struggled into my office dragging this stuffed burlap bag. "Please make it stop," she begged. "I'm going down for the last time."

Now, Widow M was a bright lady. Actually that was part of her problem. She knew she had to keep her money safe, so, out of caution, she'd opened savings accounts at three different banks—just in case FDIC reduced the insurance that backed her deposit at a single institution. She had one checking account, a separate account for certificates of deposit, and two brokerage accounts. She wasn't going to put all *her* eggs in one basket.

Of course, she also received an income by mail. It arrived by check: two annuities, Social Security, a pension, interest from a bond, and several dividends from three stocks. Plus, she got the usual stuff, like utility, book club, and Visa bills.

Is it any wonder she was drowning? She received 20-plus statements every 30 days. Multiplied by 12 months in a year, that's 240 papers stuffed away by year's end. In truth, it was closer to 700 or more. First, she didn't realize that 12 statements would arrive for every account she opened. Nor did she expect each statement to be several pages long. Confused, she saved not just the statements, but every enclosure, return envelope, and even the envelopes in which the statements had arrived.

"Why didn't you toss out the papers you didn't need?" I asked.

"But which are those?" she asked, her eyes wide. "I couldn't tell so I kept it all, just in case. But now," she continued with tears in her eyes, "when I need something, I can't find it anywhere! I'm overwhelmed."

She came to me, the "expert" to rescue her. Instead, I showed her how to rescue herself.

Get Ready to Take Control

All over the country, nasty little people with thick glasses and computers are staying up nights thinking of new ways to print reports. Like it or not, you're the target. If your papers and filing system are out of control now, brace yourself. It's going to get worse.

Don't get me wrong. I believe in communication and information and confirmations and applications and solicitations, but please, if we can't have them in digestible doses, at least let us prepare ourselves to dispense with the chaff and organize the wheat. This avalanche is sweeping us away in confusion. Maybe it's a governmental conspiracy for full employment. I mean, look at the line of experts waiting to go to work for us: bankers, investment advisers, accountants, financial planners, insurance agents, lawyers—need I go on?

You are convinced, I hope, that there is absolutely nothing wrong with you. Good. Stand up straight and start your days off with a nod of approval for that woman in the mirror. Now, before we turn our attention to those questions I threw at you early on, you'll need to do a little preparation.

It's Time for Action

I can't go through your finances first-hand and I can't tell you how much money you need to live on. But that story will out in due course. For now, it's first things first.

We're going to go through your files and dump the clutter. Don't bother making excuses. You do have time. It is not a two-week job. It is not overwhelming, nor is it hopeless. You cannot do it *later*. Like ignoring a leaky pipe, the longer you delay, the more damage will be done. You could find your house under water.

So now, we clear the area and lay a foundation. Are you rolling your eyes? Don't wimp out on me. This step is crucial to every other that will follow. Collect all your business papers from the past 12 months. A heap is okay—don't worry about neatness or order. Each paper will emerge in the right spot. But, I have to warn you, you'd better clear the dining room table—and the floor.

Chapter 3

*S*orting through Your Clutter

Procrastination Is a Drag

If you're facing a gargantuan stack of that collected stuff, congratulations! You're on your way. Don't wait for the rest of us. Skip ahead in this chapter to "Now That You're Motivated."

If you're still on the couch, I've dished up a helping of encouragement and prodding for you. Don't go off on a guilt trip because you need a push. Inertia is a tough enemy. It took me almost a full year before a friend's prodding convinced me to exercise. Now I swim three days a week and feel terrific. Think of me as that friend. You're going to feel terrific, too.

It's not easy to tackle a year's accumulation of stuff. I have a relative who pooh-poohed the idea of this book. "Don't think anyone will read it," she said. "Women may be disorganized, but they get along okay. I do." (This from a woman who carries unpaid bills around in her purse.)

But I can't fault her, or you. Who wants to make what seems like a heroic effort if the need doesn't feel urgent and the job sounds impossible? Thinking you can tackle this later, like giving up smoking tomorrow, is active procrastination. (Now that's an oxymoron.) Procrastination can lull us into some sticky spots. But, wow, we can find superhuman strength from the whisper of *motivation.*

Urgency Zaps Us into Action

Once upon a moonless night a man ran through a cemetery. In his rush, he tripped and fell deep into an open grave. Afraid and unable to see in the dark, he leaped up at the walls again and again. He shouted until he was hoarse and clawed at the freshly dug earth until his fingers bled. But the walls were too straight and too high. And no one came. Hopeless and exhausted, he collapsed into a corner and slept.

Later that night, a second man ran through the dark cemetery. And, as luck would have it, he tripped and fell into the same open grave. Frightened, he, too, jumped and clawed at the dirt walls, shouting and screaming at the top of his lungs, "Help! Help me! Please, someone! Anyone! Help!"

The first man, startled awake by the screams, decided to save the stranger from ripping his fingers and losing his voice, as he had himself. Struggling to his feet, he groped his way along the dirt wall and waited for the man to catch his breath. Then, feeling sympathetic, he put his hand on the man's shoulder. "It's no use, friend," he whispered in his raspy voice. "You'll never get out."

But he did.

What would *you* do? You're alone, trapped in an open grave, shivering in the ink-black night. It's dead silent. Suddenly you feel a hand on your shoulder and hear a voice whisper in your ear. Yikes!

That's motivation. The story is from psychologist Dr. Norma Barretta.

Here Comes the Nudge

Are you married? Statistics say women have at least a 60 percent chance of being widowed. Yes, you may be in the lucky 40 percent group, but you have a 50 percent chance of getting divorced. Hah! After all these years? you ask. You are not making this easy.

Okay, then, what if you have to take care of your husband through a long illness? Are you going to dump papers on his sick bed and shake him? "Honey! Wake up! You have to tell me what to do with these bills." I hope not.

Maybe your husband won't get sick and maybe you'll never be in a jam. It's possible. It's also possible that, even though you know subconsciously there is a railing on a stairway, you've never reached for it. If you catch your heel or stumble, however, won't it be nice to have it there to grab? That's security.

And if you are on your own? Single isn't safe. Here come the big guns. The House of Representatives Committee on Aging says we, women, can expect to spend 17 years of our lives taking care of our children and 18 years of our lives taking care of our parents or our husband's parents. And that includes taking care of their *financial concerns*.

Now are you convinced that you must get off the couch and do this? I mentioned the above statistic to my neighbor, and it sent her into a real funk. She got that sad, faraway look in her eye. I knew she was remembering how her mother had nursed her father for two years following a paralyzing stroke. He never recovered. She knows only too well that her mother was—and still is—helpless with money.

This is all about you and your life. It is urgent.

Now That You're Motivated

The first move is now.

We're going to take that paperwork you collected and sort it, all of it: mail, bills, receipts, everything you've saved for household, financial, and business affairs, over the past 12 months. If it's too big a job to tackle all at once, do it in chunks—just don't quit halfway through. You deserve the rewards this step will bring. (See Figure 3.1.) Remember, you have the advantage of being familiar with your own papers. Imagine the challenge this job would be for someone else, like your son or daughter or sister or friend. Or, if the situation were reversed, imagine being faced with their papers, files, mail, and bills. Where would you start to sort it out?

Here's what to do: First, dump everything in one massive pile. Then get hold of Paul Bunyan's wastebasket, a stack of scrap papers, a pen, and space to spread out. This is grunt work, but keep that reward in mind. See yourself smiling, relaxed, and confident, basking in the glow of self-determined security.

FIGURE 3.1   From Clutter to Categories

Ready? Use the scrap papers to mark categories, one paper per category. You don't have to think them up. This is a three-step, no-brainer exercise.

1. Take the top paper off the pile. What does it say? Let's suppose it's an electric bill. Okay, there's your first category: UTILITIES.

2. Mark the scrap UTILITIES. Lay it down and place the electric bill beside it. For now, we don't care about the date on the bill, the amount, or whether it's paid or due. We're done with it. If we come across the phone bills, gas, water, sewer, etc., they'll join this same category.

3. Go on to the next paper. Suppose it's an insurance statement. Give it the category label INSURANCE, and plop it down. For now, we don't care whether it's an insurance bill, a statement, or general information. We don't care if it's car insurance, house insurance, or life insurance. Anything pertaining to insurance goes into the insurance category *except . . .*

   Wait! Here's the exception: If it's medical insurance, make a new category, MEDICAL. Everything medical belongs there: doctor, hospital, prescriptions, medical insurance, etc.

You get the idea. Keep going. Taking one paper at a time, work your way through that awful stack. If you just can't fit something into an existing category, make a new one. There aren't any rules. Make as many categories as you want. And don't stop to read for anything but category identification for now. This is a once-through-and-done step—KISS: Keep It Superbly Simple.

Here are some suggestions for categories if you get stuck:

Annuities	Loans (monies owed or due you)
Bank Accounts (safe deposit box)	Medical (all medical information/bills/insurance)
Brokerage Accounts	Miscellaneous
Car (including repair records, etc.)	Paycheck (his/hers)
Clubs/Hobbies/Charities	Pension/Social Security
Credit Cards	Professional/Business
Family Information	Real estate/Mortgages
Insurances	Taxes/Save for Taxes
Other Investments	Utilities

It is like a game of solitaire. You play until the stack is all used up (see Figure 3.1).

The categories titled Family Information, Miscellaneous, and Professional/Business, will probably take on lives of their own. Not to worry—set them aside. We're focusing only on family *money* matters now. Go back and replay solitaire with each of those three nonmoney stacks later. Suggestions for doing this are shown in Figure 3.2. Since those categories represent specialized—but separate—aspects of your life, they deserve their own spaces. Stashing such "other" information among your money files defeats our purpose, like putting fresh milk in the cupboard and canned goods in the fridge.

By the way, no papers in the Miscellaneous stack are vital to business or they already would have fallen into a specific category. Get that box out of sight. Quick!

FIGURE 3.2   Playing Solitaire with the "Other" Stacks

FAMILY/PROJECTS (File Label)	**PROFESSIONAL/BUSINESS**

APPLIANCES   (Categories/Hangers/Dividers)
   Warranties   (Manila File Folders)
   Instructional pamphlets
CORRESPONDENCE
   Cards, letters
FAMILY INFO
   Genealogy
   Health records–kids
HOBBIES
   Stamps
HOUSE PLANS
   Ideas, articles
   Contractors
   Furnishing ideas
MAPS
   All our road maps
NEIGHBORHOOD WATCH
   Handouts from meetings
SOUVENIRS/MEMENTOS
   Bobby's stuff–pictures
   Peg's stuff
   Harry's–birthday cards
   Sheila's–weekend in Fla.
CLUBS/ACTIVITIES
   AAUW–phone list
   Church–nursery schedule
   Lions–project
   Little League–apps.
   Scouts–badge info
SCHOOL
   Car pool–phone list
   Chaperone info–rules
   PTA–committee stuff
TRAVEL
   Airline benefits/freq. flyer
   Airline tickets (used)
   Ideas: places to go

CORRESPONDENCE/HARRY
   Résumes
   Contracts
   Projects
CUSTOMER PROJECTS
   Samples
   Addendum
   Forms
IDEAS
   Clippings
   My notes
PROJECTS
   Pro forma
   Schedules
   Customers
REPORTS
   Monthly
SAVE FOR TAXES
   (Use expanded file)

For the MISCELLANEOUS category, wait one week. Then go through this stack. Then, either follow the next step or assign to a WHEN I'M BORED basket, or deposit in the circular file (that's the wastebasket).

Spot the Clues to Your Financial Persona

Okay. With the eye of Sherlock, take a glance at the categories lined up in front of you. Without reading one paper, you can already deduce some basic facts.

If Credit Cards has collected only 12 single sheets, for example, then you are a pay-by-cash person. Your habits won't be disclosed through credit card debt. Instead, examine your checking account. It will probably be the best source to learn the what, who, and when of your spending. If, on the other hand, the Credit Cards stack looks like the Leaning Tower of Pisa, take your cue from that. The statements are detailed and give a good profile.

Now scan across the other stacks. The higher a pile, the more likely it is an important aspect of your financial picture. Its details will unfold as we go along. And, by the way, any misplaced papers will find their way to the right spot, too.

Meanwhile, do you see a picture beginning to emerge? Each step will tell you more. And it will be that easy. Congratulations on coming this far. It's a major move. Give yourself a pat on the back and take a coffee break.

These general categories you've created are equivalent to the library's 50,000 volumes that were arranged under its master alphabetical order (in Chapter 1). And you know how ineffective that was by itself! We can't stop here, but it's a super beginning. You are one giant step closer to fingertip answers.

Chapter 4

*K*ey #1:
Using the File Index

*F*ight that urge to shove these messy piles into file folders just to get them out of sight. That's a symptom of the phobia. Don't succumb. What you see around you may look like clutter in a different form, but it's temporary and friendly. It won't swallow you up. Look at the stacks as a seamstress eyes her pattern pieces. Cut out and scattered about, they seem hopeless—okay, they're an eyesore. But you know how beautifully they'll all come together.

And no matter how many categories you have, don't be alarmed. You cannot have too many. The fact that your state has hundreds of towns isn't important. Being able to zero in on exactly the right one—instantly—now that's important. Zeroing in on exactly the right paper is what we're going to achieve. It's called fingertip access. Work with one category at a time and put the others out of sight. Just don't let the little devils comingle. And don't look so serious. This is going to be a joyful experience.

Make the First Investment

It's time to buy a stack of *file folders* and *hanging files*. If you are unfamiliar with these office supplies, let me tell you the difference. The manila file folders fold over and protect several papers.

The hanging files, which we'll call "hangers" to avoid confusion, are those indispensable wraparound dividers (some are sold under the Pendaflex trade name). Each hangs suspended from side rails in the file drawer, hugs a group of manila file folders, and holds up a special tab for easy identification. These are a must.

Think of the relief at finding the very paper you need, with one glance and one motion, never to root, hunt, or shuffle again. You'll have no more reason to procrastinate. We're making your financial life easy.

Hangers aren't necessary, you say?

Have you ever loaded a file drawer with only manila file folders? They are pathetically shy. The minute the drawer closes, they slip down to the drawer bottom, trying to hide under one another. When you open the drawer, instead of an orderly file, you find a slumped, curled embarrassed mess. By themselves, file folders are a hopeless group. House them in hangers and they remain separate and gain stand-tall discipline.

Do as you like. But, minding your own business means setting up your affairs in a businesslike manner. Can't you spend five bucks and treat this with the importance it deserves? You'll find them at your local office supply store.

Put the "Cats" in Place

Take the insertable plastic hanger tabs and slip in the names of the main categories you have established (taken from the scrap paper labels). Now, insert the tabs onto the hangers. Using alphabetical order, stagger the tabs left to right, repeating to form a diagonal lineup. Okay. Hang the hangers in a cardboard box for now.

Finished? How does it look? Orderly? Businesslike? Is it easy to spot a category quickly? Good. Set the box aside.

Now, Bring on the "Kittens"

You'll be glad you cleared the floor. Those scrap paper categories are about to have "kittens." In a matter of moments, you'll see the daunting piles of clutter transformed into a precious resource. And it will be out of sight. Grab a fresh supply of scrap paper, manila file folders, and a clean sheet of paper, and let's get started. We'll start with Utilities. You have already labeled a file hanger Utilities, identifying it as a main category, and set it aside. Now let's get into details:

1. Take the top paper off of the Utilities pile. Let's suppose it's an electric bill. Okay, there's your first subcategory (I call it a "kitten." Get it? Cat-egories . . . kittens . . .)

2. Anyway, label this kitten's scrap paper Pacific Power Co/ Electric or Elec/PAC Pwr. Which do you think of first, *electric* or the company *name?* Make your label reflect the way your mind works. It matters.

   Lay the label down and place the electric bill beside it. Any paper that has to do with the electric company belongs in this kitten.

3. Continue sorting through the Utilities pile until all the papers are distributed into kittens.

Perhaps you're not convinced you need such detailed labels. A lady from my workshop protested, "I'm not marking down both the company and the service. I can remember them." She's right; it seems unnecessary. You might have the name on the tip of your tongue, today. But, what about next week?

It's said that Einstein never tried to remember what he could look up. So why should we? Use good reminders.

Besides, what if you were ill and somebody had to stand in for you? How would your substitute billpayer know these details if you kept them only in your head? We're putting together a no-fail system here. Instant answers. No memorization required. Put whatever you need on that label.

If you need examples of utility kitten file labels, try these:

- ABC Serv/Gas
- AT&T/Telephone
- City Serv/Water/Trash
- First Co/Cable TV
- PAC Pwr/Electric

Now, let's get them out of sight and continue:

4. Work in an orderly manner. Once sorted, place each utility kitten inside its appropriate manila folder. That's the folder labeled after its scrap paper title (such as PAC Pwr/Elec). You'll have one folder—which holds all related bills, statements, reports, and so forth—for each type of utility.
5. Next tuck each utility kitten file folder inside the general Utilities hanger. Each hanger should hold nicely all the folders related to its category. If not, use two hangers for that category or buy a larger double-capacity hanger.

That's all there is to it. The utility kittens have found a home. If you want to find the electric bills, they'll be easy to spot. Nice and neat, huh?

Do the same for each category. Name, sort, and file its kittens. It's our last game of solitaire. When you have labeled and placed all the file folder kittens into their appropriate general category hangers, rehang them in your box or file drawer. Before you rush out and buy a filing cabinet, though, please read Chapter 10.

Remember Widow M? She started out just like this, sorting and saving. And you know what happened to her. But, don't worry, you won't need a burlap bag, because this is where we part company.

Key #1: The File Index

Here are the four steps for developing our first key—the file indexing:

1. On a clean 8½" × 11" sheet of paper, write or type the word *Index.*
2. Take a manila file folder and title it Index.
3. Then take a file hanger, color the tab with a yellow marker and mark it Index.
4. Give it a home.

The paper goes into the folder, the folder goes into the hanger, and the hanger goes into the file box. This Index hanger stays in the front of your files—always. It's one of the five keys to building your power base. Think of it as the library's card catalog. The yellow tab on this hanger makes it stand out. You'll spot it in a second.

Now create your file Index (see Figure 4.1). List both the general categories and their kittens on an Index sheet. Do a scratch copy first, then redo it in alphabetical order when the entire file is completed. This is your private reference sheet. Make it reader-friendly—print, indent, use arrows or asterisks, or colors—whatever you like. Leave a space between categories for new additions, because your information will change. This file will expand and contract like a living thing. Your index must give it "breathing" space.

The Index ends hunting parties. No more self-blame because you can't remember which file holds last year's HMO pamphlet. You won't have to *remember*. Finding anything in these files will be fast and painless. Just like your own Yellow Pages.

"So if I'm not home when my husband has to hunt something up, he'll be able to find it on his own?" a client asked.

"That's the idea," I told her.

"It's a miracle," she said, "because he can't even find his socks."

FIGURE 4.1   Setting Up the File Index

A   **ANNUITIES**. . . . . Hanging file
1st Ins Corp. . . . . Manila folder
   Applications/Beneficiary information . . . . Papers filed
   Statements
   Correspondence
NYL Ins Co
   Applications/Beneficiary information

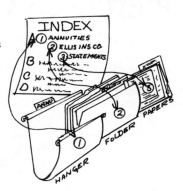

B   **BANK ACCTS**
First Community
   Statements
   Safe deposit box list
Credit Union
   Statements
   Newsletter
Mortgage/Real Estate: *see REAL ESTATE

BROKERAGE ACCT
Main Stream Corp
   Statements—current year
   Confirms—current year
      (For prior years, see long-term file)
IRAs (Harry/Sheila)
Joint Acct (ours)
Kids' Acct(s)

C   **CAR**
Loan—Harry's
   Documents/Statements
   Repairs/Warranty
Loan—Sheila's
   Documents/Statements
   Repairs/Warranty

CLUBS/HOBBIES
Country Club
   Statements
Racquet Club
   Statements

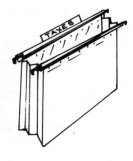

CREDIT CARDS
AmExp—Statements/Benefits/Fliers
Visa—Statements/Benefits/Fliers

Continue in this manner through the alphabet, allowing space between
categories for new additions. Remember to keep this Index at the front
of the filing cabinet, at your fingertips.

Chapter 5

Key #2: Creating Your Cross-Referenced Card Index

*I*s this tool necessary? Yes. Buy yourself a generous-sized card index. This is the second key to your success. It will change your life. You can't conduct an efficient business without tools. Remember how exciting it was when we finally got call waiting and redial on our home phones? We're taking another great idea from business. Why should the corporate world have all the convenience?

No kidding: A card index is as crucial to your files as the coordinated list of cities and grid are to every road map. We're moving far beyond the services of the library's card catalog now (or its computer replacement). Key #2, the home card index, is the trained librarian at the reference desk. It's the traffic cop at the intersection. It's the emergency 911 dispatcher. Once you have one, you'll never want to be without it.

Ever worked in an office? Remember what was on your desk? Computer, calendar, memo pad, calculator, telephone, and those neat little cards for phone numbers and customer details like birthdates, children's names, special things they like—sure, you remember. And if you were a secretary, you heard the boss's impatient: "Hey, Betty, what was the name of that sales rep from Axel Manufacturing? That guy I hustled out of here yesterday. Got a number for him?" In only seconds, you placed the number in his hands. Problem solved and business saved. All thanks to you and your smart use of . . . was it a Rolodex?

Before our enlightenment, it appeared that my husband and I were competing for the biggest heap of reminders at the end of a work day. Emptying our pockets was like throwing a ticker-tape parade. We quickly learned that an office can't survive without the card index to hold the endless and unpredictable miscellany. The same is true at home.

I now have three Rolodexes at home. I keep the miniature version next to my bedroom phone for personal phone numbers—family, neighbors, and friends—plus a few emergency numbers.

My favorite card index is a life-sustaining giant on my desk. At last count, this "brain" held more than 500 cards. It's a revolving wheel of instant information that forms the glue of my life.

The third is a smoky-gray plastic encasing 3″ × 5″ cards, next to my computer. I use that one for business contacts and instant recall for computer functions and computer experts.

Curing "Headache #37"

Let's see how this key can provide expertise for the boss of your business—you! Suppose you get a call about a lawn service in February. Poor businessperson, you say? Right: Who cares about weeds in February? But four months later the rains come, the sun is warm, and weeds are springing forth. Yikes! The yard is out of hand. Now you need the lawn service—fast.

So, where's that darned phone number? You scratch your head and sort through a pile of assorted notes and saved pamphlets. You scribbled it down somewhere—just in case. Can't find it four months later? Nuts. Do you try your luck with the phone book? That was the old way. Forget those nail-biting moments.

Here's a replay using the new way, when your fingers flick right to the answer:

You get a call about lawn service in the middle of February. With the Rolodex *next to your phone,* and its lavish supply of double-sided cards, you simply pop out a card while you're on the phone. Jot down the number, name, and details about the caller. When you hang up, you've got a *master* that reads: **"Terra Firma Co/** lawn care/Tony, eves 331-4598/guarantees his work."

Take a brief—but important—moment to decide how to file it. Can't decide? Okay, try this: pop that card into **T.**

FIGURE 5.1 Don't Forget to Cross Reference!

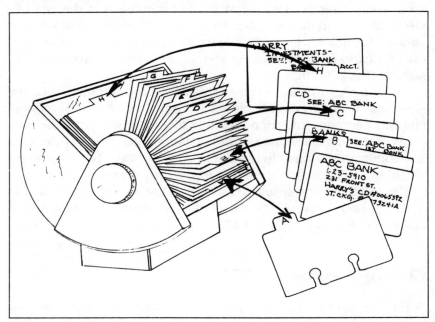

Wait! Now take four more cards. (Don't worry, you'll never run out.)

Snap one in **G.** It reads **Gardening**–see Terra Firma. Snap the next one in **L.** It reads: **Lawn care**–see Terra Firma. The next one goes in **B.** It reads: **Backyard**–see Terra Firma. Snap the last in **W.** It reads: **Weeds**–see Terra Firma.

Voilà. You've cross-indexed this card in one minute's time. I'll bet you'll find Tony's name and number in the spring. And next year, too.

Make It Personal

If your mind comes up with different trigger words (like *grass* or *planting* or *husky-voiced Tony*), make additional cross-references. The success of your system depends on how well you reflect your own thought patterns. There are no rules. Make it fit you.

Make it fun! Four months or a year later, you can dazzle everyone, but mostly you'll amaze yourself. Think of the rewards if you are a woman on your own: No more rescues needed from colleagues or family or friends who have secretaries or "superior" memories. Watch their eyebrows shoot up when you come to *their* rescue. You'll be a force to be reckoned with.

Imagine the rush of the holiday season. Your husband is in the next room, dashing off a few cards to his special friends. "Where did you put my old army buddy's address, *dear*?" he asks. You know that tone of voice. He expects the worst. "You didn't toss it out, did you? *Did you*?"

Did you?

In the future, list the army buddy as *What's-his-name*. And if you need a hint, I can think of a great cross-reference for the old. . . .

Who would have thought a Rolodex would make for a happier home life? And the same benefits accrue to caretakers and caretakees, too. Is that serendipity or what?

Electronic Update

Are you always on the go? Instead of a desk-type Rolodex, try a pop-in-your-purse electronic version. One woman professional, who survives on a tightwire freeway schedule between home, family, and business, said she uses her electronic reminder for everything from grocery items to thoughts on contract negotiations.

Take a look at your local store. There are organizer/reminder products from various manufacturers in a wide range of prices. As with computers, organize your system first. And, one word of caution: if you intend to load it up with confidential information, be sure to choose a model that allows a password for access. That way, on the off-chance that you lose or misplace it, you won't be giving your life story to the finder.

While we're on the subject of powerful, get hold of a simple calculator. A calculator makes for cheap, reliable, no-math money control, exactly what every successful business needs.

Would a Computer Be Easier or More Convenient?

The good news is that today's home computers often include a card index system. The bad news is that when you need a name or number *now*, the computer may be turned off. That makes a simple job complicated. It forces a decision. Will you turn on the computer and plow through the layers? Or put off the call until later? For instant answers available 24 hours a day, take the simple path—the see-it, touch-it Rolodex.

Would a computer make record keeping easier? Nope. Think KISS (keep it superbly simple). All we need is two sheets of paper we can curl up with on the couch. Information at our fingertips. No late-night keyboard clicks, computer beeps, or booting up required. What you see is what you've got.

However, if you want to computerize, you're in the right place. The system we're setting up will make it a successful transition. No matter how you cut it, even with computers, garbage in equals garbage out. There's no magic. First, you have to understand what you're about.

Forbes magazine published an eye-opener article in its August 29, 1994, Technology Supplement, about sophisticated corporations who have lost millions, yes, m-i-l-l-i-o-n-s, because they paid for complex computer systems without first having worked out their own specific processes. They computerized their confusion, or as *Forbes* called it, their "private catastrophes."

So remember, this is important stuff we're doing here. What you used to suspect was your personal shortcoming is really a universal problem, dumped on all of us by the times. The resulting phobia, with its clutter and confusion, strikes everywhere. By the way, once we complete our system, you might see if those screwed-up corporate giants can use your help.

Keep track of how much your supplies cost. The Rolodex and a simple calculator are the best investments you'll ever make. As a matter of fact, your total cost of supplies is less than one dinner out. Even Jack Benny would be a fan. And in case you're wondering, I have no tie-in with any manufacturer; I'm just passing on information about products that can make life easier. And that includes our own, like the keys and forms found in Appendix A. The forms are too small to be used as is, so make enlarged photocopies. Paperclip the originals in the Appendix and give the copies a home in a file folder.

A Promotion Is in Order

Let's do a checkup. So far we've collected, sorted, filed, and indexed—all secretarial duties. But every business needs an accountant, so it's time to switch hats. Give yourself a raise and a promotion. Congratulations: You are now the accountant in your business. Your first assignment? To organize a financial map for your business.

Don't be put off. You can do this while dinner's in the oven. If you're holding down a job and raising a family at the same time, relax. This won't require large blocks of time or energy. The aim here is to unburden you, not pile it on. An accountant arranges numbers in a logical order so they can be mined for answers. That's what we're about.

And, as Martha Stewart says, "It's a good thing."

Chapter 6

*K*ey #3:
Tracking Money with the Living Expenses Form

*W*e've completed that important first step toward a power base: Clutter has been transformed into a budding resource. Let's review our progress:

- We have hanging files labeled as general categories (the cats).
- Inside the hangers, we have manila file folders labeled as sub-categories (the kittens).
- Inside the folders, we have detailed statements and papers, arranged by date.

Not so? If your papers aren't arranged by date, don't worry—they soon will be. This system self-corrects.

Now let's put that resource to work. Clear some space and have in front of you:

- Files
- Rolodex
- Photocopied Living Expenses form (For a sample completed form, see Figure 6.1. For a blank form of this and other forms referred to in this book, see Appendix A.)
- Pencil, red pen, black pen

If you haven't already done so, hang your files. It makes no difference now whether you use a box or a file drawer. Later on, we're going to look at permanent ideas.

Divide and Conquer

Before we can lump expenses together, we need to take them apart and see how they fit into the overall scheme of your financial life. This can be done by following four simple steps:

1. Take out all the file folders that hold information on expenses.
2. Sort the folders into two groups:
   - Fixed expenses—any payment that does not change, such as the following:

Mortgages	Insurances
Loans	Property taxes
Estimated taxes (Do not include income tax entries unless you pay estimated taxes.)	Utilities (Some utility payments may vary. Include those under Variable.)
Cable TV	Sewer/Trash

   - Variable expenses—everything else:

Car/Transportation	Hobbies
Child care	Medical
Clothing	Miscellaneous
Entertainment	Travel
Food	House/Pool/Yard maintenance
Utilities: gas/electric/ telephone	

To avoid getting lost in nickel-and-dime expenditures, group the miscellaneous Variable items under general headings. This is *not* a budget, so we don't care whether you spent $4 on film, $30 on golf, or $15.85 for lunch. A ballpark total is what we're looking for. On the other hand, pie-in-the-sky won't do you any good. Make the numbers accurate enough to give yourself a sense of what you *actually spend.* The Living Expenses form is about you and for you. You'll depend on it. Make sure it's a true picture. Let's continue:

FIGURE 6.1   Sample Living Expenses Form

LIVING   EXPENSES   199....

Items (Fxd)	Jan	Feb	Mar	Apr	May	June	July	Aug	Sept	Oct	Nov	Dec	YrTotal
Hlth Ins													
Car Ins													
Mf Lfe Ins													
Est Taxes													
K Svg Mtge													
Bnkr Mtge													
Charity													
Cable TV													
Wtr/trsh													
Total Fxd													
Items (Var)													
Elec/gas													
Telephone													
Doctor													
Pharmacy													
Hospital													
Dept Store													
Cdt cards													
Food													
Travel													
Gas/car													
Other													
Total Var													
Total Grnd													

3. Refer to the Living Expenses form. Notice the column on the far left side labeled Items. Notice that the top half of the form is labeled Fixed, and the bottom half, Variable.

4. List both types of expenses items in that column as shown in Figure 6.1.

We just set up an Indexed filing system, but that doesn't mean you're already organized—only that you put things out of sight. Is it really necessary to copy these items onto the Living Expenses form? Yes. Then, we're making an ordinary budget after all? No.

If you want a budget, work that out on your own time. This is something new. We're weaving a web to manage *living information.* You might think bills are bills, and there is no difference if they are *fixed* or *variable.* But think back to a time when you had a money crunch. Maybe your tires were so bald that you gave up your last bit of cash for four new ones. Then before you enjoyed 100 miles of cushioned ride, the mail produced a bill for a forgotten insurance premium—as hefty as the cost of those tires.

You probably said, "Oh, god. I forgot it was due this month."

And then you whipped out the checkbook and the dreaded juggler's cap, blaming yourself all the while for not remembering. Well, who needs that? You won't be caught off-guard again.

The Proof Is in the Demo

Look at the completed Living Expenses form shown in Figure 6.2. It shows a look back over nine months of "my" expenses. Later, when you see a full year presented, you'll discover that the Living Expenses form is much more than a history of where the money went. It's a powerful *manager* for today and tomorrow. But, I don't want to get ahead of myself.

For now, see what it tells you about my money. I predict you'll be an expert on my past expenses in less than five minutes. And your own? Try three minutes.

But don't take my word for it. See how long it takes you to answer these questions:

- How much did I spend in June? See *A*, the figure at the bottom of the June column: Grand Total.
- On what dates are my mortgages due? See *B*, the notation in the left margin: 15th and 1st.
- Are taxes included in the mortgage payments? See *C*, the notation in the left margin.

  Wait a minute. You're looking at *C* and it says *PITI*. Sounds like some in-house code. Sorry, time out while I translate a short cut. PITI (pronounced P-I-T-I) is an abbreviation for a mortgage payment that includes *p*rincipal, *i*nterest, *t*axes, and *i*nsurance. PITI is used by lenders, escrow agents, title companies, and the real estate population. And now you, if you like shortcuts. (See Chapter 7 for more on mortgage details.)
- When are estimated taxes due? See *D*, the entries to the right of Estimated Taxes: Jan-Apr-June-Sept. (See Chapter 7 for more on estimated taxes.)

Are you encouraged? All that information and only one piece of paper.

If the Living Expenses form passed the test, you learned details about *my* finances like an expert. But, look again. There's more. For example, did you notice that I own a house on Ash Street? And

FIGURE 6.2   Living Expenses Form—Sample

LIVING EXPENSES 199....

Items (Fixd)	Jan	Feb	Mar	Apr	May	June	July	Aug	Sept	Oct	Nov	Dec	YrTotal
Hlth Ins	$386			$386			$386						$
Car Ins						$300							$
Mf Lfe Ins						$400							$
Est Taxes	$2300			$2300		$2300			$2300			due Jan	$
Svg Mtge	$482	$482	$482	$482	$482	$482	$482	$482	$482				$
BnkMtge	$300	$300	$300	$300	$300	$300	$300	$300	$300				$
Charity			$150			$150			$150				$
Cable TV	$25	$25	$25	$25	$25	$25	$25	$25	$25				$
Wtr/trsh	$24		$24		$24	$24	$24		$24				$
Total Fxd	$3517	$807	$981	$3493	$831	$3957	$1217	$807	$3281				$
Items (Var)													
Elec/gas	$80	$75	$20	$25	$25	$25	$60	$90	$40				$
Telephone	$35	$50	$25	$20	$50	$65	$50	$25	$20				$
Doctor			$120	$100	$17			$86					$
Pharmacy	$50	$50	$50	$50									$
Hospital			$280										$
Dept Store	$20		$60	$85	$15	$40		$10	$90				$
Cdt cards			$120	$65				$80					$
Food	$350	$350	$300	$355	$400	$300	$350	$310	$340				$
Travel				$2400		$220			$3000				$
Gas/car	$30	$10	$10	$35	$35	$20	$20	$30					$
Other			$45										
Total Var	$565	$535	$1030	$3100	$542	$670	$480	$631	$3490	$	$	$	$
Total Grnd	$4082	$1342	$2011	$6593	$1373	$4627	$1697	$1438	$6771	$	$	$	$

if asked, you can reveal what the mortgage costs. My expenses are an open book. Does this prove the point? There is nothing wrong with you. You are smart enough. It was your old "system" that muddled your thinking.

On with the New

So much for what is and what was. Let's look ahead. Are all your expenses listed? Good. Let me show you how to make all three keys work for you.

First, take a file. Let's start with Car Insurance.

Okay. Think fingertip. The mail arrives. Oops. Is this a mistake on the car insurance bill? What to do? You'll have to make a phone call. What a pain. Will you put the bill aside until . . . later?

Not if you make it easy to solve. Go to Key #2, the Rolodex.

With Rolodex card in hand, locate a recent car insurance premium notice from your file. Scan it for vital statistics such as:

- Company name/address
- Phone numbers: main office/customer service/emergency
- Agent name/home phone/secretary
- Policy number(s)/applies to which car?

If you can't find the information, call up the agent. Now.

Okay. Record those items on one Rolodex card. This is your *master.* Feel free to use both sides of the card.

If you already know how to use these cards, but don't use them, maybe your entries aren't styled to you. Do you forget where you jotted down those lifesaving items? The key is to make the Rolodex a dynamic tool. Mere alphabetical order isn't enough; we need that *cross-referencing.* It's magic, and it's a no-brainer.

Skip ahead if you don't need other suggestions for *cross-referencing.* The following is for that too-busy career-mother-volunteer who told me she felt brain dead when it came to thinking up a linkage. So, for her and other running-as-fast-as-you-can women, here's an idea for cross-referencing car insurance:

1. Pop your master card in **S,** since it reads:
   Stalwart Ins/Harry's car ins
   Policy #7-854129/

Agt Blaine Tessor/Betty 777-1111
Cust Srv 800-234-5678/24 Hr 800-777-7777
8888 Harker's Blvd, Ind. 12345

2. Under **C,** pop in a second Rolodex card that reads:
Car Insurance—see Stalwart

3. Under **H,** pop in a card that reads:
Harry's car insurance—see Stalwart

4. Under **I,** pop in the fourth card that reads:
Insurances:
Car—see Stalwart
To which you can later add:
House—see . . . .
Life—see . . .
Medical—see . . .

5. Or if your mind freezes when the worst happens?
Make out a fifth card filed in **A** that reads:
Accident—see Insurances

If your partner's mind locks onto *catastrophe* and *SOS?* Add those cards for him. This is your private and personal system, so make your own can't-miss entries.

One-Touch Filing

Since efficiency experts tell us to handle a paper only once, let's try it. While you still have the car insurance statement in hand, co-ordinate the next layer. This is the necessary and detailed information that has been so annoying to hunt for in the past.

1. On the statement, find and circle these two items:

Date Due   **Please Pay This Amount**
Jun 10 95 $300.00

2. Next, find the summary message. It will read something like this: **Full payment by date due continues this policy in force until:** *Dec 10 95.* This policy expires on the date due if premium is not paid.

Since the date due is June 10 and the expiration date is December 10, six months later, we know the premium is paid semiannually (SA). We also know that the amount of this payment is $300.

Those are the questions most likely to be asked when you make a phone call about your policy. Be ready with factual answers at your fingertips.

The Key Rules

Rule 1: Refer to your Rolodex contact card. It lists the bare essentials to get you to the right person at the right place in the shortest time.

Rule 2: Refer to the Living Expenses form, that single sheet of paper, for crucial and extensive details. Once that right person is on the line, you need back-up details for informed discussions and decisions. How can you put yourself in that nice position? Do the following:

- In the margin of the Living Expenses form, next to the car insurance entry, note premium due dates and payment schedule. For example, "Jun/Dec 10" and "SA" (see below).
- Using the red pen, put a bright red *dot* in each month of the year that a payment falls due. In this example, payments are due in June and December (B).
- Using the black pen, enter (in the appropriate months) the payment(s) *already paid.* In this example, the payment paid was $300, and it was made in June (C).
- Using pencil, enter (in the appropriate months) the amounts *coming due* over the rest of the year. In this example, the payment coming due is $300 and it is due in December (D).

	Items (Fxd)	Jan	Feb	Mar	Apr	May	June	July	Aug	Sept	Oct	Nov	De	YrTotal
	Hlth Ins													
	Car Ins SA						S300						$300	$600

LIVING EXPENSES 199....

Now we're finished. Put the car insurance file away.

Follow this same procedure for each Expense entry, Fixed and Variable. See the sample shown in Figure 6.3. Meanwhile, test out this portion of the Living Expenses form.

FIGURE 6.3 Living Expenses Form with 12 Months Completed

LIVING EXPENSES/ 199.... (as of Sept)

Items (Fxd)	Jan	Feb	Mar	Apr	May	June	July	Aug	Sept	Oct	Nov	Dec	YrTotal
Hlth Ins	$386*			$386*			$386*			$382*		↓	$1,544
Car Ins												$300* $400*	$600
Mf Lfe Ins												$400*	$800
Est Taxes	$2300*			$2300*		$2300*			$2300*			due Jan	$9200
K Svg Mtge	$482*	$482*	$482*	$482*	$482*	$482*	$482*	$482*	$482*	$482*	$482*	$482*	$5784
BnkMtge	$300*	$300*	$300*	$300*	$300*	$300*	$300*	$300*	$300*	$300*	$300*	$300*	$3600
Charity			$150*	$150*		$150*			$150*			$150*	$600
Cable TV	$25*	$25*	$25*	$25*	$25*	$25*	$25*	$25*	$25*	$25*	$25*	$25*	$300
Wtr/trsh	$24*		$24*	$24*	$24*	$24*	$24*		$24*		$24*		$144
Total Fxd	$3517	$807	$981	$3493	$831	$3957	$1217	$807	$3281	$1193	$831	$1657	22,572
Items (Var)													
Elec/gas	$80*	$75*	$20*	$25*	$25*	$25*	$60*	$90*	$40*	$60*	$70*	$90*	$640
Telephone	$35*	$50*	$25*	$20*	$50*	$65*	$50*	$25*	$20*	$50*	$35*	$73*	$500
Doctor	$50	$50	$120	$100				$86					$306
Pharmacy			$50	$50	$17						$50		$367
Hospital			$280										$280
Dept Store	$20		$60	$85	$15	$40		$10	$90			$200	$520
Cdt cards			$120	$65				$80				$50	$415
Food	$350	$350	$300	$355	$400	$300	$350	$310	$340	$300	$350	$500	$4025
Travel				$2400					$3000			$1000	$4920
Gas/car	$30	$10	$10		$35	$20	$20	$30		$20	$20		$205
Other			$45			$220						$50	$315
Total Var	$565	$535	$1030	$3100	$542	$670	$480	$631	$3490	$430 EST.	$535 EST.	$2265 EST.	$4,373 EST.
Total Grnd	$4082	$1342	$2011	$6593	$1373	$4627	$1697	$1438	$6771	$1423	$1366	$3922	$36,945

What Have You Got That You Didn't Have Before?

You now have fingertip power. Here's how it works:

- *Problem:* Mail arrives. You find that mistake in the insurance bill.
- *Solution:* Reach for your *"keys."*
  - **Flip** open the **Rolodex** for instant information on insurance company names, phone numbers, and policy numbers.
  - **Slip** the **Living Expenses form** out from the *front* of your files for facts, activity, and status.
  - **Spot** the red dots. Instantly, you know in which months the payments fall due.
  - **See** the inked entries. You know which payments have been made, when they were made, and the amounts.
  - **Find** the penciled entries. You know when future payments fall due and the amount to be paid.
  - **Make** your call.

How long did that take? A minute?

I love going through an actual trial like this. I see women's eyes light up with, "Heck, I could take care of a problem right now!" The rewards are immediate.

Now, take some time to finish your own Living Expenses form.

You may get an unexpected jolt once you've completed estimated expenses for all 12 months. Add the columns. Take a look at the Fixed totals. Did you realize you spent that much even before you got out of bed in the morning? And you can't get rid of any of them. That eye-opener is the birth of insight.

When Is Cash Not Spendable?

What you see is *not* what you can spend when it isn't *extra*. Turn a suspicious eye on that enticing stash built up in your savings account. Is it needed for next month's estimated taxes? Or for the annual insurance premium due in three months? And all this time you've been thinking it was your ticket to a skiing trip. Don't give up—set a future date, enter the savings needed on the Living Expenses form at so much per month. When the date arrives, enjoy it guilt-free—and send me a postcard.

Before and After

Now you know how simple it is to use this key. Start out January with a clean Living Expenses form. Again, here's how it works:

1. List all items.
2. Place a red dot in each month a payment will fall due, January through December.
3. Pencil in each payment amount due for the entire year.

When you pay bills, the Living Expenses form becomes your checkup sheet. As you write a check, replace the penciled numbers with ink.

KISS: Ink, it's paid; pencil, it's due. If a cost goes up, you'll spot it. You'll see that the numbers you expected to pay (entered in pencil) are different from those on the new bill. Isn't that a "wow"? It's a built-in nudge to find out why the numbers changed. Is it an error on the bill? Is the service altered? Is the cost higher with no increase in service? Get an answer now.

Seeing Month by Month

Suppose you'd like to make a special purchase and pay cash. When is the best time to do it? The Living Expenses form can tell you in which month your expenses are lowest. Total each column—in pencil, of course. What you've got is a real picture of your living expenses. It's a one-year, month-by-month slice of your life. Are expenses less in March? June? October? Is there a month in which you can cut back?

Whether you like what you see, I can't say. But has it ever been so easy to see? I wonder if Congress has a Living Expenses form?

The 12-Month Picture

Using your calculator, add *across* the columns. Do you have the grand totals? Good. Time for a reality check. Did you realize that you spent that much in a year?

Looking at the Future

Now look ahead. Seeing an entire year in advance makes it possible to plan. These numbers expose some powerful facts. For instance, those *fixed* expenses won't go away. They pay for necessities. If you want to cut down, chop away at the variables. The nice life to which you have become accustomed is supported by the *variable* expenses.

Any surprises? If you've never before had a clear picture of *how* you handle your money, you'll love the Living Expenses form. It really does manage. A couple sitting in my office stared at their fixed expenses, looked at one another, and announced, "We'll sell the house!" Without realizing it, they had been sacrificing to maintain a lifestyle that suited their long-gone large family. Now they live in a more modest home and the kids get postcards from Europe.

It's not uncommon to see young homebuyers take on a huge family home too soon (and the burdensome mortgage that goes with it) and retirees hanging on to that large home too long (when maintenance costs climb). The goal is to make your expenses fit your priorities.

You can put the Living Expenses form to work for you. Start by answering these questions:

- In which month are your total expenses highest? (Did you add each month's Fixed and Variable subtotals together?)
- What are your annual mortgage costs? (Include PITI. Did you get vital statistics from your mortgage statement?)
- How often do you pay car insurance premiums? (Did you find the dates on the statement? Did you jot down the code? *A* [annual], *SA* [semi-annual], *Q* [quarterly], or *M* [monthly]?)

On the first try, finding answers can be slow. Know why? Habits. If you pay homeowners insurance and property taxes separately, maybe you wrote only *PI* next to the mortgage entry. Then, because of old habits, let's say you started to hunt through the insurance and tax files for the other figures. Thumbing through, you suddenly remember, "Hey, I don't have to do this anymore!" So then you look back at the Living Expenses form. Sure enough, the answers are there: under Insurance—House, and under Taxes—Property.

Now try this one: What's the total you spent from January 1 to the end of March? Pft! That's nothing, right? Just whip out your calculator and add those three figures at the bottom of the columns.

All finished? How long did it take? Do you think any of your friends could answer that question? You've come a long way since the first chapter.

Pillow Talk

The Living Expenses form is key to your mental and financial health. You'll use it constantly. Keep it at your fingertips. When you get that midnight worry, tiptoe down the hall to your files and see the facts on your Living Expenses form. Here's where it goes:

1. Insert the Living Expenses form into a manila file labeled Expenses.
2. Pop the folder into a hanging file with a yellow tab labeled Expenses.
3. Place the hanger in the front of your files, next to the Index. You can't miss it.

Next, we'll take a minute to clear up Living Expenses form details about the mortgage and taxes.

Chapter 7

*U*nderstanding Your Mortgage and Taxes

"*W*ow! He got a little chin music!" Abbreviations and buzzwords pop up in so many places; they're a language unto themselves. If we don't understand them, we miss out. Don't you feel curious, left out, or uneasy when others around you seem to be in-the-know? Well, this week I found out about "chin music." It means the pitcher threw the baseball too close to the batter's face! And now I'll tell you about a "loaded" abbreviation—loaded with meaningful information for us, that is. And it also will put you in-the-know.

The Language of Mortgages

In Chapter 1, I asked whether you knew *when the mortgage was paid and what was included in the payment.* The abbreviation used in the Living Expenses form example, PITI, tells the whole story. Here it is:

PI—Principal and Interest

Your loan number is on your Rolodex. Call your lender. Put the loan officer to work. He or she will tell you when the mortgage payment is due, what the interest rate is—whether it's a fixed or variable rate—and what your payment includes.

Here are suggestions for other questions to ask your lender:

- Does the lender write the check that pays your homeowners insurance? Property taxes? If so, ask for an explanation of that impound account.
- Are you eligible for a discount if property taxes are paid by a certain date?
- Have you qualified for that discount?

Take advantage of the lender's service. The lender has all this information right at hand, on his or her computer.

T—Taxes

Now take out the county property tax statement from your Real Estate hanger. Find the answers to these nine questions:

1. If you write the check for your property taxes, are you eligible for discounts if taxes are paid by a certain date?
2. Have you qualified for those discounts?
3. Do you have receipts for taxes paid?
4. Is your loan number accurate?
5. Can you find the legal description of your property?
6. What makes up your property taxes?
7. What portion of the property value is assigned to the land? (This figure is subtracted from total property value when you take homeowners insurance. You don't insure land, only the improvements.)
8. What is the assessed value of your property? How does that compare to today's market price?
9. How much do you pay for schools or libraries?

Don't memorize the information. This is just to get a general understanding of the what, why, and how of property taxes. If you do not have a "taxes paid" receipt, call your lender or the tax collector to confirm that payment was made.

By the way, if you sell real estate and take back a mortgage, you must find out whether your buyer pays the property taxes in a timely manner. There is an easy way to protect yourself. For minimal cost—which you can assign to the borrower—you can arrange for a legal notice to be sent to you if the taxes are unpaid. Ask the title company to file a "Request for Notice" on your behalf.

Keep cumulative property tax records in your Real Estate hanging file, using a manila file folder titled to the *street address* of the property. Include the receipts for improvements and landscaping— I mean, naturescaping.

Twenty years later, when you sell your home, you will want to tally up the total cost of deductible improvements. These deductions can increase your "pocket profit" on the sale of your home. Keeping those records in one permanent file will make it easy. It also will help you track what's happening to your property taxes year by year. Who knows? It even may affect your vote on local issues.

I—Insurance

If your homeowners insurance is paid separately, you labeled a House Insurance or Homeowners Insurance manila file folder and slipped it into the Insurances file hanger. Take out a recent statement or the policy. If you don't have the information on your Rolodex, find the policy number and the deductible right now. Circle the deductible.

Next, jot the deductible down as a margin note on your Living Expenses form. If you have not already done so, enter both the policy number and the deductible on the Rolodex card. When you're deciding how much "cushion" money to set aside (see Chapter 11), include the total of all your deductibles, including car and medical insurance, too. While you've still got the policy in hand, phone the agent to clear up any questions about your coverage. Be certain he has your policy information in front of him as you talk.

Here are some suggested questions you should ask:

- How much and how often are premiums paid?
- Is there a discount for a different payment schedule?
- Does the policy include an inflation index?
- Is the policy written as *replacement cost* insurance? For example, what would the policy pay to replace a five-year-old couch destroyed by fire? Despite its age and condition, would the insurance replace it with a new couch at today's prices? Ask. It's a key question.

PITI—it spells principal, interest, taxes, and insurance—the whole of what your house costs you. If you haven't done so, jot down that PITI, PIT, or PI code alongside the mortgage payment on your Living Expenses form.

And there's your answer to everything you ever wanted to know about the mortgage payment—at your fingertips.

Behind-the-Scenes Tax Information

Finding the answer to another question from Chapter 1 will put more fingertip answers on the Living Expenses form. The question is about estimated taxes: *Do you know when the estimated taxes are due?* By the way, it's not just those retired ladies who pay estimated taxes; the self-employed also estimate taxes.

Zeroing in on the due dates for estimated taxes is not hard work. If your stockbroker doesn't supply you with an annual calendar showing them, call the Internal Revenue Service (listed under United States Government). You'll likely find yourself on hold for a long while, listening to a plethora of phonemail prompts. And if you happen to speak with a representative who's not forthcoming, don't be put off. Hang up and try again. There are excellent representatives, and you deserve good service.

If your accountant's time is not too expensive, ask him or her to explain about paying estimated taxes. A little rule here, a little rule there—geez, life ought to come with an instruction book.

IRS How To

Actually there is an instruction book for estimated taxes. Call the IRS and request form 1040 ES. It has a worksheet to help you arrive at an estimate. It also includes coupons to send with the payments.

The usual payment dates begin with April 15, followed by June 15, September 15, and January 15. The January payment covers the last quarter of the previous year. If a due date falls on a weekend or holiday, push the date ahead to the first banking day.

Now take out your Living Expenses form. Using red dots, mark the due dates for your estimated tax payments. You can now toss out the IRS booklet.

About Those Tax Returns

In Chapter 1, I also asked if you could *locate the last tax report you sent.* For permanence, set up your tax returns in a special file hanger or separate drawer. If you can lay your hands on them within a few seconds, I promise you won't procrastinate looking something up. Don't forget to note their location on the file Index. As a backup reminder, use your Rolodex.

A CPA friend advises her about-to-retire clients to use the collected returns to check the accuracy of Social Security's record of their lifetime earnings. Not a bad idea for us all, since Social Security income is based on that record.

An attorney told me he keeps his other records for three years, as the IRS suggests. I keep some longer. If you have space, consider retaining the special ones. Old files are not only great histories of real estate or business, they are indispensable when you decide to sell. If you file the tax returns and stash those mountains of receipts in the garage, note their location on your file Index, too.

It's hard to believe answers to those Chapter 1 questions seemed hard to get at when we started, isn't it? Now look at yourself. You're ready to take on the world.

So, what's next? The other half of your financial life.

Chapter 8

*K*ey #4:
Profiting with the
Income Monitor

Forms and Reforms

You want to buy a house. "Are you qualified?" That's the first question a successful real estate agent wants answered. The agent takes out a form and asks, "What do you earn? What do you own? What do you owe?" You answer and fill in the numbers. Result? The agent knows if she's gotta *live* one: a ready, willing, and able buyer.

Have you known someone who withheld information for fear the agent would call night and day? Touché. That's how buyers know they've got a live one, too!

But how about credit cards and mortgages? Someone is forever deciding if we're worth the risk. It's routine. They simplify their decisions by using forms. We expect it and accept it. Why is that? Because we know *they* must make smart decisions quickly and accurately. Well, so do we.

We need a form that can help us make quick, smart decisions for our private lives. One that cuts right to the quick. A form we can trust

There is a comfortable feeling about home life that invites us to make casual decisions and carry details and figures around in our heads. It's a misleading notion that we can do this successfully.

That's the reason it's important to put these figures down on paper. Let me tell you a story about the pitfalls of keeping financial matters in your head, instead of writing them down. My neighbors had an avoidable flap that went something like this: "Well," the wife explained, "Harry sold our old car to the yard man. But he only made the one payment. So, after a few weeks, Harry confronted him. The yard man was insulted. He said all along he planned to use his yard earnings to work off the bill. Then Harry got all huffed up, because he intended to use that money right away. It was a real mess. If we'd only known it would take a year to get our money! But they shook hands. It worked out okay."

"Still use that gardener?" I asked her.

"Uh, well, he couldn't fit us in anymore."

Key #4: The Income Monitor

Putting information on paper is a first step. The next step, and equally important, is putting it in a shape that makes it a snap to read. In Figure 8.1, you'll find a form that you cannot be without. Alone, it oversees your income. Coupled with the Living Expenses form, a powerful tool emerges. It's the difference between limping along with only your left shoe on versus running like the wind when you wear them both. Using the pair makes you a winner:

Living Expenses form + Income Monitor = Power Base

1. Clear some space and have in front of you:
   - Your Rolodex
   - Your own Income Monitor (Photocopy the blank form in Appendix A.)
   - Files
   - Pencil and red pen
2. Take out the files for Income.
3. Sort the files into two groups, as we did with expenses:
   - Fixed income—any payment that does not change. Include any income over which you have no control. That's anything "locked in," such as the following:

Social Security	Pensions
Salary (earned income)	Annuities

FIGURE 8.1   Sample Income Monitor

INCOME MONITOR 199....   (as of Sept)

Held (Fixed)	Qty	Item	Peace of Mind	Jan $	Feb $	Mar $	Apr $	May $	Jun $	July $	Aug $	Sept $	Oct $	Nov $	Dec $	Year Total
1st Bank	---	Soc Sec	Jim/dir dep/3rd	972*	972*	972*	972*	972*	972*	972*	972*	972*	*	*	*	*
1st Bank	---	Soc Sec	Jane/dir dep/3rd	640*	640*	640*	640*	640*	640*	640*	640*	640*	*	*	*	*
1st Bank	---	Pension TL Corp	Jim/dir dep/1st	1000*	1000*	1000*	1000*	1000*	1000*	1000*	1000*	1000*	*	*	*	*
Ash St ppty	---	rental (lease)	3-1-95 mail/1st	525*	525*	525*	525*	525*	525*	525*	525*	525*	*	*	*	*
Harris Ins Co	1	Jim's annuity	by mail 15th	185*	185*	185*	185*	185*	185*	185*	185*	185*	*	*	*	*
TOTAL FIXED INCOME--------$				3322	3322	3322	3322	3322	3322	3322	3322	3322				
A G Edwrds	400	Abbott Labs	.68/sh div		68*			68*			68*			*	*	
"	134	Ameri-tech	3.68/sh div		123.2			123.2*			123.2*					
"	200	Black & Decker	.40/sh div			20*			20*			20*				
"	50	IBM	1.00/sh div			12.50*			12.50*			12.50*			*	
"	151	Interste Power	2.08/sh div			78.52*			78.52*			78.50*				
"	100	Marriot	.28/sh div	7.00*			7.00*			7.00*			*			
"	175	Niagra Mohawk	1.00/sh div	43.75*			43.75*			43.75*			*			
"	684	Quaker Oats	2.12/sh div	362.5*			362.5*			362.5*			*			
TOTAL VARIABLE INCOME----$				413.2	191.2	111.0	413.2	191.2	111.0	413.2	191.2	111.0				
GRAND TOTAL INCOME-------$				3735	3513	3433	3735	3513	3433	3735	3513	3433				

- Variable income—everything else, including the following:

  Bank accounts   Rental real estate
  Brokerage accounts   Other investments

  Include every income or account you do control. These are the items you can sell, buy, or borrow against.

  All sorted? Good.

4. Starting with a bank account file folder, take out a recent statement.

5. Copy the vital statistics onto a master Rolodex card and make the cross-references. Here's one idea for a master cross-reference:

   Investment things—
   see—   Banks   Pension
          Brokers   Salary (earned income)
          Insurances   Social Security

   Did I forget anything? Suppose that from this master card you flip to Banks. The Banks card would list the three banks where you have accounts. Choose one and flip to the individual bank card for details.

   Shape the information on your Rolodex to funnel down to specific information fast, like the computers at the library. Are your cards complete? Good.

   Wait! Don't file that bank statement! Handle a paper once and get double results.

6. First, turn to the sample Income Monitor (Figure 8.1). (*Note:* If you are not yet retired, use figures of your *take-home* pay as income.) The form is completed for nine months, so you can look at the past and present income. Later, we'll look at the future.

   The Income Monitor appears to be similar to the Living Expenses form, but notice it has four columns along the left side: Held, QTY (quantity), Item, and Peace of Mind.

   Why the four new columns? Because this form lists and tracks details of individual items. The Living Expenses form groups miscellaneous items under a general category.

7. To begin, imagine each Income file folder as a mystery basket. We know that each basket contains *fruit* (investments). What we don't know is:
   - *Where* each basket is kept
   - *How many* pieces of fruit are in it
   - *What types* of fruit it contains
   - The *condition of each* one

   Since each piece contributes something special to our diet, we must identify, examine, and track each one.

   Refer to the Held column. Under Held, enter the place in which a "basket" is held. For instance, suppose your basket is at First Bank. Enter First Bank in the Held column.

8. But, what's *in* the basket? Under the QTY (quantity) heading, enter the amount of each item:
   - Do you have *one* CD at First Bank? If so, enter 1 in the Quantity column and First Bank under Held.
   - Do you have a savings account and a checking account at the same place? If so, make a separate 1 entry for each Quantity. Use ditto marks under Held.
   - Do you have additional CDs at a single bank? If so, list each CD on its own line and use ditto marks in the Held column.
   - Do you have CDs at several banks? If so, list each as a separate item. Enter 1 under Quantity. Enter each bank's name under Held.

   Once you have completed this Income Monitor, you'll never be confused about which CD is at which bank. You won't wonder about maturity dates, interest rates, or interest payments. It's true. Do this once and you're done! By the way, do you count on the CDs for income? All the more reason to include them on the Income Monitor.

   But, if you track your checking and savings account interest in your checkbook and it gets absorbed without notice, don't include it on the Income Monitor. We're setting up a quick-look snap-to-maintain tool here. It is not necessary to note every penny. Actually, if you add every tiny odd dollar, you'll defeat our purpose. You don't want a big bookkeeping job every month. Keep it simple. Focus on the funds you depend on for income.

9. Now go to the Peace of Mind column. This is the cure for midnight worries. Like a best friend, it will remind you of critical but easy-to-forget details.

   What should you remember about your CD? Here are some questions for CD Peace of Mind:
   - How much money is invested? ($30,000)
   - When did I invest in the CD? (1/2/96)
   - When will the CD mature? (12/31/96; 1 yr)
   - What's the interest rate? (5 percent)
   - How much is that in dollars? (.05 × $30,000 = $1,500)
   - When does it pay? (SA/semi-annually)

   The Peace of Mind column becomes an always-available instant summary of what you did with your money and what to expect. Do you know where to find those answers?

   Make it easy. For each CD, have at hand the bank statement, a notepad, and a master Rolodex card.

   Now call your bank (see Held column) and follow these guidelines:
   - Ask for your call to be directed to the person who can answer questions on an *existing* certificate of deposit.
   - Be ready with your account number (see Rolodex master).
   - Use the questions above as a guide. Fill two cups with one pouring. As you jot down answers, ask where you can find that same information on the statement in your hand.
   - Circle the information with a colored marker. Next time, you won't have to call.

   Getting answers for the Peace of Mind column is easy, once you have the right person on the phone.

   Now make that information *work* for you. For instance, your Peace of Mind column might have abbreviations like these: $30M/1 yr(1-96/12-96); or 5%/SA/J-D/$750 per. Make up your own code.

   Note: On the Living Expenses form we used red dots to remind us of bills. On the Income Monitor the red dots are *income* reminders.

10. Place a red dot in each month an income payment falls due. To remember when your six-month CD will mature, put a *double* red dot in the month of the final payment.

What if it matures the following year? Develop your own footnote system. Try asterisks or crosses, and the like. Use the back of the Income Monitor for long notes or explanations. This is your private reminder.

11. Now, in the appropriate months, *pencil* in the amount of each payment you will receive for the entire year.

Got it? Later, when you get that money, replace the entry in ink same as before: pen for payments received; pencil for payments expected.

Refer to the completed Income Monitor in Figure 8.2.

Bonuses: Time-Saving, Eagle-Eye Management

Using the Income Monitor is a no-brainer way to slash the time it takes to confirm income payments and sharpen money skills. Here's how:

1. The mail arrives. *Before* you open the bank statement, refer to your Income Monitor. See a red dot entered for this month? If so, you should find the payment credited on this month's statement. Okay, now you know what to look for.
2. Open the bank statement. Go directly to credits. Is the payment there? Good.
3. Ink in the entry on the Income Monitor. You're done.
4. File them both, the statement and the Income Monitor.

If the expected payment does not appear on the statement, make a call. Using the information in front of you, and the phone number from the Rolodex, you're all set. Ask to speak to the person who handles statements.

Surprisingly, this system ends nagging. Your being-cared-for parents, Harry, or you can check the bank statement and, with one glance at the Income Monitor, each would know if the payment had been credited. This is especially nice if someone else is standing in for you. No questions needed. How's that for a bonus?

Treat bills the same way. If the Living Expenses form shows a red dot this month and no invoice arrives, make that call. There's no reason for lapsed insurance or penalties on balances.

FIGURE 8.2   Completed Income Monitor

Held (Fixed)	Qty	Item	Peace of Mind	Jan $	Feb $	Mar $	Apr $	May $	Jun $	July $	Aug $	Sept $	Oct $	Nov $	Dec $	Year Total
1st Bank	---	Soc Sec	Jim/dir dep/3rd	972	972	972	972	972	972	972	972	972	972	972	972	11,664
1st Bank	---	Soc Sec	Jane/dir dep/3rd	640	640	640	640	640	640	640	640	640	640	640	640	7,680
1st Bank	---	Pension TL Corp	Jim/dir dep/1st	1000	1000	1000	1000	1000	1000	1000	1000	1000	1000	1000	1000	12,000
Ash St pply	---	rental (lease)	3-1-95 mail/1st	525	525	525	525	525	525	525	525	525	525	525	525	6,300
Harris Ins Co	1	Jim's annuity	by mail 15th	185	185	185	185	185	185	185	185	185	185	185	185	2,220
TOTAL FIXED INCOME-------$				3322	3322	3322	3322	3322	3322	3322	3322	3322	3322	3322	3322	39,864
A G Edwrds	400	Abbott Labs	.68/sh div		68			68			68			68		272
"	134	Ameri-tech	3.68/sh div		123.2			123.2			123.2			123.2		493
"	200	Black & Decker	.40/sh div			20			20			20			20	80
"	50	IBM	1.00/sh div			12.50			12.50			12.50			12.50	50
"	151	Interste Power	2.08/sh div	78.52		78.52			78.52			78.50			78.50	314
"	100	Marriot	.28/sh div	7.00			7.00			7.00			7.00			28
"	175	Niagra Mohawk	1.00/sh div	43.75			43.75			43.75			43.75			175
"	684	Quaker Oats	2.12/sh div	362.5			362.5			362.5			362.5			1450
TOTAL VARIABLE INCOME----$				413.2	191.2	111.0	413.2	191.2	111.0	413.2	191.2	111.0	413.2	191.2	111.0	2861
GRAND TOTAL INCOME------$				3735	3513	3433	3735	3513	3433	3735	3513	3433	3735	3513	3433	42,726

INCOME MONITOR 199.... (as of Sept)

Accountant Stuff

Continue with your Rolodex master cards and cross-references. Then fill in the Income Monitor (with dots, payments, and reminder notes) until you have completed each file Item. You only have to do this job one time, so don't be timid about quizzing bankers, insurance agents, pension reps, trustees, stockbrokers, accountants, attorneys, and other experts, for your Peace of Mind column. You'll thank yourself a thousand times during the year.

Now for the totals. Add the Fixed Income. Add the Variable Income. As we did before, add the columns down, across, and together. Then enter the grand totals, both monthly and annual.

Next make a hanging file for the Income Monitor. Color the tab yellow. Place it in the front of your files—at your fingertips—because you'll use it constantly.

Wait! Are You a *Preretiree?*

Although the already-retired woman might consider all her income as disposable, that's not the case with a preretiree. The working woman must split her income two ways—into monies that can be used now (disposable/spendable funds) and monies that must remain untouched and put to work for a secure future (put-aside funds). Monies put aside have a way of getting into trouble if they aren't tracked.

Luckily we have a form to make the preretiree's double effort a simple one. See the Preretiree Income Monitor in Figure 8.3 and a form titled Monies Put Aside from Payroll in Figure 8.4. Give them a minute of your time and you'll see that they answer three crucial questions:

1. *How much of your income is spendable?* The Preretiree Income Monitor is modified to answer this crucial question for you. See Total Spendable Income in the first column. This is the cash flow that supports your current lifestyle.

2. *How much money have you set aside to be invested for your future nest egg?* It's crucial not to let these dollars fade into a murky haze. Switch to the form titled Monies Put Aside from Payroll. This companion form tracks every *con-*

FIGURE 8.3   Completed Preretiree Income Monitor

PRE-RETIREE INCOME MONITOR EXAMPLE 199....

Held	Qty	Item	Peace of Mind	Jan $	Feb $	Mar $	Apr $	May $	Jun $	July $	Aug $	Sept $	Oct $	Nov $	Dec $	Year Total
SPENDABLE																
Broker Jt Acct	1	Bill's comissn	SS mkt 1st15th	2300*	2450*	3100*	2400*	3500*	2200*	4000*	3100*	2700*	EST.* 2100	EST.* 2100	EST.* 2100	33,350
" " "	1	Bill's bonuses	qrtrly M-J-S-D			250*			265*			340*			210*	1,065
" " "	1	Barb's pay ck	fixed 1st15th	1500*	1500*	1500*	1500*	1500*	1500*	1500*	1500*	1500*	1500*	1500*	1500*	18,000
1st Bnk savings	1	rental income	1st by mail	525*	525*	525*	525*	525*	525*	525*	525*	525*	525	525	525	6,300
TOTAL SPENDABLE INCOME---$				4325	4475	5375	4425	5525	4490	6025	5125	5065	4,125	5,025	4,735	58,715
INVESTMENT INCOME																
Broker: living	400 shs	Abbott Labs	.68/sh reinvstg		68*			68*			68*			68		272
trust account	134 shs	Ameri-tech	3.68/sh reinvstg		123.2			123.2			123.2			123.2		492
@ brkr his IRA	200 shs	Black & Decker	.40/sh reinvstg			20*			20*			20*		20		80
" " "	50 shs	IBM	1.00/sh reinvstg			12.50			12.50			12.50			12.50	50
@ brkr her IRA	151 shs	Interste Power	2.08/sh reinvstg			78.52			78.52			78.50			78.50	314.08
" " "	100 shs	Marriot	.28/sh reinvstg	7.00			7.00			7.00			7.00			28
1st Bnk Jt Acct	$30,000	CD/5% 1yr	to 12/31 pays SA						750* 31st						750 mty	1,500
ABC Ins Co	1	Barb's annuity	Jan5400 @5.4%												ann* reprt	291
TOTAL INVESTMENT INCOME---$				7.00	191.2	111.0	7.00	191.2	861.0	7.00	191.2	111.0	7.00	191.2	841	3,028
GRAND TOTAL ALL INCOME---$				4,332	4,666	5,486	4,432	5,716	5,351	6,032	5,316	5,176	4,132	5,216	5,576	61,743

tribution made for your future, identifies the account, notes whether it is pretax or taxable, and includes matching corporate funds, the dates, and amounts. Okay, you know where your spendable money goes, but do you know where the put-aside money goes, and, the most important point of all, whether it is growing as hoped? That's the third answer the form provides.

3. *What's happening to the money set aside for your retirement?* Go back to the Preretiree Income Monitor (Figure 8.2), to the lower half of the first column titled Investment Income. This section records the income coming from your Monies Put Aside from Payroll (Figure 8.4), while reminding you that it is *not* spendable. It tells you how much is invested, where, and the account in which it's held. In a later chapter, we'll track your overall financial status so you'll know what those put-aside monies have been up to.

As we go along, you'll see how the Monies Put Aside from Payroll form plays a key role in helping you achieve that future lifestyle. By the way, you can also use Figure A.13 in Appendix A to get a handle on how far along you are on the path to your retirement goal. It's quite handy when you're estimating what your retirement income will be.

Need a Booster?

Did we miss anything? Oh, yes. Maybe there is income from the stocks and bonds held in your brokerage account. How do you extract Peace of Mind answers from a brokerage firm statement's gobbledygook? It must come as no surprise that one of the most-asked questions is on how to understand those statements. Designed by demons to satisfy in-house needs, those monthly reports could make anybody's eyes spin.

But don't despair: the next chapter unravels their mysteries.

FIGURE 8.4 Monies Put Aside from Payroll

PRE-RETIREE MONIES PUT-ASIDE FROM PAYROLL 199....(Income Monitor supplement)

Held	Qty	Item	Peace of Mind	Jan $	Feb $	Mar $	Apr $	May $	Jun $	July $	Aug $	Sept $	Oct $	Nov $	Dec $	Year Total
Bill's compny	1	401-K pre-tax	began 1990	115 *	112 *	155 *	120 *	175 *	110 *	200 *	155 *	135 *	150	150	150 *	1,727
same	- -	same " 1:2	compny matched funds			191 *			202 *			245 *			225	863
Barb's compny	1	401-K pre-tax	began 1991	75 *	75 *	75 *	75 *	75 *	75 *	75 *	75 *	75 *	75	75	75 *	900
same	- -	same " 1:2	compny matched funds						225 *						225	450
thru Barb's compny	1	Deferrd Annuty aft-tax	payroll deductm	100 *	100 *	100 *	100 *	100 *	100 *	100 *	100 *	100 *	100	100	100 *	1,200
TOTAL PAYROLL MONIES --$ PUT-ASIDE FOR INVESTMENT				290	287	521	295	375	712	375	330	555	325	325	775	5,140

Chapter 9

*B*reaking the Code of Your Brokerage Statement

Is It a Plot?

Will the investor who understands a brokerage statement, please stand up? Just as I thought—not a one. That's what comes from firms who make their statements be all things to all people—both on the inside and outside of their business. What we customers get is an all-occasion, one-size-fits-all computer spawn. It may be unavoidable, but, too often, it's overkill.

I grant you, the answers we want are on the statement, all right, just like the town of Bird-in-Hand was in Pennsylvania. But, where's the map to lead the way? We'll make one.

Answering the Five Essential Questions

This once-and-only time, have at hand:

- Pencil
- Scrap paper
- A brokerage statement
- Five colored felt-tip pens (red, green, blue, orange, and black)

Wait. Do you see what's printed on the back of the statement? "A guide to your statement." Before you clasp it to your breast like newfound gold, give it a read-through. Is it in Greek? Forget I mentioned it. Set the statement aside.

We're going to do a little role-playing to tame this jungle of information. Assume you represent the brokerage firm. Your job is to design the brokerage statement from the viewpoint of the investor. How do you begin? There are five essential questions that you will need to answer:

1. Who Is Handling My Money?

Every customer wants to know who she is dealing with. Jot down this first requirement on the scrap paper as: Section 1: Introduction (who, what, where).

Now, with the statement in hand, take a look at the first page. It's all there, just as you asked, grouped together for your convenience:

- Firm name and address
- Broker name and phone number
- Statement dates: (01/29/94 to 02/25/94)
- Your name and address
- Your account number and type
- Your Social Security number

Can you find everything? Portions may be hiding in the heading.

Next, let's categorize this information so it catches your eye at first glance:

1. Using a red felt-tip pen, circle all this introductory information.
2. Using the same colored marker, write, 1. Introduction, inside the circle.

2. Am I Worth More This Month Than Last?

That's the bottom line, isn't it, especially if you own stocks? Jot down this second requirement: Section 2: Summary (Comparison/Summary/Review/Snapshot).

Okay, looking again at page 1, find a heading such as Comparison, Summary, Review, or Snapshot. There may be several subheadings—income summary, account summary, retirement summary—and you should include them, too.

1. Using a green felt-tip pen, circle all the comparison/summary information.
2. Still using green, write, 2: Summary inside this circle (or use whichever label explains it best for you).

3. How Is My Money Being Invested?

I mean, if you look in the newspaper for quotes, can you decipher which stocks or funds you own? Many are listed and many sound similar. Your brokerage statement should list and give details on everything you own, including broker CDs and the like. Jot down this third requirement: Section 3: Items in My Account (Account positions/Holdings/Assets held).

Now you're into the body of the statement. Find a heading titled Account Positions, or Holdings, or Assets, or something similar. Each firm uses its own title. Find it? Notice that this section covers the entire list, *every item,* in your account, and may continue onto the next page or so. Scan down the list until you come to Total Account Value (or words to that effect). That's the end of the list.

1. Using your blue marker, enclose this list in a single circle, extending it for as many pages as needed. Include all columns.
2. Label this with a big blue 3: Items in My Acct.

Can you see the statement beginning to separate into categories?

4. What Happened This Past Month?

Did you buy or sell anything? Was your purchase recorded? What about stock dividends or interest on your bonds? And didn't that CD mature? Were the payments credited to your account? On time? Even though you trust in the company's honesty, mistakes happen. I've had lots of clients admit they go nuts trying to keep track. We can fix that. Jot down: Section 4: Activity (Transactions/What happened this month).

The Activity section includes everything that happens, whether generated by you or by automatic payments coming into your account. Find headings like Activity This Period or Transactions.

Since this section tracks both what you *did* this past month and the *cash movement* (just like a bank statement), look for a heading like Ending Balance. That's the end of the activity list. The amount of activity you or your investments generate will determine the length of this section.

1. Use bright orange to circle this list. Include all columns.
2. Label this circle as 4: Activity.

You'll see other figures to the right of these listings; for now, ignore them. This is our once-and-done, find, circle, and label stage.

5. How Much Did You Earn This Past Month?

It would be a great time-saver if payments *into* the account were separated from all the other information. Jot down this fifth requirement: Section 5: This Month's Income (money in your pocket, or this month's interest and dividends).

Move further along on the statement to locate headings for Income Detail. This section does separate and list only those investments that *paid* you this month. Since it omits other activity, it is *not* a list of every item in your account. This is that time-saver section you hoped for, a month's income at-a-glance.

1. Enclose this section in a black circle.
2. Label it 5: This Month's Income, using the same black pen.

Does your statement answer the investor's five essential questions? If you are a client of any of the major securities firms, the answer is "yes." Also, if your account includes a checking account, charge card, loan, or outstanding orders, there will be additional sections. Make them visually friendly, too. Enclose them in color and label them.

Now, step back and take a look at the whole statement. What do you think? Feel like a lion tamer? So much for the jungle.

Instant Benefits

Being at ease with the brokerage statement smooths out bumps of insecurity. Hearing well-intentioned platitudes, whether from an adviser or spouse—"Don't worry about it, I'll take care of it" or "Don't worry about it, we're fine"—doesn't make for middle-of-the-night peace of mind. Every woman likes to *see* that all is well—in black and white. That's a fair request; yet a woman on her own may feel too intimidated to speak up. With couples, the uneasiness breeds arguments.

She says, "If you can't show me what we've earned, just put the money in the bank! It's simpler." He asks, "Don't you trust me?" Phew! Your knowing where to look for answers is a godsend. And just because your elderly mother can no longer do her own book work doesn't mean she doesn't care, either. Being able to pinpoint the right detail on a brokerage statement is worth a thousand comforting words.

Power Base Details

Now that we've set up categories on the brokerage statement, let's extract the details we want for our Rolodex. First, find the vital statistics and transfer them to your Rolodex master card. See Section 1: Introduction (circled in red).

While you're in that category, underline the account number and the statement date. It will come in handy when you review your statements in sequence.

By the way, note the account title and type on the Rolodex master card. Here are some examples:

- An individual retirement account:
  BROKERAGE ACCT—(#1 of 5)
  Sarah/**IRA**/#321-45678-012
  AG Edwards/1111 E First/Your City
  Frank Broker/123-456-7890
- A Joint Account:
  BROKERAGE ACCT—(#3 of 5)
  Sarah & Harry/**Jt**/#321-87654-012
  AG Edwards 1111 E First/Your City
  Frank Broker/123-456-7890

The *type* is an IRA. The *title* is who owns it. You can create a string of cross-references for multiple accounts. For instance, suppose at brokerage firm A you have two IRAs (one for you and one for Harry), a joint account, your sole account, plus the one you have with your daughter. For simplicity, make one general cross-reference card. This master card might read:

Brokerage Accounts: (5)
    see—Brokerage—Harry's IRA
    see—Brokerage—Sarah's IRA
    see—Brokerage—Sarah & Harry (JT)
    see—Brokerage—Sarah (Sole)
    see—Brokerage—Sarah & daughter (JT)

Tip: If you title five cross-references as Brokerage Account, code each one individually as #1 of 5, #2 of 5, #3 of 5, etc.

Make the Key Connectors

Wait! Don't file that statement away. We've got to take information back to the Income Monitor (see Figure 9.1).

1. From Section 1: Introduction on the statement, take the brokerage firm's name. Enter it in the Held column of the Income Monitor.
2. Find Section 3: Items in My Account (circled in blue). Easy to spot? Okay. Circle these subtitles:
   * Quantity
   * Description (of each item)
   * Estimated annual income

These columns are "kittens" under the main category.

3. On the statement, place an asterisk next to each item that has an entry under the Estimated Annual Income column. Not all investments pay income. Skip those that do not. Include all dividends or interest credited to your account, whether you spend it or not. Skip stocks and bonds that don't pay dividends.
4. Next, copy only the asterisked items to the Item column on the Income Monitor.

FIGURE 9.1   Income Monitor

INCOME MONITOR 199.... (as of Sept)

Held (Fixed)	Qty	Item	Peace of Mind	Jan $	Feb $	Mar $	Apr $	May $	Jun $	July $	Aug $	Sept $	Oct $	Nov $	Dec $	Year Total
1st Bank	---	Soc Sec	Jim/dir dep/3rd	972*	972*	972*	972*	972*	972*	972*	972*	972*	972	972	972	11,664
1st Bank	---	Soc Sec	Jane/dir dep/3rd	640*	640*	640*	640*	640*	640*	640*	640*	640*	640	640	640	7,680
1st Bank	---	Pension TL Corp	Jim/dir dep/1st	1000*	1000*	1000*	1000*	1000*	1000*	1000*	1000*	1000	1000	1000	1000	12,000
Ash St ppty	---	rental (lease)	3-1-95 mail/1st	525*	525*	525*	525*	525*	525*	525*	525*	525	525	525	525	6,300
Harris Ins Co	1	Jim's annuity	by mail 15th	185*	185*	185*	185*	185*	185*	185*	185*	185	185	185	185	2,220
TOTAL FIXED INCOME-------$				3322	3322	3322	3322	3322	3322	3322	3322	3322	3322	3322	3322	39,864
A G Edwrds	400	Abbott Labs	.68/sh div		68*			68*			68*			68		272.-
"	134	Ameritech	3.68/sh div		123.2*			123.2*			123.2*			123.2		493.-
"	200	Black & Decker	.40/sh div			20*			20*			20*			20	80-
"	50	IBM	1.00/sh div			12.50*			12.50*			12.50*			12.50	50-
"	151	Interste Power	2.08/sh div			78.52*			78.52*			78.50*			78.50	314.-
"	100	Marriot	.28/sh div	7.00*			7.00*			7.00*			7.00			28.-
"	175	Niagra Mohawk	1.00/sh div	43.75*			43.75*			43.75*			43.75			175.-
"	684	Quaker Oats	2.12/sh div	362.5*			362.5*			362.5*			362.5			1450-
TOTAL VARIABLE INCOME----$				413.2	191.2	111.0	413.2	191.2	111.0	413.2	191.2	111.0	413.2	191.2	111.0	2861
GRAND TOTAL INCOME-------$				3735	3513	3433	3735	3513	3433	3735	3513	3433	3735	3513	3433	42,726

5. From the statement's quantity column, copy the amount of each item into the QTY column on the Income Monitor.
   - Sh = shares of stocks/funds
   - Dollar amount = bonds
   - Number of units = limited partnerships
6. Finally, find the estimated annual income for each item. Pencil those figures into the Year Total column on the Income Monitor. Refer again to the example shown in Figure 9.1.

If your statement does not provide this information, call your stockbroker (after the market closes). The broker has the information at her fingertips. You can ask all the necessary questions to complete the information on your Income Monitor. Don't be shy; you'll only have to quiz your broker this one time. Besides, any good broker likes working with an informed investor.

Here are some suggested questions to ask your broker:

For each stock:
- What is the dollar dividend per share? (Peace of Mind) This is the annual dividend.
- How often does it pay? (Peace of Mind)
- Which months does it pay? (Red dots)
- What is the dollar amount of each payment? (Enter each in pencil.)

Per-share $ dividend × Shares you own = Annual total

Annual total $ dividend ÷ 4 payments = $ amount per payment

For each bond:
- What is the interest rate? (Peace of Mind)
- How often does it pay? (Peace of Mind)
- Which months does it pay? (Red dots)
- What is the dollar amount of each payment? (Enter in pencil.)
- What is the maturity date? (Peace of Mind)
- What is the rating? (Peace of Mind)
- Is there a call date? (Peace of Mind/note on back)

For mutual funds, Ginnie Mae mortgages, limited partnerships:

- What does it pay? (Peace of Mind)
- How often does it pay? (Peace of Mind)
- Which months does it pay? (Red dots)
- What is the dollar amount of each payment? (Enter in pencil.)
- Is part of the payment a return of principal? (Note on back.)

By the way, do you want a report on a mutual fund? Ask your stockbroker about the Morningstar service. And if it isn't available at your public library, ask your broker to order it. (See Appendix B for more information.)

Check the Credits at a Glance

Are you beginning to see how the Income Monitor helps form a power base? In seconds, you can see how much income you're supposed to get, every single month. You can see if a check is late. Ah, but will you know if checks are credited to the account? Were they credited in a timely manner? Let's see:

- Go to the brokerage statement, Section 5: This Month's Income (circled in black).
- Look for the payments that have been credited. See them? Do the payments match up with those red dots on the Income Monitor? If so, the payments credited to your account should match the red dots.
- Update the Income Monitor. Replace this month's expected entries (those in pencil) with ink to show that they have been received. Again, the rule is: pencil for payments to come; ink for payments received.

Now for your second question: Were the payments credited in a timely manner?

- *Go to* Section 4: Activity. (Circled in orange.)
- *Look for* the dates on which the income was credited. It shows the date the money hit your account and where it went next.

Money arrives into a cash account (sort of the train terminal of accounting) before it moves into the money market. It moves out of the money market only on your instructions.

Can you see where your cash balance went? This section should show a debit to cash and a matching credit to the money market. This extra little step is sometimes confusing to investors. The only time a cash balance is a concern is if it is allowed to *sit* there. Since cash balances earn practically no interest in their limbo state, call your broker and ask why that money isn't in the money market. Your broker will realize you are on the ball if you call this to her attention. And, you are!

That's it. File the statement without looking at the other sections. Follow our financial commandment: Thou shalt not read a statement pointlessly, but shall set a purpose in mind, accomplish it, and withdraw. For now, our only purpose was to select what was needed for the Income Monitor.

Your Safe Deposit Box

Any other hurdles? Do you have income investments in your safe deposit box? That's no problem. The Income Monitor will work for them in exactly the same way:

- *Enter* Safe Deposit Box in the Held column.
- *Note* in Peace of Mind how the checks come to you. By mail? Direct deposit? Or is the income reinvested?
- *Use* red dots for the expected dates. (Your stockbroker can give you dividend and interest answers even though the items are not held in the account.)

Reinvested Income

Suppose you reinvest your dividends: are they still considered income? Yes. You don't have to *spend* the dollars to list them on the Income Monitor. Lots of people like to reinvest dividends until they decide to spend them. That's similar to rolling over a CD without spending the interest. You still want to know it's been earned and paid, don't you? So, yes, include reinvested interest and dividends on the Income Monitor.

If your living costs go up, dividends are an additional source of spendable money. You would simply notify the corporation that instead of reinvesting dividends, you now wish to receive them. In the past it was not possible to reinvest stock dividends if shares were held at a brokerage firm. That is no longer true. Check with your broker. If you reinvest dividends on shares held at the brokerage firm, their statement will show the additional shares. That's good news for you. For each stock, that's one less piece of paper that comes through the mail.

Is it true that if an investor doesn't take cash dividends, she doesn't have to pay income taxes? Sorry, not true. The IRS knows you *earned* it. Dividends are taxable when paid.

Other Statements and Income

- *Finish* up the Rolodex and cross-references for each income file.
- *Make* the one-time phone call for expert assistance on the payment information.
- *Complete* the payment details with red dots and pencil.
- *Add* the columns.

If you get stuck on other statements, call the appropriate account expert. If you can't understand their answers, hang in there. It's not you. It means the explanation was foggy. Contact the manager. There is never a time when your money should be doing something that is confusing to you.

By the way, did you notice? By building the Living Expenses form and the Income Monitor, you have just created your own system of checks and balances.

Chapter 10

*K*ey #5: Digging through Your Mail with the Bill Payment Center

*W*e could skip this chapter if the mail suddenly stopped coming. But it won't and we can't. Clutter marches on. You are *more* organized, but what good is that if there's no way to dispatch that daily delivery? In only one week there will be mail on the table, and mail on the desk, and mail on the dresser, obliterating our achievements! So we've got to do something with the mail. I have a suggestion—try it out. Dispatching the mail is what drove me to find this power Key #5.

Adding *Extra* to *Ordinary:* The Fifth Key

In a line of office equipment at the local discount store, I found a unique file box called a Bill Payment Center (by Fellowes). (See Figure 10.1.)

At first glance, it looks like any other ordinary file box. But the Bill Payment Center is a real powerhouse. It isn't designed to simply *store* files and whatever else gets stuffed into it. This well-thought-out item picks up on our desire to just get stuff out of sight. It satisfies the urge to procrastinate. And it gets rid of clutter without problems. Seems too good to be true, doesn't it?

FIGURE 10.1   Bill Payment Center—Key #5

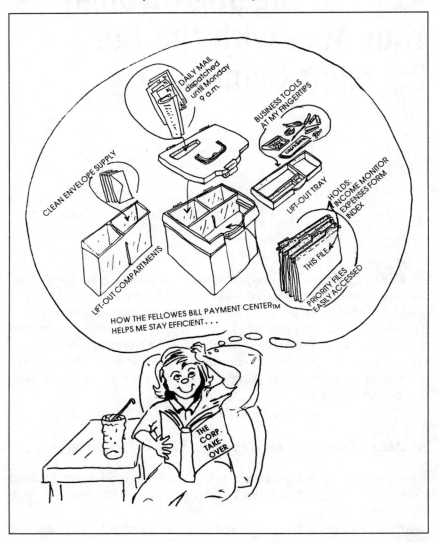

The secret to the Bill Payment Center's effectiveness is the slot in the lid, coordinated with inside service and support compartments. That's all there is to it.

How could a slot in the lid of a file box suppress clutter? That's a fair question. Now I have one for you. Where do you keep your car keys? Chances are, on the way into the house, you drop them on the entry table along with your purse. On the way out, you pick them up. Am I close? Most of us do the same. We keep often-used essentials at our fingertips. Why not do the same thing for often-paid bills? The Bill Payment Center, with its slot, provides an instant drop-off spot for important mail. It's safe and convenient. It's at your fingertips.

This portable file box whose praises I am singing is made of a smart-looking durable plastic that fits unobtrusively under my desk. It comes in a variety of colors and costs about $10. Before you run to the closet for a shoe-box substitute, let me tell you more about it, and how it aids in the victory over mail clutter.

After you open the security lid, you will find a divided tray just beneath. The tray has the capacity to hold every essential needed to pay bills and update records—postage stamps, pens, calculator, checkbook, and so forth. At your fingertips.

Lift out the tray and you find three separate compartments below. One compartment holds the mail (or to-be-filed papers) dropped through the slot in the lid; the second stores clean envelopes for correspondence and bill paying; and the third, and largest, is designed to hold files for monthly bills and accounts.

I know you have too many files to use this as a file cabinet substitute. We all do, but that is not its purpose. Before we go further though, I have another question for you: Do you keep your dyed-satin heels in the front of your clothes closet? My guess is you don't. Because these shoes are for special occasions, they are most likely pushed to the back of your closet or stored in a box—definitely not at your fingertips. On the other hand, I can guess that your sneakers, slippers, flats, business heels—any shoes you wear regularly—are lined up at the front of your closet where you can get at them in a second.

You have set priorities. It's something we do unconsciously about many things. We stack everyday dishes conveniently above the kitchen counter and place special serving pieces in the dining room. Regular bath towels are at our fingertips; others lay carefully folded in the linen closet. If we didn't automatically set priorities in our daily lives, keeping first things first, we'd likely end up like old Uncle Stanley. He's forever on his knees, head in the refrigerator, rooting through the pities to find his horseradish. If you're wondering about *pities,* they're leftovers. You know, it's a pity to save and a pity to throw out—like those papers that come in the mail.

When Less Is More

Now, let's streamline the business side of our lives following these simple seven steps:

1. Collect the files (hanging files, too) for the bills you pay frequently—monthly, bimonthly, quarterly. Add to them the files for income you receive.

    Tip: For a shortcut, check the red dots on the INCOME Monitor and Living Expenses form. You'll know exactly which files to collect.

2. To that stack, add files that hold the Index, Income Monitor, and Living Expenses form.

3. Now make up new files titled Entertainment/Dues, Miscellaneous, and Save for Taxes. Add these to the stack. All together, these files make up your most active, *priority* files.

4. Hang the priority files in the Bill Payment Center. Voilà! Your most-used files are prioritized and portable—and at your fingertips.

5. Station the Bill Payment Center at a convenient spot for drop-in use. Retrace the steps you follow now when the mail arrives and set the Bill Payment Center in a spot that does not force a change of your habit. Where do you sit down to look over the mail? I use a nearby desk so my Bill Payment Center sits under it—out of sight, and at my fingertips.

6. Now in the regular file cabinet, in which you house your permanent files (that's everything else), set aside a *priority* section at the very front of the drawer.

7. Label new file folders and hangers to *duplicate* those you just inserted in the Bill Payment Center. Hang the duplicates in this priority section of the file cabinet. These *priority backup* files will absorb the in-depth information needed to support the active priority files in the Bill Payment Center.

Why Bother with Duplicate Files?

We duplicate the priority files because it is the secret to maintaining clutter-free, fingertip ease—permanently. Remember our motto: once and done! Your files need breathing room. For example, suppose you set up a nice clean file for your health insurance, an HMO. In it are all the current statements and necessary papers. The file fits nicely in the Bill Payment Center. It's neat and simple. But, as we all know, nothing stays the same. A few weeks pass and along comes the mail with new HMO backup information. Three hefty booklets! Where can you put them? Should you toss them?

One booklet lists all available health providers. Seems you should keep it on hand, just in case. The second explains in detail how the program operates. Hmm . . . probably should keep it for reference. The third is more stuff you don't want to read right now. Just get them out of sight. But where?

They don't fit in the priority hanging file and folder you set up. Do you stuff them in anyway as you might have in the past? How long will it be until you look at them again? How often will you look at them? You want to keep them, but these booklets are not priority. *Warning:* They are the beginning of that old clutter. The answer? Stash them in the duplicate *priority backup file* in the filing cabinet. Your problem is solved. When the time comes that you need to review them, you'll know exactly where they are. Meanwhile they aren't in the way of active business. Phew!

Let's consider an example of how this system might work for your auto insurance files:

- *Priority:* Current statements, pertinent notices for this year; filed in the Bill Payment Center—at your fingertips
- *Priority backup:* Original policies for current coverage, correspondence affecting current coverage (can include several years' information); filed in the front section of permanent file cabinet—easily accessed
- *Historical backup:* Documents, records, history of coverage and policies; stored in the back of the bottom drawer in file cabinet or in garage—rarely accessed

Now you no longer have to shuffle and root through a jumble of stuff to find one paper.

Save the final section of your main file cabinet for *truly* inactive files—souvenirs, old letters, and anything you want to hang on to. Or if you have a commercial business, or special interest, devote a whole file drawer to it. Allow the same levels of priorities and include a special Index for these categories.

Now, update your financial Index. Your files are ready.

Here Comes More Mail—Are You Ready?

You used to handle it the old way: The mail arrived. You flipped through it, pulled out what looked interesting, and parked the rest until later. Am I close? Then you would make a little stack, knowing you'd get back to it—later. Everybody does that, too. But when the next batch of mail arrives, is the first stack still—you know, waiting?

You get busy with other things. Maybe the second day's assortment of mail adds to the first pile? Or maybe you have a way of stacking the new mail in a fresh stack so you can tell which came first? There's nothing wrong with you. That's a habit of human nature. Why fight it? Let's work with it.

We aren't robots. We like to take time and glance at the goodies. Maybe there's a happy surprise in the mail. If not, why waste time deciding what to do with each piece? It's easier to walk away. So what's the solution?

Try this for two weeks when the mail arrives:

1. Immediately:
   - Open and extract checks.
   - Move the checks to your wallet (for that quick trip to the bank).
   - Save the envelopes (as a reminder that you received the check).
   - Once you update your Income Monitor toss the envelope.
2. Next:
   - Sort out first-class nonpersonal mail (including those retained envelopes). Take a second to glance at the return addresses, but don't meander *aimlessly* through these. You know what they are.

- Drop the whole lot into the Bill Payment Center slot for safe holding.

3. Stack personal letters next to your coffee cup to be read— after completing these brief steps (that took you less than a minute). Don't forego the pleasure of reading them. Personal letters are a rare treat. Enjoy.

    By the way, you've never tossed those personal letters on that "later" pile, have you? At least not until you've read them? What about afterwards? Do you then set them aside until later? No more. Once you decide to answer those letters (no matter when), they become priority business.

4. Drop already-read personal letters through the slot. When you sit down to do the bills and filing, the letters can be answered. If you put birthday cards down that slot, maybe you would never buy another "belated" one. It helped me. My friends smile at me again.

5. Next, deposit magazines on the coffee table. What's left? Junk mail.

6. Toss the junk mail into the trash. Ouch? You can't throw away junk mail without looking at it? Okay. Will you try a When I'm Bored basket? You'll know it's all there waiting for you when you're in the mood to investigate that surprise catalog item or free offer.

Phew. We did it. Everything is dispatched. Enjoy your coffee and letters.

Never Say "Later"

What's been dropped in the slot is top priority. It's safe and out of sight. Nothing will be lost or scattered. No guilt. No worry.

Does out of sight equal out of mind? That's a legitimate concern. A friend told me about the disastrous family reunion she was hostess of. She'd forgotten to pay the electric bill. Her husband's family never liked her anyway, she said, and—well, we need reminders.

When do you tend to your bills and filing? Do you set aside a special day and time, or take care of each bill as it arrives?

Make a Date

Pin down a *definite* day, time, and place, to take care of business. Never think that you'll do it later. It's too vague. Later never comes. Instead, tell yourself "Monday, 9 AM, at the desk." Be definite. Name a time and place you can mark on the calendar.

See yourself sitting in the chair, the convenient Bill Payment Center at your fingertips, the aroma of hot coffee emanating from your favorite mug. Visualize it now. Because the Bill Payment Center is portable, you might imagine yourself beside the pool, an iced tea at your side. It's your movie.

Got the picture? See the clock in your scene? Is it 9 AM? Good. Now, when you drop envelopes down the slot, your brain thinks, "These bills are safe and ready for me until 9 AM Monday."

Still worried that you might forget? Tie the bill-paying job to another routine activity, something you *never* skip, like grocery shopping or the weekly laundry. Those chunks of time between loads of wash are too brief to go anywhere and too long to sit idle, tapping your foot. But they might be perfect for your new simplified way of doing bills and correspondence. By noon, clothes, finances, and the cat litter can be all cleaned up for the week.

If you need a visual reminder, try this client's suggestion. Draw a smiley face—a boy or a man—with needle hair. Give him a tee-shirt lettered: B-I-L-L. Add a cartoon balloon over his head that says "Pay Me!" Put him on the fridge.

We have alarms on clocks and buzzers on ovens, so who's to say Bill shouldn't be on the refrigerator? Or on a golf bag or on the calendar?

It's Time

It's 9 AM Monday. Here's the drill: Before you open that first envelope, scan the Income Monitor and Living Expenses form for red dots. Do you see which bills and checks are due this month? Good. Let the dots save your time.

Suppose the brokerage statement lists 20 account items but you have only five red dots that represent activity. You just eliminated 75 percent of the usual effort. Record payments for the five dots. You're finished. Do the same for bill payments you make to others.

This is a quick and accurate, no-brainer system. If a check or expense entry isn't on the statement, the Income Monitor or Living Expenses form entry remains in pencil. If it's past due, make a phone call.

Toss those easy-to-lose credit card receipts down the slot, too. When the statement arrives, you're ready. Check them off, pitch out the ones you no longer need, and drop the others in the Save for Taxes file. No clutter. You can have flowers on the dining room table again.

Chapter 11

*F*inding Emergency Money in Minutes

So Long, Phobia

Has our organizing effort been worthwhile? You bet. You can't compile the Living Expenses form and the Income Monitor without gaining financial insight. I don't know what your situation is, but you do, and that's what we're about. Do you know how few people have their ducks in a row? Give yourself a pat on the back.

The next time you call up about your savings account, you'll have the Rolodex open, the phone number dialed, and a smile on your face. You'll be ready, with names and facts at your fingertips.

But it's not only that. How about those dizzying monthly statements you used to save but never read? You've nailed that coffin shut, too. No more glazed eyes. Who cares if statements are one-size-fits-all? You know the secret: Zero in on a specific item and ignore the rest. One more difficulty dispatched.

Ready, Set, Go!

Everything is in place. Now, let's tackle another important question from Chapter 1. Take out these three of your keys:

1. Income Monitor
2. Living Expenses form
3. Rolodex

You are the president and owner of this well-managed business. That means you're in the driver's seat. Got a notepad?

Let's find out how to shop for money answers as fearlessly as we do for shoes. When needed, you'll call reliable sources, ask smart questions, compare choices, and make sharp decisions. Best of all, as you see the answers emerge (and they will emerge), you'll begin to trust yourself. Feeling confident? An actor once told me nervousness makes for the finest performance. House lights up!

Here's the question: *It's January. You need $2,000 for a dire emergency. Where will you find it?*

If you don't understand investments, you'd probably go straight to your savings. Good choice. Whether you understand investments or not, it makes sense to look in the easiest place first. You have fine instincts; trust them.

If you find that extra $2,000 in savings, write a check. Your emergency is over.

If you are hesitating, you have to wonder why. Is it that nagging inner voice, preying on your uncertainty? Maybe you're suddenly wondering if that $2,000 in savings is really *extra* money. Let's find out.

Key In on Details

1. Lay your Income Monitor and Living Expenses form side by side.
2. Zero in on the grand totals from both forms (Income and Expenses) for January. That's the bottom number on the Income Monitor, where you added up all of January's income. On the Living Expenses form, it's all of January's expenses.
3. Jot down those totals, assigning them to four columns: Month/Income/Outgo/Balance. Our purpose is to *see* the

flow of money as in Figure 11.1. (There is a blank form for you to photocopy in Appendix A.)

4. Using your calculator, subtract January's outgo from income. The balance is your *net* cash flow. It can be plus or minus.

Income – Outgo = Balance (either + or –)

5. Repeat steps 2, 3, and 4 until you see at least six months' cash flow, January through June.

Suppose that in January, you spend more than you earn. Your balance is a minus answer. Does that mean you can't touch that $2,000? No.

Here's an old saying I just corrupted: Jumping to a conclusion based on one month's cash flow is like the blind man describing an elephant after touching only its tail. You need to grasp the whole picture.

Take a good look at the six-month picture of your money. Can you take $2,000 out of your savings today? Consider these questions before you decide:

- Is the money needed to make up income shortfall?
- Is it being held for a large payment coming up?
- Will it be replenished naturally over the coming months?
- Can you soon replace it from another source?

Picture Money in Buckets

Figure 11.1 illustrates a cushioned cash flow across one full year. Like our other forms, the Cash Flow worksheet is a shortcut to answers. It allows you to see how money flows. Visualize your savings account as a bucket and your money as a liquid.

We'll start with an empty bucket. Now imagine a spigot above it. Turn it on. A flow comes into the bucket. That's steady and predictable income. As it fills the bucket, it forms a financial *cushion*. On the example, you can see the bucket filling up.

Now imagine a spigot attached near the bottom of the bucket. When you turn that on, the flow goes out of the bucket. That's the uneven and often unpredictable outflow of expenses. At times, the cushion runs low. It may even gush out.

What happens if you start the year with an empty bucket? Well, if your furnace breaks down, there's no ready cash to pay the repair bill. Instead of an annoying repair, you've got an emergency. The financial world calls that dry bucket a state of *illiquidity.*

Illiquidity can create a crisis. It forces you to scrounge around looking for money in a hurry. For comfort and flexibility, stay liquid. Maintain enough cushion money to cover unforeseeable expenses. Easily said? Yes, the challenge is figuring how much is enough!

There's an easy way to find out how much cushion you need. On this example, I jotted down 12 months' income and outgo, subtracted, and did a running balance. You can see what happens each month.

The buckets show what the numbers prove, that the level of liquidity is constantly changing. In the illustration, January begins with $2,000 in the bucket (your cushion account). The level drops in January, April, June, and September. Is that a problem? No.

Fluctuation is normal. Look at the month of December. By the end of the year, the bucket is filled up four times higher. Financial life is lumpy. When you look at the whole year, you can see that the drop in January is not a threat.

How much cushion is enough? There is no precise answer, but it should cover at least common situations. First, try to allow for the typical unexpected events, such as replacing tires or having the garage door repaired. Add to that the cost of deductibles. Find this figure by adding together all cash outlays for which you are responsible *before* your insurances kick in (home, auto, health). Add the cost of copays in the event of hospitalization.

Finally, if you depend on a wage that might be unexpectedly disrupted, add three months' living expenses. If you rely on pensions and Social Security that are not likely to be disrupted, you can cut that to 30 days' living expenses. Use the Living Expenses form, Income Monitor, and Cushioned Cash Flow worksheet to make this easy. As an extra, include travel money. It won't be touched unless you're on your way.

Every business sets up a credit line to see it through lean periods. Your financial business is no different. This cushion account, which provides you with liquidity and financial flexibility, is your private credit line. You won't be forced to borrow or sell in an emergency. And, you don't have to pace the floor at 2 AM when the cushion is low. Just look ahead. You can see that the dip is temporary.

FIGURE 11.1   Cushioned Cash Flow Worksheet

CUSHIONED CASH FLOW   199...

MONTH	INCOME -	OUTGO=	NET CASH	
January	3735-	4682=	(947)	dip into cushion
February	3515-	1342=	2173	add to cushion $
March	3433-	2011=	1422	" " "
April	3735-	6593=	(2858)	dip into cushion $
May	3515-	1373=	2142	add to cushion $
June	3433-	4327=	(894)	dip into cushion $
July	3735-	1697=	2038	add to cushion $
August	3515-	1438=	2077	" " "
September	3433-	6771=	(3338)	dip into cushion $
October	3735-	1633=	2102	add to cushion $
November	3515-	1311=	2204	" " "
December	3433-	2127=	1306	" " "

	Jan -	Feb +	Mar +	Apr -	May+	Jun-	Jul +	Aug+	Sept-	Oct +	Nov +	Dec +
Carry frwrd $2000	(947)	2173	1422	(2858)	2142	(894)	2038	2077	(3338)	2102	2204	1306
	1053	3226	4648	1790	3932	3038	5076	7153	3815	5917	8121	9,427
Cushion $ 1053												$9,427

Too often, widows fear they are sliding into a bottomless pit when the cushion gets low. Looking ahead on the Cushioned Cash Flow worksheet is free therapy that brings peace of mind.

When the Cushion Isn't There

If your cash flow numbers show that you can take $2,000 out of your savings, write the check. You've examined your situation and satisfied yourself that you won't be caught short. If the numbers show that you can't touch the $2,000, you need to look elsewhere.

Where should you look? Some clients have confessed to selling mutual funds for quick and easy emergency cash. Good idea? Not so hot. It can be a high-cost solution. (See details in Chapter 15.) When and if you look to your other assets for emergency money, there are a few things you need to know—before running for outside help. These include:

1. What to ask about each investment
2. Who to ask
3. How to compare those answers to find out:
    *   which choice gives you money fastest?
    *   cheapest?
    *   easiest?

Let's decide what to do.

Selling Is Easy—Is It Best?

You can sell an asset and end the emergency. But should you borrow instead? Do you feel confident to decide on your own? Do you know how to borrow against your own assets? Or who to ask?

It's tough to get the right answers unless you ask the right questions. And how do you find the right questions? It's like applying for that first job to get experience, when no one will hire you unless you have experience! Truth is, too often investors sell a perfectly good investment just to get the whole dilemma over with. We're going to put the picture in focus. Your decision, your choice, will be made with confidence. Stay with me, there's a shortcut.

Read through the sample Looking for Cash (Borrowing) chart in Figure 11.2. In the left column are ten must-ask questions. Across the top are different investment types. In the blocks are general answers to get you started.

Remember, take the information in this book and make it your own. Every rule has an exception. Every rate changes. Basics remain the same, but make your own chart for up-to-date accuracy in details. Photocopy and complete the blank Looking for Cash forms in Appendix A. One is for borrowing (Figure 11.2); the other is for selling (Figure 11.3). You can use the blank forms to:

- List your own investment types.
- Make the calls to the "experts."
- Jot down abbreviated answers.

Don't forget to protect this chart. It will be easy to understand, important, and confidential. When it's completed, place it in a labeled file folder. File the folder inside the file hanger titled Investments.

Calling Glitches

Making calls is not as easy as it sounds. Who's the expert on the other end of the phone? We make a call, explain what we want, and sit on hold. We get passed on to someone else, repeat our story, get put on hold. We tell it again, get put on hold—geez. By the time we've listened to all of the elevator music and commercials and questions, our ears are numb, and we've forgotten why we phoned. It's easy to bag it and hang up. Why is it so tough to get the answers?

I wish we could smooth out the bumps, but it's an imperfect world. You might as well know what the answer search entails. As my sister reminds me when I'm faced with tough stuff, "You can handle it. You st-rong woman!" I pass it on to you. Just laugh and keep plugging. Here's what 45 minutes on the phone with bank personnel brought me:

Call #1: Computer greeting, "If you want . . . punch 4, if you want . . . punch 3, if you want . . . punch 5. Now enter your account number." I didn't have an account number. I called again: ten minutes—t-e-n—on hold. Finally, I reached a live person.

FIGURE 11.2   Looking for Cash (Borrowing)

Questions for borrowing	Passbk Savings	CD	Stocks	Bonds	Mutual Funds	Defer. Annuty	Whole Life Ins	Real Estate
Can I borrow against it?	avail. cash	gen. yes	yes/if stk. eligible	yes/ but muni int taxable	maybe	no/but int may be avail	yes/if has cash value	yes/if has enough equity
How much can I borrow?	------	% of value	changes/ up to 50%	varies: to 75% val	depends	w/d % int (no bor)	see last statement	% equity
How soon can I get the money?	Immed.	1-2 days	2 days	2 days	depends	w/d int 10-14 days	10-14 days	allow sev wks
Do I have to sign papers?	------	yes	yes	yes	yes	yes/ask for cash w/drwal	yes	yes/note trust deed etc
Are there up-front costs?	------	if sell CD	no	no	no	w/dwl penalty?	no	yes / % of loan
Are there other costs?	------	lose % of interest	yes/float int ea day	yes/float int ea day	same as stocks	w/dwl is IRS txble	yes/talk to agent	yes/ask title offcr.
Must I make payments during the loan period?	------	no	if value drops lots	if value drops lots	if value drops lots	cannot repay	co does in-hse	gen yes monthly
Do I still earn (interest or dividends) during the loan period?	------	yes/ reduced	yes (div)	yes (int)	yes/if any	------	yes but ln offsets	ppty val not impaired
What happens when the investment matures?	------	rec prin /net int	does not mature	rec prin /net int	does not mature	lower retire inc	dth bene reduced	due on sale
Provide these figures: a. what I will have at maturity with loan? b. what I will have at maturity without the loan?	------							
Speak to:	Teller	Accts supv.	stockbrkr	stockbrkr	stockbrkr	insr agnt stkbrkr	insr agnt stkbrkr	real est loan officer

*************************LOOKING FOR CASH***********************************

FIGURE 11.3   Looking for Cash (Selling)

Questions for selling***	Passbk Savings	CD	Stocks	Bonds	Mutual Funds	Defer. Annuty	Whole Life Ins	Real Estate
Can I cash out or sell a portion?	yes/withdrawl	usually/ask	yes	sell min block/ask	yes	make withdrwl	withdraw cash val	yes
How soon can I get the money?	immed.	w/n week ask	w/n week ask	w/n week ask	w/n week ask	approx 2 weeks	approx 2 weeks	close of sale
Are there selling costs?	-------	no	yes	yes	depends/ask	no	no	yes
Are there penalties for selling?	-------	usually/ask	market value risk	market value risk	market value risk	under age 59 1/2	withdrwl ask	market value risk
Will the proceeds be taxable?	-------	profits	profits	profits	profits	profits	profits	depends ask CPA
How much will I net?	-------	ask for figures	ask for figures	ask for figures	ask for figures	ask for figures	ask for figures	ask for figures
Do I have to sign papers?	-------	ask	no	no	no	yes	yes	yes
***								
Speak to:	Teller	Accts supv.	stockbrkr	stockbrkr	stockbrkr	insr agnt stkbrkr	insr agnt stkbrkr	real est loan officr

EACH INSTITUTION'S POLICIES MAY DIFFER AND
EACH INSTITUTION'S POLICIES ARE SUBJECT TO CHANGE

*******************LOOKING FOR CASH***************************

Call #2: Receptionist did not want to answer questions and did not know who would. I figured she was a temp; at least I hoped so.

Call #3: Got a live one. Our conversation went like this:

Me: "I have an existing CD at your bank. Can I borrow against it?"

Rep.: "No, we don't lend on CDs."

Me: "Do you offer loans on *any* accounts?"

Rep.: "Yes, we have a 'savings-secured' loan available."

Me: "What qualifies as 'savings-secured'?"

Rep.: "Umm, a certificate of deposit."

Think of it as a game—a treasure hunt. All my calls weren't disasters. Several banks had the information. From two, I was delighted by knowledgeable answers.

Since my questions were only an exercise, I was persistent and calm. But, if I'd been strung out by an emergency? Yikes. Prepare yourself. I think it was the great financier Bernard Baruch who said, "I can't cross a bridge until I come to it; but I always like to lay down a pontoon ahead of time."

You must find the right spokesperson. On every phone call, identify your purpose and ask for a representative by name or title. If you reach an informed live person, the odds for success skyrocket.

This is what I found:

- At the bank, I had success with the new accounts person, the new accounts supervisor, a personal banking officer, and a financial services officer.
- At the brokerage firm, it's easier. Just ask for your stockbroker.
- At the insurance agency, ask for your agent.

Warning: Don't look to a receptionist. Her job is to smile and serve as a traffic cop.

Dig in your heels. Persist politely. There's nothing wrong with you. It's these computerized-disorganized (is that an oxymoron?) times. Do it your way. Don't digress. You aren't buying anything. You don't have time to hear about other products or ideas. Focus and go.

After the Call Is Over

Take a quick glance at the finished chart. Compare the choices. Can you eliminate some choices at first glance? Most? All? You may not have to do the entire chart to find the best answer. Look at all sides of a question. Just because you *can* do something (like borrow against investments), doesn't mean you should. Financial experts can show you what can be done and how to do it. That's their contribution; also, it's their business.

Now make your contribution in the best interest of your business. Take the experts' numbers and filter them through your emotions (Would you worry or lose sleep?); your attitudes (Do you suspect complications? Will you lose control?); and the pressures of your situation (Do you trust them to watch the account?). Just one "no" is a red flag. Take it as a warning that this is not the choice for you. Like the carpenter, think twice, act once.

Should you consider taking a margin loan on your stocks? Only if it's obviously quicker and cheaper. If you borrowed in January and could repay the loan by August, when you have extra cash, borrowing against stocks may not seem scary. Just remember, even a steady stock can bounce around in value and you can't control the direction of the overall market. Therein lies the downside of this loan.

Be sure you understand the margin call. We'll use a single share of stock to see how a margin loan works. Suppose you own a $100 stock and borrow the maximum the brokerage firm permits. Let's say that's 75 percent of its value, or $75. The stock certificate with its remaining $25, or 25 percent value, is left in your brokerage account as security. (The idea is similar to the real estate lender requiring a 20 percent down payment before lending you 80 percent as a mortgage.)

If the stock market stumbles and your $100 stock drops drastically—say to $75—the brokerage firm's security is gone. You now have an unsecured loan. That will be quickly remedied. The firm will notify you to immediately put up money to reestablish the firm's position of safety. This means you'll have to find some fast cash, which is what got you into the margin loan in the first place.

Suppose you've evaluated your situation and the margin loan makes sense. No one can give you a more expert analysis. The facts—the best place to borrow and how and when you'll repay—are on the charts you've put together. Trust yourself and your expertise. Then, once the facts convince you intellectually, check in with your emotions. Uneasiness means don't do it. Confidence means go ahead.

Whether you withdraw cash, borrow, or sell, you'll have made the decision on your own—with understanding.

Chapter 12

*U*sing the Five Keys for Instant Answers

A young professional gave me a glowing report. "I bought this great house as soon as I got the job," she said. "It has a fabulous view. Now I'm furnishing it just the way I've always dreamed." I asked how many years she had been with the firm. "This is my first," she grinned. "Actually, it's been only five months."

A few days later we met again and completed two keys, the Living Expenses form and the Income Monitor. In only five months she had spent seven months' income. "But how did this happen?" she gasped. "I can't believe it! I never thought . . . " The cause is less important than the shock that brought her to her financial senses. As she sat looking at the two forms, I asked one question: "What have you spent so far this year?"

Sound familiar? This was the second question asked in Chapter 1: *"Your accountant called. What have you spent so far this year?"* You can get that answer in a minute. Take out your Living Expenses form and calculator. Then, supposing this is the end of March, add together the grand totals for January, February, and March. You can do this while your accountant is still on the line. Not too shabby for a spur-of-the moment quiz, hmm?

That's fingertip expertise. Your accountant will wonder how you did it. Compare that answer to what you have *earned* so far this year. That's an instant fiscal checkup!

Now let's move on to the tough questions about what happens when trouble hits home. This information is not just for married women, by the way. These are common questions that might affect any family member or even a friend or neighbor who needs your help. For example: *Your husband is seriously ill. What happens to his pension and/or Social Security if he dies? Do the payments end? Are they reduced? If so, by how much? Do you know the steps to take to find out? What would your total income be if you were widowed? Would it be* enough?

The Irrevocable Income choice

Up until a few years ago, a working man could choose to take—without his wife's input—the maximum retirement pay offered for his lifetime. It seemed a good move. He retired, income flowed, and family life went on as usual—as long as he lived. But when he died, the pension died with him, leaving his widow flat broke. It was a disaster for her.

Today, the Equity Act (please note it was passed as recently as 1984!) requires the wife's input. If she agrees to his choice for the maximum payout for his life only, she gives notice that she is *aware* that she will receive no further pension upon his death.

This is how it works: The employer notifies the employee of this option when it's time to make retirement decisions. The following is an excerpt taken from a letter sent by a corporate benefits department to an employee. The italics are mine.

> . . . If you are presently married, the normal form of payment is a 50% Joint and Survivor benefit unless you elect otherwise. This form of payment would provide *continuing payment to your spouse* or beneficiary in the event of your death, but with reduced payments to you during your lifetime . . . The retirement Equity Act of 1984 requires that *both you and your spouse sign and notarize* the enclosed Joint and Survivor Annuity *Waiver* Form if you elect a form of payment *other than* a Joint and Survivor Annuity.

A wife would not sign the waiver if they agreed to adopt the normal, preferred, *Joint and Survivor* option. That means the pension payments are based on two life spans. When the retiree dies, the survivor continues to receive checks.

If your Harry retired before 1984, perhaps he chose the payment for his life only. What's done is done; that cannot be changed. But, if he's not yet retired—and unless you are *absolutely* certain you won't need his income if you are widowed—take the Joint and Survivor option.

Okay, let's assume you will continue to receive income under the Joint and Survivor option. That next question is: Will the income be enough? We can't answer that unless we have real dollars to work with. Let's get them.

The Pension Interview

If your husband is retired, call the pension department of his former employer. Have in hand his Social Security number, birthdate, and identifying information from his pension checks. If he is not yet retired, have in hand the annual report on his prospective pension benefits. Don't forget to jot down these details in your Rolodex.

Speak to an employee benefits representative. Be patient: Wait until that person has your husband's file in front of him. You need specific information.

Here are some points to cover:

1.   Confirm that your husband's pension payments are set up as Joint and Survivor.
2.   Can the representative estimate the payout? (This can also be found in the company's annual *benefits report* to your husband.)
3.   What happens to the payout at your husband's death?
4.   What percentage of his income will you receive as his widow? How much is that in dollars? If he has had prior marriages, does that affect the payments?
5.   Will the payments continue for your lifetime?
6.   Are health benefits continued for your lifetime?

Note the answers on the front of a manila file folder labeled Pension. Include the date of the call and the person contacted. Keep the file folder handy for our next step.

What Will Social Security Provide?

Both you and your husband probably receive the free annual Social Security report titled *Estimate of Social Security Benefits.* Despite that, call the Social Security office to ask about your benefits as a widow. The phone number for Social Security is 1-800-772-1213. Enter it in your Rolodex. Have ready your husband's Social Security number and birthdate. Jot down answers on the front of your Social Security file folder.

Ask the representative what income you will receive as a widow. Here's what I learned from one representative: A 60-year-old widow receives approximately 71 percent of her husband's monthly payment. At 62 she'd receive about 82 percent. The 65-year-old widow receives the full payment. *But the widow under 60 is not eligible for payments.* (Ask what happens if disability is involved.)

Social Security also has a booklet called *When You Get Social Security Retirement or Survivor Benefits.* It discusses marriage, divorce, disability, and lots of other situations—and it's free.

Often, women believe they'll get two Social Security checks, but it doesn't work that way. Call them and get your answers first hand. You may have a choice between your check or his, but not both or a combination of both.

Put Your Keys to Work

Now you have real dollar amounts to work with. Take out the Income Monitor and the Living Expenses form. We'll see if your widow's income is enough. Got your calculator?

Figure your situation two ways (use blank forms):

- When your Harry retires, will there be enough income?
- If Harry died, would you have enough income?

Too many couples have never sat down and discussed this in detail. Scary, huh? To find out how this will affect you, follow the next three steps:

1. On the Income Monitor, think "retirement scenario": Substitute Social Security and pension figures for Harry's present salary.

2. On the Living Expenses form: Business costs will be gone; subtract them out of the Living Expenses form.
3. Side by side: Subtract total expenses from total income.

You did it. Not such a big job, was it?

Can Harry afford to retire? Good. Show him the figures. In his deepest deep he may not believe he'll ever be able to. Won't he be surprised if you can show him he can? Next thing you know you'll be setting a date and looking at travel brochures.

Now, for peace of mind, take a good look at the "what if you are widowed?" scenario. Repeat the same steps on the Income Monitor and Living Expenses form, adjusting the income and expenses accordingly. Subtract total expenses from total income.

Okay. Is the income enough?

I know this is gruesome conversation. Some women don't like to tell their husbands they're examining financial life without them. But I think a man is relieved to know the woman he loves will be okay. It's as if he'd still have his arms around you.

Widows Need Cushions, Too

Before we go further, do a Cushioned Cash Flow worksheet for each of the two scenarios. Take a look at the buckets. Do you have a cushion in the retirement scenario? And what does the cushion look like for the widow scenario?

Will your income be enough? Yes? Great. Enjoy peace of mind about your finances. If the answer is no, you will be faced with decisions. You may not like them, but at least they're out in the daylight. Let's see if there's a way to beef up the income.

Reconsider your widow's income and expenses. Did you trim away excess variable expense? For instance, you wouldn't need two cars. That reduces repair, gas, and insurance costs. Go over each item.

How about the fixed expenses? Test each one. If you can't shave costs without making drastic changes in your lifestyle, then let's look elsewhere. Don't be afraid to know the facts. Maybe you can replace the lost income. There's no time like the present to learn about investments and other risk management.

Refer to the chart How Long Will Your Money Last? in Appendix A. It shows what happens to your money over time, when a specified portion of principal is regularly taken. If you must gradually dissipate your savings, seeing the results played out in black and white may help you sleep at night, worry-free. If this is a choice you'll make, set down details, including taxes or any other hidden costs that can affect the process. Meantime, let's consider another strategy that does not touch principal.

A Way to Replace Lost Income

Suppose the picture painted by the Income Monitor and Living Expenses form shows that you would have a monthly shortfall of $500 as a widow. Is there anything to do now to avoid it? Possibly.

Is your husband in good health? At 6 percent, $100,000 produces $6,000 a year in income. That's $500 a month. You need $100,000. Where can you find it? This is a classic situation to consider insurance. Maybe your husband could be insured for a $100,000 term life insurance policy. Reliable companies issue policies that guarantee no premium increase for ten years. Do you have $130 or so extra spending money available each month for premiums? Let's find out.

The Keys Help Again

Take another look at the cushion in Figure 11.1 as an example. At year's end, there is an excess that might be applied to an insurance premium.

Now look again at the Income Monitor and Living Expenses form for your retirement scenario. Will that cushion be called on for living expenses? No? Then there's your answer. Yes, you have enough money available to pay an insurance premium and ensure your financial security if you are widowed. By the way, will your mortgage be paid off in a few years? That money will then be available for living expenses. Insurance is one idea to consider.

Another idea is to build up your savings. That would help replace the income shortfall. How do you decide?

Use your calculator. You'll find in Figure 11.1, based on saving the extra money at the end of the year, that Harry would have to live another lifetime to save $100,000. Well, maybe you won't need that much. But, what if you decide to build your security through savings and he dies after one year of retirement? Or five?

It's a real risk for you. Too few savings and too little time. In a situation like this, life insurance is the better choice. It guarantees payment of a lump sum. Your lifetime income will be assured.

Real Caring

Talking life and death is hard, but I think you're in for a pleasant surprise. Financial security is a gift we give each other. You'll feel good knowing your husband will be financially okay. Give him a chance to feel the same about you.

Show him the Income Monitor and Living Expenses form scenarios you worked out. Once he sees Now, At Retirement, and As a Widow, in black and white, he'll be pleased you've worked it out and relieved that you can talk about it freely with each other. Seeing the facts together will give you both peace of mind. No financial planner could do better.

Chapter 13

*C*onsidering Bonds

*W*hile we're on the subject of income, let's talk about bonds. Suppose you've been enjoying income from a bond that was chosen by someone else—your husband or maybe a family member who left it to you in a will. Since the bond has performed true to its reputation for convenience and dependability, all you've had to do is cash the interest checks! Well, all good things come to an end. The bond has matured and the lump sum sits in your account, earning little. What do you do? That real-life dilemma brings us to another Chapter 1 question: *A bond matures. Can you choose a proper replacement?*

Women need to know how to choose an appropriate bond. Otherwise, when a bond matures, they run for cover in the money market or savings account. That's a double-dip negative; not only is it a costly choice, it's also risky. I've seen women's bank accounts exceed the security level of FDIC insurance while at the same time their income shrinks because they settle for the scant interest paid.

Would you put up with *anything* to avoid making a choice? Sorry, but when you have to make a choice and don't make it, that *is* a choice. If uneasiness is the cause, let's replace it with confidence—plus a higher income.

Basics Go a Long Way

Sidestep bonds for a moment. Think about the common every-day ability to walk. Suppose you didn't know how. How would you learn?

How *did* you learn? By understanding the detailed physical movements of taking a step? Did you memorize which leg muscles expand and contract; which joints move; how weight shifts from foot to foot; how to maintain balance? You get the point. A clingy novice would be frightened by too many technical facts. To take that first step you'd have cried for help—for an *expert* to be at your side, in case you stumbled.

Well, each of us did have someone at our side for support when we took those first steps. Not an expert in physiology, just some-one to get us pointed in the right direction. Once we caught onto the basics, the rest was up to us. And we're doing just fine!

It's the same with investing; only instead of muscles, bones, and balance, we face explanations of products, formulas, and trends. No wonder we run to experts or hide out in the familiar old-time savings account. The very thought of choosing bonds—or stocks—calls up shivers.

Some people take walking to sophisticated levels: they run, dance, or ski. But simple walking provides a basic all-purpose way of getting where you want to go. So the aim here is not to turn you into sophisticated high rollers of the financial world, but to show you how to quickly master basic all-purpose, solid investing skills. They'll take you where you want to go.

What It Means to Own, Lend, or Borrow

If we followed Benjamin Franklin's advice, "Never a borrower or a lender be," this country would grind to an instant halt. Owning, lending, and borrowing are part of our routine. They *are* our rou-tine. Except for spending, all we can do with money is own, lend, or borrow. And you've already done all three.

You *own* your house, you *borrowed* to buy it, and you have a savings account or CD, which actually is a *loan* to the bank. You might not think of these everyday transactions as *investing*, but they are. And Wall Street investing is doing more of what you al-ready do.

A stock certificate represents *ownership* in a corporation. A bond certificate represents a *loan* made by you. All else, every investment we hear about, involves either of these two activities— lending or owning—or a fancy combination of both. And now you have the basics.

But if that's all there is to it, how can we account for the mountains of magazine articles and newspaper advice columns and how-to books? You've heard about selling the sizzle? We wouldn't want Wall Street without Madison Avenue glamour and mystery, would we?

Investment Spawn

There are at least hundreds of investments. Your stockbroker may come up with a new idea every week. You're no dummy, but maybe it makes your head swim. Well, your stockbroker's ideas aren't really new. They are newly titled, fancied-up versions of owning and lending.

A fool and her money are soon sought after. If you don't have direction in your financial life, the sound of a fresh investment idea is tantalizing. To ward off foolish mistakes, decide where you want to go. Create your own map and follow it. Stay with mainstream places and people. Stay with simplicity in investments. You'll get where you're going.

Bonds Have Been Around a Long Time

You would invest in a bond for two basic reasons: It pays income and, at maturity, your investment money is returned intact. That's the promise of a bond. It's the real-life vehicle that satisfies that investment maxim: Get a return *on* your money and a return *of* your money.

Are bonds safe? Some are and some aren't. There are questions to ask, all based on the answers to these questions:

- Will this bond pay the promised interest payments?
- Will you get your money back when it matures?

Maybe you'd rather close your eyes and rely on the stockbroker's say-so? Please, never do that. And you don't have to go the other extreme and argue either.

Like the loan officer at the bank, you must also ask questions. Who wants to borrow your money, for how long, for how much, and what sort of risk are they? You are a smart investor. Don't take your stockbroker's opinion for the quality of the borrower. Follow familiar routines. If you were at the local department store, you'd look for product labels, right? You favor certain manufacturers, especially if they have proved reliable in the past. Relying on a label is better than expecting a salesperson to know if a toaster is wired safely.

You can check out bonds the same way. Would you buy an electric appliance that wasn't UL-approved? Would you prefer an appliance that carries the reputable Good Housekeeping Seal of Approval, despite the sales pitch you hear about brand X? If you choose brand X and it fails to perform, you are the one who's stuck, not the retailer. It's the same with bonds.

Luckily, bonds are rated for quality by independent entities. Ask the broker about ratings. Just like the appliances at the department store, there are many nonrated choices around. A nonrated bond may be great or not so great. We just don't know. Shopping among nonrated issues is akin to taking that chance on brand X. The only bonds you want are those that are *rated.*

A rating is determined by the bond issuer's ability to perform: to pay interest and principal to the bondholder—that's you. The rating assesses the likelihood of default, exactly what you need to know. It's like an inspected toaster.

Where Are the Ratings?

You don't have to dig to learn the ratings on bonds, this is where your stockbroker does her stuff. Every reliable broker (in a reliable firm) has up-to-the-minute rating information at their fingertips. The best-known and nationally recognized rating agencies are Standard & Poor's Corporation and Moody's Investors Service, Inc. Don't bother to memorize those names. Ratings are publicly available, known, and used industrywide.

You can collect information on bonds without investing. What I mean is, like any purchase, sometimes the retailer doesn't have what you want. That shouldn't keep you from asking, looking, and learning. Good salespeople (all stockbrokers are salespeople) will be interested in finding what you are looking for. They will contact you when the specific item you want is available. And, like anything else, if you have changed your mind in the meantime, that's your right. You are in charge.

When the broker asks what kind of bond you want, be ready with your requirements. Let's find out what they are, one step at a time:

1. How is this bond (issue) rated?   Don't be timid, the reliable stockbroker expects this question. As a matter of fact, she should first ask you what rating you want.

At this moment, you may not be able to name a rating, but you do know you want something *safe*. The highest ratings are *triple A* (AAA), *double A* (AA), or *single A* (A). Bonds rated *C* indicate the highest degree of speculation. As Mark Twain said, "There are two times in a man's life when he should not speculate: when he can't afford it and when he can." Enough said. Don't waste time looking at a broker's entire inventory.

2. Why does a reliable brokerage firm offer risky bonds?   The firm is a retail store that serves shoppers from around the world. There is something for everyone.

Since you are looking for the safest choices, ignore everything except those rated A or better. Don't misunderstand: Even a AAA rating is not a guarantee; it does, however, indicate top quality.

3. Does the broker offer bonds with guarantees?
Yes. Ask for *insured* bonds or U.S. government-*guaranteed* bonds. On an insured bond, the issuer (not the brokerage firm) has bought insurance to cover both principal (your investment) and interest payments (earnings on your investment) in case some unforeseen problem arises.

4. Why would you choose insurance instead of the U.S. government guarantee?   The interest payments on U.S. government bonds are subject to federal income tax. If the insured bonds are municipal, they are *usually* income tax free. Always ask.

Hometown Bonds

Again, a tax-free bond is a *municipal* (muni) bond. As you know, every level of government needs more money—local governments, state governments, and our federal government. When they want to repair or build, they borrow.

It's the same process you and I go through to buy or build a house. We borrowers shop the lending marketplaces: banks, savings and loans, credit unions, etc. We obtain a mortgage by promising to pay back the principal and interest for 30 years. We pass creditworthy standards (probably with a AAA rating) and sign loan papers (a legal IOU). At the time we *issue* the IOU, the bank lends the money. They are the debt holder, and they are also the *investor.* They look forward to 30 years of income from us. Meanwhile, we build our house with the loan proceeds.

Actually, all around you are other homeowners who have issued IOUs to their lenders. Since the banks enjoy support from our payments, it seems a shame that we can't name them as an exemption on our income taxes. You know, like a dependent aunt?

Now, go down the street from the bank to another marketplace that puts borrowers and lenders together—the securities firm. Here the process is the same but the characters switch roles. Now you become the investor-lender and debt holder (bond holder), and the municipality becomes the borrower who issues the legal IOU (the bond certificate). Your money flows through the brokerage firm to the borrower.

Follow the money path on this bond:

1. You invest in Center City's Burnham Highway bonds.
2. Center City uses the money to pay for construction of a crosstown freeway, called Burnham Highway.
3. Each day you drive downtown on Burnham Highway, you toss a quarter into the scoop at the toll booth.
4. Your quarter goes to pay interest to Burnham Highway bond holders.

That's a *revenue* bond. Your quarter is the revenue. Have you ever paid the Pennsylvania Turnpike tolls? On behalf of those bond holders, I thank you.

Because you can't sit across the table at a town meeting and discuss these projects, the bond certificate tells you the story. It describes the project or other purpose the money will be used for. It tells you where the money will come from to pay you back. It tells you when the bond will be fully paid and how much interest it will pay until then. It will even tell you if the issuer can pay off the bond early.

Other Bond Types

Sometimes interest and principal are paid from taxes or special assessments. General obligation (G.O.) bonds are secured by the full faith and credit of a government body with taxing power.

A U.S. government bond is an IOU backed by the U.S. government. If you hold U.S. government issues, you are one of the lenders that support the debt you hear about on the evening news. The U.S. Treasury needs us—and our money. I'm sure you're glad to help out. How big is the debt today?

Did you know that, counting one dollar a second, it takes 11.57 *days* to count to $1 million; 31.69 *years* to count to $1 billion; and 31,688.09 *years* to count to $1 trillion? As of the first week of August, 1996, the national debt was reaching $5 trillion, almost five times that 31,688.09 years of counting. Imagine paying 5 percent on $5 trillion. We are.

The broker can help you select bonds of corporations, such as IBM or AT&T. Their debt issues are called *corporate* bonds. Unlike most municipals, corporates are taxable, just like a CD or U.S. Treasury bond. If you want to delve further into bonds, see the suggested readings in Appendix B. Our focus here is the what, why, and how of choosing.

Ready to Name a Rating?

Let's say you have decided that you want to choose a bond from your broker. First, you want it to be a AAA tax-free bond. Good. Maybe that's what you had before. Now, what bond maturity do you want? That depends on when you want your money back. Typically, the longer the term, the higher the rate. With a CD, you give up access to your money for the term you select and it remains tied up. Have you ever been stuck? My neighbor's car gave out and he had to ride the bus for six weeks while he waited for a CD to mature. It added an hour to his commute, but he decided it was better than cashing in the CD early and losing money.

It's the same with bonds—any kind of bonds—all bonds. Even though a bond is safe, insured, or guaranteed by the U.S. government, you might lose money if you cash it in early. Never forget that. Use the five keys and Cushioned Cash Flow worksheet to avoid inappropriate choices.

Are there set penalties for selling a bond before maturity as there are for CDs? No, but there is a risk of price change. That mystery will be cleared up later in this chapter.

Back to Hometown Bonds

Refer to the article in Figure 13.1 to learn how bonds originate. Then, here's an assignment: If your town decides to build new schools, roads, or, perhaps, a water treatment plant, ask your stockbroker about the bonds. It's a great way to learn the behind-the-scenes story firsthand. Also notice how much your taxes jump to pay for those school bonds and road bonds. And then, remember, if you become a bond holder, you'll be paying yourself! Small world, huh?

How to Be Liquid and Safe

The most talked about and probably least understood aspect of bonds is the impact of the maturity date on a bond's value. Suppose you buy a bond at its face value (par) and two months later it is worth 15 percent less; should you feel uneasy? That's what we're going to find out. Understanding this point is crucial to successful investing.

So far, you can tell the stockbroker you are looking for a municipal bond that is tax free, AAA, and insured. Now she asks what maturity you want. Think about it: How long should you lock up your money?

Should you go for the term that pays the highest income? Maybe, and maybe not. Your choice will depend on your situation. You have to live with the decision for a long time. Remember my neighbor who set a financial trap for himself by tying up his money in a too-long-term CD? When he needed to get at the money to buy a

FIGURE 13.1 The Birth of a Bond Issue

Ashland to vote on school bond

By GORDON GREGORY
of the Mail Tribune

ASHLAND — On March 12 voters of School District 5 will decide a $20.9 million bond issue to, among other things, expand the overcrowded middle school and replace the ancient Mountain Avenue complex at the high school.

In unanimously approving the bond issue at Monday night's regular monthly meeting, the school board embarked on what it hopes is a 50-year effort to renovate and upgrade all district buildings and facilities. It anticipates that similar bond issues will go before voters roughly every decade.

"It's a continuation of many steps," said board member Alan DeBoer, who noted that a bond issue approved 10 years ago for the high school library ends next year.

If approved, the money from this bond would be used to:

■ Build a 280-student addition to the middle school. Many sixth-grade students still attend class in the district elementary schools, or at a church adjacent to the middle school. The addition would not eliminate what many see as a need to replace the entire middle school building at some point.

■ Tear down and replacing the high school theater complex that also contains a number of classrooms and the school cafeteria.

"It's the school building . my grandmother went to," board member Kent Provost quipped of the 90-year-old complex.

"It is an old building crumbling away."

It's also been determined to be the building most likely to collapse in an earthquake.

■ Add a music facility to Briscoe Elementary School. The old music building has been condemned and students use a nearby church for music class.

■ Spend roughly $2 million on new buses and roof repairs, expenditures that would otherwise come from the stagnant general fund budget.

■ Buy enough new computers to equip all classrooms with multiple computers.

If approved, the bond would raise taxes about $1.55 for each $1,000 of a property's assessed value. That would tack about $230 onto the annual property tax bill on a $150,000 home.

Bond supporters point out that the library levy of some 40 cents per $1,000 of value will end next year so the impact will be buffered.

While Ashland residents almost always approve school funding measures, the defeat of a bond to deal with middle school overcrowding several years ago worries some. That loss has been attributed to a lack of community education.

Source: Reprinted courtesy of *Mail Tribune,* Medford, Oregon.

new car, he was faced with a penalty for cashing in the CD early. He avoided the CD penalty only because he delayed his new car purchase. But solutions to a cash squeeze aren't always so simple.

Get the Whole Picture

Before you invest $10,000 in bonds, let's see how this investment works. While there is no penalty for selling a bond before it matures, a bond's value is subject to *market risk.* You recognize that. It's what you suffer through when you sell real estate.

You buy a house for a specific price. Will you sell it for the same price? Who knows? The buyer's offer will be affected by what's going on at the time, such as: Are mortgage rates low? Are loans easy to get? Are there other houses for sale that are in competition with yours? Because the sale of your house is subject to market risk, its exact sale price is unpredictable. You may profit, break even, or suffer a loss.

Now switch back to bonds. You invest $10,000. Will you get your $10,000 back? Yes, on the maturity date. What will you get if you sell before then? Who knows? The buyer's offer is subject to market risk, such as: Have interest rates moved? Is the rate on your bond competitive? Are rates stable? Is there a large inventory in competition with your bond? As a result of influences like these, you profit, break even, or suffer a loss.

But the similarity ends there. The *difference* between real estate and bonds is that bonds escape market risk on the date they mature. Real estate is forever subject to market risk because it does not have a maturity date.

Our goal for investing is to eliminate the unknown. Select bond interest you can live with and maturities you can wait for. We'll see how to do that later on in this chapter. In the meantime, to make sure it doesn't happen to you, take a look at what happened to hypothetical investor "Sheila" and her bonds.

Buy More Than Rates

Sheila decided to put $10,000 in AAA-insured municipal bonds. Her stockbroker told her that five-year bonds were paying 3 percent. "Are you *happy* with 3 percent?" the broker asked.

"Not really," Sheila replied.

"I didn't think so," the broker laughed. "Let's see what else we've got—here's an issue at 6 percent."

"That sounds better," Sheila agreed. But as she handed over her $10,000, she noticed that the 6 percent bonds didn't mature for 20 years. Was that important? She hesitated. Would the competitor across the street have short bonds at 6 percent? "Ah, hold up on that," she said. "I'll be right back."

So off she went to compare. But it was no surprise when, across the street, she found pretty much the same choices she'd just seen. The major brokerage houses are tapped into the same mainstream marketplace. Their information is up-to-the-minute and covers the whole market. And, since the municipal market is competitive and active, everybody knows what's going on. That's to the investor's advantage. But be careful—get competitive quotes about identical quality, type, and maturity. Compare apples to apples.

Satisfied that the major brokerage firm where she was sitting was a good place to do business, Sheila took out her calculator. She wanted to know what the 6 percent interest rate meant in dollars and cents (.06 × $10,000 = $600). It meant she'd earn $600 a year. She decided that was okay. The $600 would buy a video camera this year, computer next year, a fax machine the following year, and so on. Well, it was enough. So, with a shrug, she decided the maturity date wasn't all that important. The deal was done. She owned and still owns $10,000 AAA-insured, 20-year, tax-free munis at 6 percent.

Did she make any mistakes?

Sheila has held the bonds for five years of their 20-year life. All has gone well. The interest payments have arrived as promised. But now she needs a new car, and because she forgot to set aside a *liquid* cushion account, just like my errant neighbor, she must cash in these bonds. Will she get her $10,000 back? We'll see.

I mention to Sheila that I happen to have $10,000 to invest in bonds.

"Want to buy my AAA-insured bonds?" she asks.

That would work out nicely, wouldn't it? If I pay her $10,000, I'll get 6 percent income on the bonds, and she'll get the cash for her new car. Let's see if it's a smart investment for me. I need up-to-the-minute information. I flip open my Rolodex and call my stockbroker to do a little comparison shopping. You know how values change. My stockbroker knows what's happening in the financial world.

"What's today's interest rate on a 15-year AAA-insured municipal?" I ask my stockbroker.

You might think I've made an error, asking about 15-year bonds, because the bonds Sheila will sell me are 20-year AAA-insured bonds. But her bonds have only 15 years left to run. I want to know what others of like maturity are paying. That's how I can tell what interest rate to expect. It's that apple thing again.

"Rates are up," the broker tells me. "Today, 15-year AAA-insured municipals are paying 12 percent." (I wish.)

Wow! Today I can get twice as much interest on my $10,000 if I invest in 15-year bonds. Suddenly Sheila's don't look so good.

Take out your calculator. Figure the interest paid on 12 percent bonds. (.12 × $10,000 = $1200) Wouldn't you rather have $1,200 in income instead of $600?

There is nothing you and I can do to avoid movements in interest rates. Market forces cause the Federal Reserve to act on rates in an attempt to influence our economy. Our job, since we are on the receiving end, is to find ways to withstand the impact of those movements. That means making investment choices with built-in flexibility. Otherwise, the squeeze will come.

Let's get back to the $10,000 bond investment and see how the squeeze occurs. Once Sheila learned that current 15-year AAA-insured bonds are paying 12 percent, her hackles go up. "You mean I'm *stuck* with 6 percent? Then I got taken by that stockbroker?"

Did she? I don't think so. Sheila succumbed to the delicious lure of the highest rate. Dieters know all about that weakness. At the tempting sight of gooey chocolate layer cake, they shove their hands in their pockets and chant, "A moment on the lips, forever on the hips." Curb your financial appetite. Once you take that *highest* rate, it's yours to the end. No pun intended.

In the heat of the moment, 6 percent looked good. So good, compared to a mere 3 percent, that Sheila forgot to think about that 20-year maturity date. Twenty years! That's longer than an '80s marriage.

Where were you 20 years ago? Changing diapers, maybe? Was your income the same as today? Have your taxes or cost of living increased? Do you live in the same house? Has its value changed? Remember $35,000 houses and 14 percent CDs? How about 35-cent ice cream cones? Who could have guessed everything would be so different? Or so expensive?

No one knew for sure, and that includes the experts. The only reliable guarantee about the future is that it holds more changes. The secret to choosing successful investments, especially bonds, is to be ready to take advantage of those changes. Build in flexibility.

It's a painful eye-opener to be locked into a *fixed* investment when all about you is changing. You may suffer financial injury from which you can never recover.

The Cost of Illiquidity

What's going to happen to Sheila? Maybe I'll buy her 6 percent bonds. "Let's bargain," I tell her. "Will you take $5,000?"

She's insulted. "No thanks, friend, I'll sell through my stockbroker," she says.

Good move.

Her stockbroker quotes a similar price, saying, "Sorry, that's today's market." So Sheila decides to take her chances with me. "Will you pay me $9,000?" she asks.

"No, sorry," I tell her. "$5,000 is my best offer. To get a 12 percent return on your bonds, I'd have to buy them for $5,000. ($600 ÷ $5,000 = .12.) No reasonably informed investor would settle for less than the going rate." That means her $10,000, 6 percent bonds are worth much less on today's market. But, six months from now, who knows? If a drastic occurrence sent interest rates plunging to 2 percent, her 6 percent bonds would sell at a profit.

"So my safety efforts, choosing insured AAA bonds, have done nothing for safety of principal after all." Sheila throws up her hands.

"Not true," I remind her. "Your interest payments are protected. The entire principal will be paid at maturity."

"But, if I sell now, when I need cash," she reasons, "those numbers on paper will turn into real dollars and slip through my fingers. Gone forever. I'm going back to my savings account."

Sheila is convinced that security lies in a savings account. In truth, a large part of security depends on *flexibility.* Make it a cardinal rule, clad in iron, to set aside *liquid* cushion funds. Figure out your cushion needs from the Cushioned Cash Flow worksheet. Bonds are long-term investments. Keep cushion money short term, as in money market accounts and 90-day Treasury bills. If you select the appropriate investment, you create your own guarantee to avoid a cash squeeze. We'll discuss some examples later on in this chapter.

Liquidity Creates Opportunity

If Sheila had accepted the lower interest on the five-year bonds, they would have matured and she'd have her $10,000. With the $10,000 in hand, she could reinvest $5,000 in new bonds at the current higher rate. Happily, that would pay her $600 annual income. With the remaining $5,000, she can shop for her car. That's doubling her financial opportunities—and all because of flexibility. Instead, because she cashes in the 20-year bonds early, she loses $5,000, gives up the $600 annual income, and still has only $5,000 to use toward a new car.

There's more to an investment than the highest rate. Every choice must fit your situation.

Sheila's AAA-insured bonds were safe, but they were not liquid. If you force yourself to sell early, that's not a bond problem; that's an *investor* problem. And it's widespread. Even the government has trouble with this concept. Unfortunately, the following story does not describe a hypothetical mistake by a hypothetical government. It's real. Notice what our government experts did with the Social Security trust fund.

In October, 1982, the Associated Press reported that the Social Security trust fund suffered a book loss of $212 million because government securities were sold *before maturity.* Being squeezed gave the government gurus tough choices. Would they borrow needed cash at the high interest rates then prevalent or would they sell their long-term bonds at a loss? It seems the Treasury Department decided it was cheaper to sell the old (long-term) bonds at a loss. They cashed in both government bonds and mortgage certificates with a face value totalling $1.35 billion and took a loss of $212 million, or 16 percent. Then they had to borrow anyway. For the first time in history, the article reported, Social Security borrowed $1 billion to $2 billion from the disability and Medicare funds.

Please note: Our U.S. government not only lost Social Security funds on that sale, but it lost what that money could have *earned* for the future. Consider this: They lost only $212 million in 1982. But the real loss is much more. If that $212 million earned only 4 percent a year, it would have brought in $8,480,000 for benefit payments each year. By 1995, 13 years later, those lost benefits would have equaled $110,240,000! Not to speak of the years to come.

You and I bail the government out for its mistakes. We're not so lucky with our own, though. Stay flexible.

Spread Your Cash Around

Let's reverse Sheila's dilemma. What if her five-year bonds had been at 12 percent and the new ones only at 6 percent? Wouldn't she have outsmarted herself? The cash would have created an *opportunity,* all right—an opportunity to reinvest for less money. How do you fix that?

You can overcome that doubt by not putting all your eggs in one basket. Diversification plays a role in protecting you. We'll get to that. But what about choosing long or short rates? The investment maxim is: Go long-term on high rates, short-term on low ones. If you can get a *legitimate* high rate on a long-term bond without sacrificing quality, grab it.

The definition of *high* is always relative. Is 6 percent high or is 8 percent? I once locked in rates at 13 percent when veteran brokers snickered and asked how I'd feel when new rates skyrocketed. I was prepared to accept being wrong and diversified enough to survive if I were. Luckily, time proved me right. Rates did drop and we haven't seen that "high" since.

Don't be afraid to make a decision based on your own good common sense. That common sense will evolve from studying your Income Monitor, Living Expenses form, and Cushioned Cash Flow worksheet. Never let all your dollars ride on one investment. Life is chancy. This $10,000 bond investment we've been discussing represents one small portion of your overall investment dollars. And it must fit into your total picture like a piece of a puzzle.

Okay, now you know the necessary basics to replace a bond that has matured. For a comfortable first-time experience, the AAA–insured municipal with a five-year maturity is a conservative choice.

Five years is not a magic number, but it illustrates the point about flexibility. To achieve increased safety and flexibility in a portfolio, select bonds of *equal quality,* but *unequal maturities.* By staggering maturities, you boost liquidity and the overall return, and create continuing opportunities for new choices. That's smart investing.

Layer Your Money

Separate your priorities into three layers:

1. The first layer is your income (earned or pension). It's the first source of money that supports your everyday lifestyle.
2. The second layer is made up of cushion funds. These monies must be available (without warning) as back-up for daily expenses, monthly bills, insurance deductibles, and unexpected expenses or emergencies. Since some return is sacrificed to maintain permanent liquidity, cushion funds are *not* considered investable monies.
3. If you have longer-term investments in place to produce additional income, call this the third layer.

Here's an example of how these layers might play out:

1. Income creates a 100 percent liquid *first* layer. Vehicles to consider for backup liquidity might be as follows:
   - Money market (Cash is available now.)
   - Savings account (Cash is available within 30 days.)
   - U.S. Treasury bills (Cash is available in 90 days.)
   - CDs (Cash is available in six months or more.)
   - U.S. Treasury bonds (Cash is available in one year, two years, or more.)
2. Using a $35,000 cushion as an example, the *second* layer might look like this:
   - $5,000 money market
   - $10,000, 90-day U.S. Treasury bill (This and the following elements of layer two are continually rolled over at maturity.)
   - $5,000, six-month CD
   - $5,000, nine-month CD
   - $10,000, one-year U.S. Treasury bill
3. You may have a *third* layer. Using $60,000 worth of longer-term bonds to generate additional income—without sacrificing flexibility or liquidity—might look like this example. Notice the bonds are the same AAA quality throughout, but the maturities are staggered. This method of arranging maturities is called *laddering*.
   - $5,000 AAA-insured municipal with remaining maturity of 3 years

- $5,000 AAA-insured municipal with remaining maturity of 5 years
- $10,000 AAA-insured municipal with remaining maturity of 7 years
- $10,000 AAA *newly issued* municipal with maturity of 10 years
- $10,000 AAA *newly issued* municipal with maturity of 15 years
- $20,000 AAA *newly issued* municipal with maturity of 20 years

You can see the maturities by developing a time line like the one shown in the following illustration. Here's how to do it:

1. Make a time line. Draw a straight line from left to right, across a sheet of paper.
2. Moving from left to right along that line, draw a series of 20 slanted parallel lines, each bisecting the time line.
3. The portion of each slanted line *above* the time line represents a calendar year. Label them in consecutive order, from 1996 to 2016. Allow enough years, from today forward, to cover the span of your own investment maturities.
4. Make a mark (asterisk) on each year an investment matures. Then, using the portion of the slanted line that falls below the time line, enter the dollar amount that comes available on that date. Repeat this for each fixed investment you own. (See the following example.)
5. The finished picture shows, at a glance, your "scheduled" liquidity, which creates scheduled flexibility in your investment choices.
6. This is an important worksheet. Be sure to include it on your file Index. Then keep your Time Line in a priority spot, such as with the Income Monitor, Living Expenses form, and Cushioned Cash Flow worksheet, labeled with a yellow tab.

Look at your time line. How many opportunities for choice have you created? Will you enjoy financial flexibility over the coming 20 years of change? Is there cash coming due for a specific event, such as college tuition?

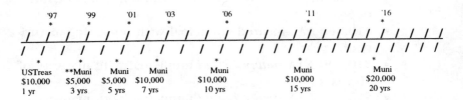

'97   '99   '01   '03   '06   '11   '16

USTreas	**Muni	Muni	Muni	Muni	Muni	Muni
$10,000	$5,000	$5,000	$10,000	$10,000	$10,000	$20,000
1 yr	3 yrs	5 yrs	7 yrs	10 yrs	15 yrs	20 yrs

*Year when bond matures.
**Interest from bonds would be reinvested as received, increasing the total portfolio value.

You Can Monitor the Ladder

Typically, short-term investments pay lower rates and long-term investments pay higher rates. If you stash everything for the short term to achieve 100 percent cash availability, you'll earn the bare minimum on these cushion funds. That's a poor choice.

If you lock everything into long-term investments, you freeze your assets. Not only are you likely to be faced with a squeeze for cash, but you will have eliminated opportunities for new investments. That's also a poor choice.

Yikes! So if you use laddering, how do you keep track of what seems to be a dizzying array of investments and maturities? Keeping up-to-date on maturities needn't be difficult. A mainstream brokerage firm includes everything on one *consolidated* statement. No scattered errands are needed and no clutter is produced. You'll like the simplicity. And, you have your Income Monitor as a guide. Remember: To stay in control of your money, you must have simplicity.

You Can Raise Overall Returns

There is another super advantage that comes from laddering maturities. Although you start out selecting the shortest terms on investments and sacrifice higher returns as a result, that doesn't last long. As the short-term bonds mature, you can reinvest that money *long* term. Over time, you'll have longer bonds and higher interest rates in the entire portfolio, without giving up flexibility or liquidity.

I'll show you why. Look again at the TIME LINE to see how laddering works that magic. Three years pass. That three-year bond matures, but the five-year bond is now a two-year, and the seven-year is now a four-year—see how it works?

You keep choosing bonds to fill in the spaces that open up at the *long* end of your ladder. It's like walking up the down escalator, only much safer.

The No-Leak Bucket

Let's say you have designated money layers for income, cushion, and investments. Are three layers of money enough to allow you to sleep worry free?

Well, actually, for security, there must be a fourth. For instance, what would you do if the house burned? It would be a *catastrophe.* You'd call the insurance agent. Neither income nor cushion money would handle a disaster and your investments could be wiped out. So, tuck insurances in as a layer for *risk management.* Your insurance coverage should at least include car, house, renter's, life, health, and so on. Okay—you've got them all?

Pleasant dreams.

Chapter 14

*A*re Stocks Too Risky?

*C*onfidence wrings the life out of old fears. With money control comes a change of attitude. Your curiosity will be rekindled. You might even find yourself wondering why a portion of your *riskable-investable* funds shouldn't go to work in the stock market.

But before you rush out to the nearest brokerage office for advice, get comfortable with the bond income. Enjoy that steady, *fixed* income without rocking your financial boat. Then, when you're ready, consider the perks of common stocks. They have a double-barreled potential, the opportunity to grow your *income* and opportunity to grow your *nest egg.* It's a chance to keep up with the times. And people you don't even know will work to help make that happen for you.

Investing in Success

Ever have a burger at McDonald's? Sure, who hasn't. Maybe everyone in the civilized world. Well, every employee—from the counter help, cook, manager, and franchise owner, straight up to the corporation president—is working diligently to help the company grow better and bigger. If you are an owner of McDonald's stock, the benefits of their efforts come to you.

Choosing shares of such well-established corporations that pass on *dividends* to their investors, is a slow, steady, quiet way to build wealth. And it works. It's like patiently passing time in a comfortable rocking chair while you await the first signs of spring in your carefully cultivated garden—the promise of what's to come, held clearly in your mind. Blossoms, then full leaf, and finally, when the time is right, the rich harvest.

On the other hand, stocks of companies that most often grab headlines and are discussed with wild-eyed fervor, offer thrills and chills of a financial circus for those who like the risks of a high-wire act. We aren't going to talk about them, though. You've picked up this book to find a solid guide to the safest (and most predictable) ways to enhance your financial comfort. So ignore that guy swinging from the porch rafters; he's not with us.

A Fool and His Money

The *1994 Statistical Abstract of the United States* tells us that, during the years 1990 and 1991, over 300,000 accidents occurred in our bathrooms. It's a risky place to be. Yet we still put two or three of them in our homes! Call on that courage; you'll need about the same amount to invest in common stocks.

Once you know what to watch out for, you can build a dependable lifetime income from common stocks. But remember, we're not talking about that guy on the porch who threw his food money into Uncle Stanley's once-in-a-lifetime hot tip. If friends would confess, you'd probably find that their moans about losing their life savings in "investments" were really caused by swallowing and following a "hot tip." Those losses, often everything they put up, are hard to avoid. Here's why.

Let's say ten exciting, aggressive, companies are fiercely competing to sell home computers. Everybody wants a computer; it's a great market. But behind the glitz and glamour is one company that supplies a crucial computer chip to all ten computer companies. Whose stock would you like to own? Which computer company will succeed? Which will fail? Who knows? Trying to choose a winner out of the ten computer fledglings is *speculation*. Ah, but owning shares of the indispensable supplier, the company which services the industry? That's *investing*.

No Guarantees

Unlike bonds, stocks are not guaranteed or insured, but an informed investor can limit her risks. You can reasonably expect to get your share of dividends and growth, if you know how to choose quality corporations.

"Hah! that's a big *if,*" a client said. "Our stocks from my father seem okay, but let my husband pick a new one and it goes to zero—well, practically."

"How does he choose stocks?" I asked.

"Hears about them at poker, or from his golf buddies. They know more than us. And, a couple times, he bought from a broker who called us up about this company with a super-hot computer game. Pfft! Another bomb. We had a big fight and went back to CDs."

There it is, the effect of the hot tip. Exciting can't-miss stock ideas flourish in the most unexpected and innocent gatherings. Running for cover when it's too late and vowing never to "invest" again—both phobia symptoms—are never far behind. Let's fix that.

Back to Square One

For two weeks, forget what you know and have heard about stocks and the stock market. Stop reading investment advice. Ignore financial television. Turn a deaf ear to tips. Ready? I need your full, unbiased attention. You're about to become a stock expert.

This business of investing requires a businesslike approach. We need more than an alphabetical list to help us find our way. Luckily, tools and professional systems that give us guidelines already exist.

I'm going to show you the ABC tools you can rely on. Actually, you can't do without them. They will give you the skills to choose a solid stock. But remember, we're taking a first step. It's direct, simple, and dependable, but not guaranteed. Don't believe anyone who tells you there's a "sure thing."

The Buck Starts Here

There's the story about the stockbroker who died of a heart attack the day the market crashed. That afternoon, a man called the office and asked for him. The broker's assistant said, "Oh, I'm sorry to tell you—Mr. Anderson had such a shock when the market dropped, he had a heart attack and died!" The next morning, the phone rang and a man again asked for Mr. Anderson. "Haven't you heard?" asked the assistant. "Mr. Anderson had such a shock when the market dropped, he had a heart attack and died."

The next day, the call came again. But by now, the assistant suspected the voice was familiar. "Are you a client of Mr. Anderson's?" she asked. "Oh, yes," the man answered. "May I speak to him?" "But when the market dropped, he had such a shock he suffered a heart attack and died!" she said with exasperation. "Aren't you the same person who has called for the past three days? Didn't I already tell you the terrible news?" "You sure did," he said. "I just like hearing it."

Investing is not a passive occupation. Why let a stranger, and maybe a young, inexperienced stranger, dictate how your life savings should be spent? Instead of just following your stockbroker's suggestions, do your homework. Develop ideas of your own. Discuss and compare. Stocks must fit into *your* situation, just as the bonds did.

Did I just lose you? If so, that's okay, it's good to know now. If the idea of doing research stops you, don't venture into the stock market. Skip the rest of this chapter and continue on with the questions from Chapter 1.

For those of you who just rolled up your sleeves, I can promise it will be an easy assignment. But before you begin, rid yourself of such self-defeating convictions as, "I've never understood this stuff." And vow never to greet a stockbroker with lead-me-any-where-and-I-will-follow questions such as, "I have an extra $10,000. What shall I do with it?'"

Okay, ready to take matters into your own hands? Let's do it.

The ABC Tools for Confidence in Choosing Stocks

Tool A: The Standard & Poor's Stock Guide

This little booklet is published monthly. Just as our one-page Income Monitor is a bible of information arranged in chart form, so too is the *Standard & Poor's Stock Guide*. It's easy to read, easy to come by, and it's a standard reference in the investment community. You can find the *Standard & Poor's Stock Guide* either on the desk of your reliable stockbroker or at the public library. If your library doesn't subscribe, request that they do so. You can also subscribe. See Appendix B in the back of this book for details.

Since your stockbroker receives an updated issue each month, ask her to pass the old one on to you. Brokers often provide current issues to their substantial clients. If your broker doesn't receive a monthly copy from her firm, you would have to wonder why not. Make it a rule to do business with well-informed experts.

Here's how to use the guide. First, set limits. Approach the guide wearing the same selective blinders you wore with your brokerage statement. See only what you need to see and get out. This is the one-size-fits-all packet of information on thousands of stocks for thousands of people. Don't get lost in it; we have no search party to send out for you. But, don't worry, we're going to spell out exactly what to look for before we open the cover.

Here's our target: From the guide's 5,100-plus-item, alphabetical conglomeration of securities, we are going to cherry-pick the stocks we might consider as investments. Just as with bonds, we want to look at only the *best* possibilities, those that are established and well scrutinized. And because, like bonds, stocks are rated, we'll focus on top-ranked issues. Not every stock in existence is ranked and not every stock is listed in this book, but the ones we want to consider are here. Forget about the others.

To keep down the eye-glazing, ignore everything but those corporations ranked A+, A, and A-. We want to glean a conservative, mainstream, acceptable list of our own. It's straightforward secretarial work.

With your guide in hand, follow along with these next eight steps. I'm looking at an S&P guide dated April 1995. The information and page numbers of the issue you're using may vary slightly.

1. Go to page 5, titled Earnings and Dividend Rankings for Common Stocks.

2. Notice the rankings (about the seventh paragraph):

   A+ = highest

   A = high

   A– = above average

   Ignore the rest.

3. Now go to the last paragraph on that page for an explanation of the rankings. Notice it states that "a ranking is not a forecast of future . . . market price performance . . ."

   That same paragraph cautions that rankings are no substitute for complete analysis. With that in mind, we'll go on to the next step. We're finished with this page.

4. Flip to page 6, and go to the beginning of the alphabetical listings. (See Figure 14.1.)

   The data is separated into 13 main columns. Notice that each stock's information reads across the two facing pages. The stock entries are numbered, from 1 through 50. These number columns are located on the left border of the first page, and on the left and right borders of the facing page. The print is small and the lines are close, so use the number as a line guide.

5. Find the column titled Com. Rank. & Pfd. Rating. It is just to the right of the corporate name. The title is an abbreviation for common stock ranking and preferred rating, exactly what we're after.

   (By the way, an explanation of each column is shown inside both the front and back cover of the guide. Save that study for another time.)

   Okay. Do you have your pen and yellow pad handy?

6. Starting at line 1, under Com. Rank. & Pfd. Rating, slide your finger down the rankings until you spot A+, A, or A–, as shown below for Bristol-Myers Squibb.

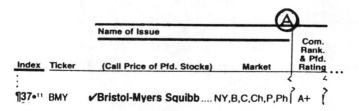

FIGURE 14.1 *Standard & Poor's Stock Guide*

34 **BOR-BRO** Standard & Poor's

¶ S&P 500 # MidCap 400 ✧ SmallCap 600 • Options

Index	Ticker	Name of Issue (Call Price of Pfd. Stocks)	Market	Com. Rank. & Pfd. Rating	Inst. Hold Cos	Inst. Hold Shs. (000)	Principal Business	Price Range 1971-93 High	1971-93 Low	1994 High	1994 Low	1995 High	1995 Low	Mar. Sales in 100s	March, 1995 Last Sale Or Bid High	Low	Last	%Div Yield	P-E Ratio	Total Return % Annualized 12 Mo	36 Mo	60 Mo
1	BORAY	Boral Ltd ADS[51]	NNM	NR	10	178	Constr'n prod/oil&gas prod'n	24½	13¼	26⅜	18¾	21⅝	19½	237	21⅝	19¾	20⅛	5.9	28	1.0	6.9	3.
2•[1]	BCU	✓Borden Chem/Plastics	NY,Ch	NR	97	7351	Produces chem & PVC resins	24	7½	26⅜	9⅞	25½	14¾	96598	18¼	14¾	18¼	19.3	5	89.3	6.1	28.
3	BWA	✓Borg-Warner Automotive	NY,Ch	NR	85	17491	Auto powertrain components	28	20½	34	21⅝	26⅛	22⅜	7363	25⅛	24	24¼	2.5	9	−16.9	...	..
4	BOR	✓Borg-Warner Security	NY,Ch,Ph	NR	74	17514	Provides protective services	22⅞	18	22	8¼	9⅞	5½	14096	8	5½	7⅞	...	14	−53.3	...	..
#5•[2]	BORL	✓Borland Intl	NNM,Ch	NR	89	8313	Design/mkt computer software	86¾	9⅝	16	6	10¼	6⅛	147702	10¼	7⅛	8¾	...	7	−38.1	−45.1	−10.1
6	BOS	✓Boston Celtics L.P.	NY,B,Ch,Ph	NR	15	27	Professional basketball team	23⅞	10⅝	24⅛	18½	21⅞	20¾	753	21¾	20¾	21	7.1	18	17.8	9.4	13.
7•[2]	BOST	✓Boston Chicken	NNM	NR	91	14000	Oper,franchise food svc strs	25½	17¾	24¼	13½	19⅞	14½	125894	18	15⅜	16¼	...	43	−15.2	...	..
8	BSE	✓Boston Edison	NY,B,Ch,P,Ph	B+	171	17198	Electric utility:Boston area	32⅝	7	29⅞	21½	25½	23⅛	11533	24¾	23⅛	24	7.6	10	−5.3	8.6	11.
¶9•[3]	BSX	✓Boston Scientific	NY,Ph	NR	133	32181	Dvlp,mfr medical devices	23⅝	9⅝	17⅞	11⅞	26⅜	16⅝	156752	26⅜	20⅞	24⅝	...	30	82.4	...	..
10•[4]	BSTN	✓Boston Technology	NNM	NR	78	8598	Voice process'g communic sys	14⅜	1 15/16	18⅝	7⅝	17⅛	11⅝	126909	17⅛	12⅞	15¾	...	32	34.0	76.3	23.4
#11•[5]	BOW	✓Bowater, Inc	NY,B,Ch,P,Ph	B−	188	27899	Mfrs newsprint,coated paper	44½	14⅞	29⅝	20⅝	37⅝	26⅜	81050	37⅝	30⅛	35¾	1.7	d	71.3	17.7	10.6
12	Pr B	7%Sr'B''PRIDES'[56]([57]23.911)	NY	BB+[58]	39	4147		....	....	27¼	21	32	23¾	13750	32	26	31	5.3	..	...	...	...
13	BWTRY	✓Bowater plc ADR[59]	NSC,Mo,To	NR	6	1035	Packaging products,services	8⅛	⅞	7⅞	6¼	7½	6	186	7½	6¼	7¼	3.2	17	13.5	10.9	21.4
14	BWL.A	✓Bowl America Cl'A'	AS,Ch	B+	19	1028	Bowling centers	12⅛	¼	10	7⅞	8¼	7⅜	357	7⅞	7⅜	7⅝	4.7	13	−19.1	−4.8	−4.5
15	BOM	✓Bowmar Instrument	AS,B,P,Ph	B−	16	645	Electromechanical compon'ts	44⅞	¼	4⅜	2½	3⅜	2⅝	1681	3⅛	2⅝	2¾	...	10	−12.0	9.0	24.0
16	Pr	$3.00 cm Cv Sr vtg Pfd([61]25)	AS	NR	..	...		72	25	56	37⅛	46	39¼	31	41½	39¼	37½B	8.0	..	...	...	...
✧17	BNE	✓Bowne & Co	AS,B,Ch,P,Ph	B+	111	9180	Fin'l,corp,legal printing	24⅜	⅜	28½	15⅜	18¼	15½	5731	17¼	15½	16⅛	2.2	11	−26.9	−0.3	10.7
✧18•[4]	BOXXB	✓Box Energy 'B'[62]	NNM	NR	42	4706	Oil&gas explor,dvlp,prod'n	19½	8⅝	14⅛	7½	11	7⅝	24007	9⅞	7⅝	8⅞	...	20	−18.4	...	..
19	BOYD	✓Boyd Bros.Transport'n	NNM	NR	12	837	Flatbed trucking services	....	....	13	9½	12¼	9½	294	12¼	11	11¼	...	13	...	...	...
20•[6]	BYD	✓Boyd Gaming	NY,Ch	NR	40	3487	Own,operate casino-hotels	26	12⅞	19⅜	10½	14¼	10½	2422	14¼	12⅝	13⅛	...	45	−12.5	...	...
21	BPT	✓BP Prudhoe Bay Royalty[63]	NY,Ch,Ph	NR	46	8572	Royalties of oil/gas prop	35½	23⅞	27	15¾	18	15⅞	5957	17½	16½	17	8.5	11	−21.5	−11.3	−0.8
22•[7]	BLE	✓Bradlees, Inc	NY,Ph	NR	80	9785	Discount department stores	20⅛	10⅝	17¼	10⅞	12	9⅝	14559	11½	10½	11⅛	5.4	22	−22.7	...	..
23	BP[illegible]XA	✓Bradley Pharmaceuticals'A'	NNM	NR	7	337	RX-OTC Pharmaceuticals	4⅛	1½	4½	2⅛	4¾	3⅝	32769	4¾	4	4	...	15	12.3	5.8	..
24	BT[illegible]	✓Bradley Real Estate	NY	NR	63	5200	Real estate investment trust	32½	13/16	19¼	13⅝	16¾	14⅞	3280	16¾	16	16⅜	8.1	16	−4.4	2.6	−3.5
25	B[illegible]	✓Brady(W.H.)'A'non-vtg	NNM	A−	51	3052	Mfrs adhesives & coatings	43	10	49	42¼	53	47	1645	53	48	53	1.5	18	18.3	18.1	11.6
26	B[illegible]	✓Brandon Systems	AS	B+	37	1910	Temp computer personnel svc	12⅞	3½	19⅛	11⅝	22½	17¼	3330	22½	19⅛	21⅞	1.3	19	76.1	49.6	34.5
27	[illegible]	✓Brandywine Rlty Trust SBI	AS	NR	1	1	Real estate investment trust	11⅛	5/16	6	1⅝	4¾	3½	611	4½	3⅞	4	e5.0	d	73.8	60.2	35.2
28•[8]	[illegible]A	Brascan Ltd Cv'A'Ord	AS,Ch,Mo,To,Vc	NR	54	8915	Canadian invest't mgmt co	31⅞	4¾	15½	11⅞	14⅜	12⅛	1426	13⅝	12⅛	13⅝	◆5.5	12	19.8	7.2	−0.1
29	[illegible]	✓BRE Properties Cl'A'	NY,Ch	NR	77	5054	Real estate investment trust	39⅞	2⅞	34⅝	29⅞	32	30⅜	2942	32	31	31⅛	8.1	14	6.0	8.2	11.6
30•[9]	[illegible]	✓Breed Technologies	NY,Ph	NR	115	11645	Mfr airbag sys crash sensors	21¾	10¾	44	15¼	29	20¼	37652	25	21¼	21⅞	0.9	11	−33.2	...	...
✧31	[illegible]EN	✓Brenco, Inc	NNM	B	50	5737	Bearings for RR freight cars	25	3⅛	14	8¼	13	10⅝	5327	13	11½	12⅝	1.9	14	32.0	33.1	16.4
32	[illegible]RBK	✓Brenton Banks	NNM	B+	27	1750	Commercial bkg,Iowa	20⅞	2¼	20½	17½	18¾	17¾	230	18¾	17¾	18B	2.4	14	4.9	9.3	17.9
33	BPTM	✓Bridgeport Machines	NNM	NR	17	1148	Metal cutting machine tools	....	....	10¼	8¼	15	9⅝	6497	15	12⅞	14¾	...	13	...	...	...
¶34•[illegible]	BGG	✓Briggs & Stratton	NY,B,Ch,Ph	B+	349	20935	Mfr small gas engines:locks	44¾	6⅞	45⅛	30½	37¾	32¼	18661	37¼	34⅞	36¾	2.7	9	...	...	...
35	CBA	✓Brilliance China Automotive	NY,Ph	NR	..	...	Minibus manufacturer in China	34¾	13½	20	7½	8⅝	5⅜	10987	8⅛	5⅜	5¾	1.4	6	−50.7	...	...
#36•[10]	EAT	✓Brinker Intl	NY,Ch,Ph	B+	385	60240	Limited menu restaurants	30⅞	1 11/16	33⅜	15	20⅞	15⅞	169499	20	15⅞	16⅝	...	18	−42.2	−0.1	22.6
¶37•[11]	BMY	✓Bristol-Myers Squibb	NY,B,C,Ch,P,Ph	A+	1251	246163	Pharmaceutical,medical prod	90⅛	3⅞	61	50	65⅞	57¾	211089	65⅞	61⅛	62⅞	4.7	17	28.6	−1.7	7.8
38	[illegible]	[illegible]	NY,B,P	[illegible]	5	4	[illegible]	[illegible]	[illegible]	[illegible]	[illegible]	[illegible]	[illegible]	....	[illegible]	[illegible]	[illegible]	[illegible]	..	...	...	...
39	BVSI	✓Brite Voice Systems	NNM	B	35	2969	Mfr voice data/audiotex sys	14¼	2½	19¾	7⅜	21⅞	15¼	16387	20⅛	15⅞	16⅛	...	24	19.4	45.4	20.9
40•[9]	BAB	✓British Airways ADS[67]	NY,Ch,P,Ph	NR	113	9848	Major int'l U.K. airline	69	16⅛	74⅛	54⅞	66⅛	56¼	14071	66⅛	60⅜	65¾	2.9	13	13.4	20.3	19.9
41	BRG	✓British Gas ADS[68]	NY,B,Ch,P,Ph	NR	71	5894	Major gas supplier in UK	54¼	8⅝	54⅛	39	49⅛	44¾	4111	48	44¾	46¾	5.2	19	10.7	9.4	12.5
42•[10]	BP	✓British Petrol ADS[70]	NY,B,Ch,P,Ph	NR	411	49154	Major integrated world oil	86¼	4½	85¼	58⅜	84⅛	75⅝	95456	84⅛	75⅞	83¾	2.4	16	40.4	21.4	11.0
43•[12]	BSY	British Sky Broadcstg Gp ADS[71]	[13]NY	NR	96	15977	Pay TV svcs U.K./Ireland	....	....	25¼	23¾	26	22⅞	21425	25¼	23⅞	24⅝	1.3	37	...	...	...
44•[14]	BST	✓British Steel ADS[72]	NY,Ch	NR	78	15340	Largest steel producer in U.K.	27¾	7	27¼	18⅛	26¼	22⅝	14112	26¼	24⅝	26¼	2.2	52	32.5	33.8	7.9
45•[15]	BTY	✓British Telecommn ADR[73]	NY,P	NR	156	9191	Telecomm'n svcs in UK	74⅞	6	71¾	53⅞	64¼	57⅞	18136	64⅛	57⅞	63¼	4.5	18	16.3	10.5	12.0
46•[3]	BBTK	✓BroadBand Technologies	NNM	NR	77	5760	Dvlp stge:mfr telecomm elec	52¼	18	33½	11	31¾	20¼	31748	26¼	21	25¼	...	d	21.7	...	...
47	BPIX	✓Broadcasting Ptnrs 'A'[74]	NNM	NR	40	3897	Own,oper AM/FM radio stations	19	14	17	10¼	18⅝	15	17931	18⅝	16⅞	18⅜	...	80	44.1	...	...
48•[5]	BWY	✓Broadway Stores	NY	NR	59	12668	Operates department stores	17½	5⅝	13¼	6¾	7½	4½	24397	7⅛	4½	6¾	...	d	−48.1	...	...
49	WS	Wrrt (Pur 1 com at $17)	NY	....	7	85		5¾	1⅜	4½	1¾	2⅛	1⅛	454	1⅝	1⅛	1¼B	...	..	...	...	...
50	BROC	✓Brock Control Systems	NNM	NR	37	1726	Dvlp sales, mkt software prod	22½	9½	25	6	7½	5¾	3787	7	5¾	7	...	64	−64.6	...	...

Uniform Footnote Explanations-See Page 1. Other: [1]NY:Cycle 2. [2]CBOE:Cycle 1. [3]CBOE:Cycle 2. [4]ASE:Cycle 1. [5]P:Cycle 3. [6]Ph:Cycle 2. [7]ASE:Cycle 2. [8]Mo:Cycle 1. [9]Ph:Cycle 1. [10]P:Cycle 1. [11]CBOE:Cycle 3. [12]CBOE,NY:Cycle 1. [13]Ch,Ph [14]NY:Cycle 1. [15]ASE,CBOE:Cycle 1. [51]Ea ADS rep 8 Ord shrs, par A.$0.50. [52]Approx. [53]Incl proceeds from sale of rts,'94. [54]Div rt min($1.20)cm thru 12-31-92,may extend. [55]Pfd in $M. [56]Dep for 0.25 shr'7%'PRIDES,Sr,B Cv Pfd. [57]Fr 1-1-97,scale to $23.50 in'98. [58]Note:'r'added to derivative/hybrid secur ratings. [59]ADR rep 1 ord shr. [60]®$0.27,'94. [61]Fr 1-1-98. [62]non-vtg. [63]Units of Beneficial Int. [64]Incl $0.23 non-taxable:©$0.09,'94. [65]3 Mo Mar'93. [66]Stk dstr of Strattec Security Corp,'95. [67]Full paym't ADR's equal 10 Ord par 25p. [68]Full pay't ADS's equal 10 Ord par 25p. [69]Fiscal Mar'91 & prior. [70]ADS's equal 12 Ord par 25 pence. [71]Ea ADS rep 6 Ord Shrs, 50 pence. [72]Full paym't ADS's equal 10 Ord par 50p. [73]Full pay't ADR's equal 10 Ord par 25p. [74]Evergreen Media plan acq, $12 cash & 0.46 com. [75]®$0.22,'94. [76]17 Wk Jan'93 earned $0.65.

Source: Reprinted by permission of Standard & Poor's, a McGraw-Hill Co.

FIGURE 14.1 *Standard & Poor's Stock Guide* (Continued)

Common and Convertible Preferred Stocks — BOR-BRO 35

Splits ◆ Index	Cash Divs. Ea. Yr. Since	Dividends: Latest Payment Period $	Date	Ex. Div.	Total $ So Far 1995	Ind. Rate	Paid 1994	Financial Position Mil-$: Cash& Equiv.	Curr. Assets	Curr. Liab.	Balance Sheet Date	Capitalization: Lg Trm Debt Mil-$	Shs. 000 Pfd.	Com.	Earnings $ Per Shr. Years End	1990	1991	1992	1993	1994	Last 12 Mos.	Interim Earnings Period	$ per Shr. 1993	1994	Index
1	1992	[52]0.608	5-8-95	3-31	[52]0.608	1.19	[53]1.252	84.3	1403	1327	j6-30-94	832	...	1095333	Je	2.41	1.47	1.02	1.28	0.72	0.72				1
2	1989	1.64	2-14-95	1-30	1.64	[54]3.52	2.06	74.1	227	170	12-31-94	120	...	36750	Dc	1.22	1.39	0.73	d0.04	3.94	3.94				2
3	1994	Q0.15	2-15-95	1-26	0.15	0.60	0.57½	14.9	216	248	12-31-94	86.8	...	±23122	Dc	...	...	pd0.12	p□1.41	2.75	2.75				3
4	....	None Since Public			...	Nil	....	16.0	143	186	9-30-94	453	...	21755	Dc	...	p1.16	p1.30	p1.50	P0.56	0.56				4
5	....	None Paid			...	Nil	....	94.0	132	103	12-31-94	23.7	...	27378	Mr	1.81	d4.29	d1.87	d2.62	E1.20	d1.64	9 Mo Dec	0.23	1.21	5
6	1987	1.50	12-15-94	12-5	...	1.50	1.50	137	167	118	12-31-94	60.0	...	6400	Je	1.23	1.69	1.19	0.80	3.61	1.20	6 Mo Dec	2.78	0.37	6
7◆	....	None Since Public			...	Nil	....	30.1	49.7	22.6	10-02-94	130	...	44093	Dc	d0.08	d0.14	d0.20	0.06	P0.38	0.38				7
8	1890	Q0.45½	5-1-95	4-4	0.91	1.82	1.76	5.33	328	407	9-30-94	1258	[55]217	45421	Dc	Δ1.60	1.96	2.10	2.28	P2.41	2.41				8
9	....	None Since Public			...	Nil	....	124	255	62.5	9-30-94	8.95	...	p149427	Dc	*0.25	*0.44	0.57	0.70	P0.81	0.81				9
10	....	None Paid			...	Nil	....	21.1	63.4	23.1	10-31-94	0.50	...	24668	Ja	0.07	d0.11	0.13	0.27	P0.50	0.50				10
11	1984	Q0.15	4-3-95	3-6	0.30	0.60	0.60	234	599	332	10-01-94	1117	8294	36691	Dc	□2.30	1.15	Δd2.64	d1.84	Pd0.59	d0.59				11
12	1994	Q0.41⅛	4-3-95	3-6	0.82¼	1.645	1.065	Cv into 0.82 com, $28.659				....	4300	...	Dc	...	...	...	....	....	....	Mandatory conversion into 1 com 1-1-98			12
13◆	1947	[52]0.133	6-16-95	4-7	[52]0.133	0.23	0.21½	342	1017	833	j12-31-93	231	89820	499227	Dc	Δ0.50	□0.44	0.38	Δ0.42	....	0.42				13
14◆	1969	Q0.09	5-17-95	4-12	0.18	0.36	0.36	7.91	9.85	4.16	1-01-95	....	...	±5744	Je	±0.76	±0.72	±0.65	±0.69	±0.66	0.60	6 Mo Dec	±0.23	±0.17	14
15	....	None Since Public			...	Nil	....	0.26	9.90	8.41	12-31-94	0.58	120	6415	Sp	d0.77	0.05	0.20	0.06	[60]0.28	0.27	3 Mo Dec	0.07	0.06	15
16	1992	Q0.75	3-31-95	3-9	0.75	3.00	3.00	Cv into 13.33 com, $1.875				....	120	...	Sp	...	...	...	....	....	....				16
17	1941	Q0.09	3-29-95	3-13	0.18	0.36	0.315	28.8	143	38.3	1-31-95	3.10	...	17389	Oc	0.49	0.84	1.65	2.05	1.80	1.54	3 Mo JanΔ	0.38	0.12	17
18	....	None Since Public			...	Nil	....	40.9	47.1	5.04	9-30-94	55.1	...	±20803	Dc	p2.00	p0.09	0.92	0.10	P±0.44	0.44				18
19	....	None Since Public			...	Nil	....	0.10	7.08	7.93	9-30-94	7.86	...	3823	Dc	p0.35	p0.30	p0.39	p0.60	Pp0.89	0.89				19
20	....	None Since Public			...	Nil	....	34.9	73.0	102	9-30-94	543	...	56817	Je	...	...	...	p0.43	Δ0.19	0.29	6 Mo Dec	Δ0.13	0.23	20
21	1989	0.39	1-20-95	1-13	0.39	1.45	1.483	Equity per shr $16.69			9-30-94	....	...	21400	Dc	3.57	4.05	3.03	2.39	....	1.55	9 Mo Sep	1.89	1.05	21
22	992	Q0.15	4-1-95	3-9	0.30	0.60	0.60	6.88	495	473	11-05-94	289	...	11360	Ja	...	p1.79	p2.25	□1.19	P□0.51	0.51				22
23	....	None Since Public			...	Nil	....	2.97	8.80	6.65	9-30-94	8.00	...	±6867	Dc	±d1.38	±d0.41	±d0.30	±0.17	P±0.27	0.27				23
24◆	61	Q0.33	3-31-95	3-7	0.33	1.32	1.29	Equity per shr $11.54			9-30-94	23.1	...	8196	Dc	0.36	0.38	0.40	0.82	P1.05	1.05				24
25	[illegible]	Q0.20	4-28-95	4-3	0.40	0.80	0.71	68.0	140	34.0	10-31-94	1.89	29	±7271	Jl	2.09	2.14	□1.16	2.33	2.55	2.96	6 Mo JanΔ	1.12	1.53	25
26◆	[illegible]	Q0.07	4-12-95	3-23	0.14	0.28	0.23½	16.4	28.2	4.64	1-01-95	....	...	4448	Sp	0.54	0.46	0.60	0.69	1.10	1.17	3 Mo Dec	0.26	0.33	26
27	[illegible]	†0.70	2-2-95	1-18	†0.70	0.20	†0.87	Book Value $6.28			9-30-94	7.50	...	1856	Dc	d1.08	d3.61	Nil	1.33	PΔd0.21	d0.21				27
28	[illegible]	gQ0.26	5-31-95	4-25	g0.52	1.04	g1.04	Equity per shr $18.51			j12-31-93	1168	11157	87790	Dc	0.40	d0.60	d1.56	1.01	P1.17	j1.17				28
29	[illegible]	Q0.63	3-23-95	3-6	0.63	2.52	[64]2.40	Book Value $22.45			1-31-95	97.1	...	10925	Jl	3.74	1.94	2.56	3.02	2.04	2.23	6 Mo JanΔ	0.97	1.16	29
30	[illegible]	Q0.05	4-24-95	3-20	0.10	0.20	0.05	22.3	120	43.5	12-31-94	1.67	...	31446	Je	*0.58	*0.08	0.13	0.59	1.56	2.00	6 Mo Dec	0.50	0.94	30
31	959	Q0.06	4-3-95	3-13	0.12	0.24	0.21	6.65	42.0	7.53	12-31-94	9.57	...	10086	Dc	0.40	0.46	0.20	0.43	0.88	0.88				31
32◆	988	Q0.11	1-31-95	1-12	0.11	0.44	0.44	Book Value $14.27			9-30-94	40.8	...	7905	Dc	1.38	1.52	1.67	1.80	P1.27	1.27				32
33	....	None Since Public			...	Nil	....	5.25	70.2	28.5	12-31-94	3.28	...	5659	Mr	...	...	[65]0.26	0.63	....	1.11	9 Mo Dec	0.61	1.09	33
34◆	1929	Q0.25	4-3-95	2-10	h[66]0.50	1.00	0.91	11.0	503	212	1-01-95	75.0	...	28927	Je	1.23	1.26	1.78	2.43	□3.54	3.89	6 Mo Dec	□1.21	1.56	34
35	1993	Q0.02	2-3-95	1-11	0.02	0.08	0.08	92.8	242	128	12-31-93	8.08	...	±17391	Dc	...	p0.34	p0.84	1.03	....	1.03				35
36	....	None Since Public			...	Nil	....	1.11	52.1	112	12-28-94	4.46	...	71832	Je	0.33	0.41	0.51	0.69	0.83	0.91	6 Mo Dec	0.38	0.46	36
37	1900	Q0.74	5-1-95	4-3	1.48	2.96	2.92	2564	6675	3739	9-30-94	639	22	510678	Dc	3.33	3.95	□4.26	3.80	P3.62	3.62				37
38	[illegible]	Q0.50	6-1-95	[illegible]	[illegible]	[illegible]	[illegible]	Cv into 4.24 common				....	22	...	Dc	n/a	n/a	n/a	....	....	....				38
39	....	None Since Public			...	Nil	....	8.25	34.3	11.6	9-30-94	0.83	...	7868	Dc	0.20	0.30	d0.39	d0.25	P0.68	0.68				39
40	1987	0.591	2-7-95	12-9	0.591	1.88	1.797	1226	2357	1928	j3-31-94	2405	...	954019	Mr	2.31	6.13	3.64	4.63	E5.00	5.86	9 Mo Dec	4.20	5.43	40
41	1987	[52]1.367	7-15-95	5-22	[52]1.367	2.43	2.387	629	4636	3904	j12-31-93	3625	...	4327000	Dc	[69]4.97	5.10	2.39	d0.98	E2.50	d1.01	6 Mo Dec	2.22	2.19	41
42	1917	0.598	5-9-95	3-3	1.117	1.99	1.755	210	8311	8357	j12-31-93	7144	12706	5451062	Dc	Δ6.72	1.68	d1.80	2.03	P5.29	5.29				42
43	....	Plan semi-annual div			...	0.33	....	0.19	405	340	p6-30-94	1447	...	±1715054	Je	...	...	...	....	p0.67	0.67				43
44	1989	0.333	1-26-95	12-2	0.333	0.58	0.32½	575	2261	987	j4-02-94	469	...	2000748	Mr	1.69	d0.30	d0.99	0.51	....	0.51				44
45	1985	1.168	2-21-95	1-5	1.169	2.84	2.704	2773	5669	5544	j3-31-94	3199	...	6211440	Mr	5.95	5.78	2.99	4.24	....	3.55	9 Mo Dec	3.38	2.69	45
46	....	None Since Public			...	Nil	....	86.1	93.8	14.4	9-30-94	0.55	...	13039	Dc	pd1.29	pd1.55	pd1.54	pd1.89	Pd1.85	d1.85				46
47	....	None Since Public			...	Nil	....	1.12	16.9	5.30	12-31-94	81.0	...	±7897	Dc	...	...	...	p0.22	□[75]0.23	0.23				47
48	....	None Since Public			...	Nil	....	16.9	1171	373	10-29-94	1103	942	45852	Ja	...	...	[76]...	d2.30	Pd0.80	d0.80				48
49	....	Terms&trad. basis should			be checked in detail			Wrrts expire 10-8-99				....	...	...	Ja	...	...	...	....	....	....				49
50	....	None Since Public			...	Nil	....	11.6	22.7	4.82	9-30-94	....	...	4875	Dc	p0.04	p0.28	p0.51	0.66	P0.11	0.11				50

◆Stock Splits & Divs By Line Reference Index [7]2-for-1,'94. [13]2-for-1,'92. [14]2-for-1,'95. [24]1-for-2 REVERSE,'94. [26]5-for-4,'91,'92. [32]2-for-1,'90:3-for-2,'94. [34]2-for-1,'94. [36]3-for-2,'91(twice),'93,'94.

Got one? The name of the corporation is to the left. In my S&P, the first listing is an A+—Abbott Laboratories.
7. On your yellow pad, jot down the corporation and its rank. Abbott Labs—A+.

Are we going to buy this stock? We don't know yet. First comes the grunt work. Stay with me.
8. Continue to find and list all A-ranked corporations.

List *all* the *A* companies for this *entire* S&P Guide? Yes, and close your mouth—you'll catch flies. If your fingers just cramped up because you're thinking, "My god, I'll have thousands!"—you're in for a surprise. This once-and-done effort will give you insight the average investor does not have. Can you spend 20 or 30 minutes on something this important? Shake your fingers—it's a short-term commitment.

I'm waiting. Pages are flying. Your list is growing. I've done this same exercise or I wouldn't ask you to do it.

All finished? The surprise is, there aren't many A companies. You probably have extracted only about 378 names from those 200+ pages.

Take out your calculator. If approximately 5,100 corporations are listed in this issue, and only 378 are ranked A or better, that's a only a little over 7 percent! (You get this number by dividing 378 by 5,100 = 7.4 percent.) Surprised?

That means 93 percent of the companies in the guide are ranked *lower* than A. Think about that. So the investor who is looking for top-ranked shares doesn't have to drown in a blur of company names. That's for the go-ahead-confuse-me person who says to the broker, "What have you got?" In stockbroker speak that's "Bring on the blizzard."

That means we ignore 93 percent of the stocks in this guide. That list in your hand represents an important group from which you will choose a stock. Keep it. Guard it. Make a file for it. When someone suggests an off-the-list alternative, just say "no."

You probably recognize some companies on your list. These corporations are a well-established, integral part of our way of life. They are familiar because you use their products and services: Albertson's Inc., Allegheny Power, Bell Atlantic Corp., McDonald's, Rubbermaid, Safeco—but scan your list and see for yourself.

Go a step further and see if our identifying top companies has any value in the real world. Check out the January 1, 1996, issue of *Forbes* magazine from your library. This issue is their "Annual Report on American Industry," in which they list ratings on 1,309 companies. Using your personally compiled list of companies as a reference, see how many of those names pop up among the year's top performing companies. Coincidence? Not likely.

Although lots of these names are as familiar as old socks, have you ever connected that you could *own* them? Since you use the products and services anyway, why not enjoy a quarterly dividend check? It's like a perpetual rebate.

How do you decide which stock you like? Here's one method: Select any company on your list. For my example, I'm going to choose McDonald's Corporation, an A+. So I'm not in this alone, let's say you choose Bristol-Myers Squibb, also A+.

Good. We've got two examples for our discussion, *no recommendation intended.* What's each company's business? Maybe, even though the name is familiar, you can't exactly say? We've got to know. Don't waste time investigating a company whose business you oppose. Maybe you hate cigarettes or don't like the damage certain chemical products cause in the environment? It takes only about ten seconds to find out if this company is one you would be proud to own. Where do you look? Once again, refer to the alphabetical listings in Figure 14.1. Locate your chosen company in the guide.

Once you've found it, move to the third column, titled Principal Business. See it below? On page 34, line 37, I see that Bristol-Myers Squibb's principal business is "Pharmaceutical, medical prod."

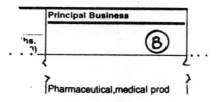

How about McDonald's? On page 124, line 18, of my issue it reads: "Fast food restaurant: franchising."

It doesn't take long to feel at home with the guide. Look up three other companies you're curious about.

Okay. We chose an A stock. We found a description of the primary business. So far so good, but our goal is to find a stock that pays *income*. Does this company pay a dividend? You don't have to ask anyone else. This is your expertise. We'll look it up.

Still in the guide, go back to that line numbered for your stock listing. Slide your finger to the right, to the fifth section. Within that section, find the heading, % Div Yield.

For McDonald's, I found: 0.7 percent dividend. Now check to see if Bristol-Myers Squibb pays a dividend. As you can see below, my issue reports that Bristol-Myers Squibb pays 4.7 percent.

Just because companies have the same ranking doesn't mean they have the same dividend policy. In this case, Bristol-Myers Squibb pays a higher dividend, but perhaps McDonald's will excel in growth of value. Sometimes the age of the company, as well as its business policies, affect dividend payout.

Still on the same line, move to the facing page. Notice the *year,* entered just to the right of the line number. See the column heading? Cash Divs. Ea. Yr. Since. Here's a chance to see what kind of a payout history this company has.

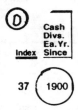

Does the above entry, *1900,* mean that Bristol-Myers Squibb has paid a dividend every year—can you believe it?—since 1900? Yes, that's what it means. Now skip to McDonald's. My issue reports that McDonald's Corp. has paid a dividend since 1976.

It took only a couple seconds to get that information. Surprised? Maybe you've discovered a different A company that you like. Maybe it's got a higher dividend and a longer track record?

You and I just had an investment expert's conversation. See how easy it is to slip into the expert mode? It's just like the lightbulb experience a friend and I had, when we realized our lunch conversation was a discussion about software for our home computers.

Only investment industry addicts talk in percentages. Let's translate the percentage into everyday dollars and cents, so we know how much those dividend checks will bring in.

Is this where your expert usually takes over? No more. This is *your* life. Still focused on the correct line number for your stock listing, slide your finger right, to the next section titled, Dividends. Okay. Go to the second subsection under Dividends, titled, Total $. This is where we find dividends translated into dollars and cents.

As shown below, there are three views given of the dividend payment:

1.   Present—So Far 1995 (what's been paid to date)
2.   Future—Ind. Rate (total payments indicated for year)
3.   Past—Paid 1994 (total paid previous year)

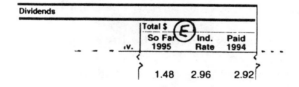

Do you see these entries? (Your guide will vary.)

1.   So far this year, Bristol-Myers Squibb has paid $1.48 per share.
2.   We can expect it to pay $2.96 per share by year's end.
3.   Last year, the company paid $2.92 total dividend per share.

Just reading the numbers aloud will have you sounding like your stockbroker. Flip to the *M* page and find out what McDonald's did. Find it?

1.   So far this year McDonald's paid six cents per share.
2.   We can expect 24 cents by year's end.
3.   Last year, they paid 23.4 cents total dividend per share.

So, had you and I owned these stocks, both our incomes would have increased from the previous year. Compare *last year* with *what we can expect* by year's end. That's the growth we talked about—at least part of it.

Turn back to your guide in Figure 14.1 once again. Staying on the same line, backtrack to the area marked with an *F,* the section titled Price Range. Look at High and Low. Find the place? This section is a look back over the past 24 years, to show history of the stock's performance.

1.   Under the subheading 1971–93, see High and Low. These numbers tell us the highest price and lowest price reached during those years.

2.   Under the subheadings 1994 and 1995, see High and Low. Here you find the highest price and lowest price reached more recently—the year just past and the current year (of the guide in your hand).

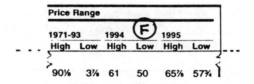

According to my S&P guide, the lowest price Bristol-Myers Squibb sold for, from 1971–1993, was 3⅞. That's under $4! The highest price was 90⅛! Imagine if you had owned it—and held it—through all the price swings of those 22 years.

Then what happened? Let's see—in 1994 the low was 50; the high was 61.

See what a great snapshot this is of a long history? And we're not finished yet. What's been happening recently? Move to the next column. Since my copy of the stock guide is from April 1995, the date I see in this column is March 1995, the previous month.

The highest price so far in March was 65⅞. The lowest price was 61⅛. The last price, when my issue of the guide went to print, was 62⅞ as you can see below.

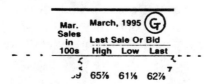

How about McDonald's? I see that so far this year it's had a high of 35¾ and a low of 32⅝; the last price is 34⅛.

Assume that we each bought our stock at *last* year's (1994) lowest price. Using the figures from the S&P guide, we can see that Bristol-Myers Squibb's shares would now be 12⅞ ahead. Rounded, that's $12.88 per share. Not bad, hmm?

Can you see where that answer came from? Let me show you:

1. Convert the fractions by using the following fractions-to-decimals reference.

    Fractions-to-Decimals Reference

⅛	=	.125	⅝	=	.625
¼	=	.25	¾	=	.75
⅜	=	.375	⅞	=	.875
½	=	.50			

2. Once the numbers are in decimal form, use your calculator to subtract.

    Here's an example of how to figure out investment results, using Bristol-Myers Squibb as a model:

$62.88	This year's last price of 62⅞	As S&P went to print
−50.00	Last year's low of 50	Price we paid
$12.88	Gain in value	Paper profit

    That's all there is to it.
    Now see what happened to McDonald's:

$34.125	This year's last price of 34⅛	As S&P went to print
−25.500	Last year's low price of 25½	Price we paid
$ 8.630	Gain in value	Paper profit

If you'd bought McDonald's at last year's low price, you'd be $8.63 per share ahead as of April 1995. Okay, try another stock. Choose any other A company. Did it lose or gain? How much?

You sound just like an expert.

Now, back to the stock guide in Figure 14.1. Find Bristol-Myers Squibb again. On the facing page, find Dividends (E). Below it, find the subheading Total $. Okay. Now below Total $, find the sub-sub-heading (still above the middle column) titled Ind. Rate (an abbreviation for *Indicated Rate*). Later, you can read the explanation for this figure inside the back cover of your S&P Guide. For now, slide your finger down to the line for Bristol-Myers Squibb.

Take that figure (2.96) and add it to the Bristol-Myers Squibb paper profit. By the way, *paper* profit means only that you have not sold the stock. You do not have the profit in your pocket, but it is recorded on paper. Once you sell, label it "pocket" profit.

$12.88 (Bristol-Myers Squibb paper profit)
+ 2.96 dividend (as reported in the guide)
For a total of $15.84 per share.

Okay, but what does that $15.84 represent? It's your *total return.* Part of the return comes from price increase. Part of the return comes from the dividends paid. When your stockbroker mentions total return, you'll know exactly what she means.

Or you could say, $15.84 is the *yield* on one share of stock. If you owned 100 shares, you'd have a *total return* of $1,584. That's $132 a month! Fun, huh? But, put your checkbook away. There's still another very big question to answer before you flash the cash.

Tool B: The Value Line Investment Survey

So far we have an A corporation, we approve of its business, and we like the dividend—it has a good payment history and it increased this year.

"So what more do we want?" you ask.

More than past history. We're investing for the *future.* We need expert input on how to look ahead. Our financial success depends on it. So here comes more help.

The *Standard & Poor's Stock Guide* warned us that its rankings are an appraisal of *past* performance. That history is important. After all, isn't that what any mother asks a prospective nanny before turning her loose on the children? But then we move on to what we can expect from her in the future. It's the same with stocks.

That's where tool B comes in. *Value Line* looks at the past and present, and based on those efforts, suggests the *future.* For more comfort from those worrisome midnight questions, think of *Value Line* as a professional second opinion.

Value Line is available at your public library, through your stockbroker, or by subscription. See Appendix B for more information.

Value Line is a weekly publication used industrywide. Every three months, a new full-page review of your company is issued. This update makes it easy to stay smart about your stocks. Once you're familiar with the format, you can scan data in minutes.

Like the *Standard & Poor's Stock Guide, Value Line* is dense with information. Lucky for us, it's written in straight English. But, because it's so rich, put on your blinders as we did before. Decide what you want *before* you dive in. Once you learn the layout, you'll love it.

How do you use *Value Line?* Take these four easy steps:

1. Using the current *Value Line* Summary and Index, Part I, find the index to stocks. (See Figure 14.2.)

   Locate the page number of the report on your corporation. You'll easily find Bristol-Myers Squibb or McDonald's or any other company you want to investigate. The Index page numbers are entered in bold print, immediately to the left of the alphabetical listings. The full-page report will be in a separate pull-out pamphlet, held in the same black binder. Go to that page. (See Figure 14.3.)

2. If we look at the full-page report, we'll find commentary about the company halfway down the page, as shown below:

BRISTOL-MYERS SQ. NYSE-BMY   VALUE LINE 1255

Ⓐ

Bristol-Myers Squibb is off to a faster-than-expected start this year. Year-over-year earnings per share increased 13% to $1.29 in the first quarter, which is well above our and consensus estimates of $1.19 and $1.22, respectively. Results were favorably impacted by the positive effect of exchange rate fluctuations, with the weak dollar increasing global sales by 2%. Additionally, the three acquisitions—Calgon Vestal Laboratories, Matrix Essentials, Inc., and the UPSA Group—were far less dilutive to profits than earlier anticipated. They reduced share net by two cents while accounting for one-third of the 16% increase in overall sales. Pharmaceutical sales increased 13% (to $1.9 billion), led mainly by a near-doubling (to $125 million) in *Taxol's* (an anti-cancer drug) contributions. The company's medical devices and consumer products businesses also showed good top-line growth, helped significantly by the aforementioned additions. **We've raised our profit estimate for 1995.** Financial results in 1994 were unaffected by exchange rates, but absent a substantial reversal in prevailing currency trends, Bristol-Myers stands to benefit through much of the year. It also appears that patent protection for the company's flagship drug, *Capoten* (with worldwide 1994 sales of $1.5 billion), has been extended by about six months (through February '96) by recent GATT legislation. The recent launch of antidepressant *Serzone*, albeit into a very competitive market, should help as well. Factoring in continued growth in *Taxol* and *Pravachol* (a cardiovascular medicine) sales, along with strict cost controls, our new estimate is $5.05 a share (up 25¢ from three months ago). **The huge drugmaker's long-term growth prospects, however, remain lackluster, in our opinion.** Its large sales base is clearly a factor. The maturity of many of its businesses is another. And so, too, is Bristol-Myers' relatively unexciting new-drug pipeline. In all, we look for its share earnings to grow at a mid-single-digit rate in 1996 and out to 1998-2000. **A good dividend gives this top-quality issue some appeal.** We also note the company's cash-rich solid balance sheet, which affords management the wherewithal to render our projections low. *George I.H. Rho*   *May 5, 1995*

FIGURE 14.2 *Value Line* Index

May 5, 1995 SUMMARY AND INDEX • THE VALUE LINE INVESTMENT SURVEY Page 5 **BI–CA**

PAGE NUMBERS
Bold type refers to Ratings and Reports; *Italics to Selection & Opinion*

1255 Bristol-Myers Squibb

	Page	NAME OF STOCK		Ticker Symbol	Recent Price	Timeliness	Rank for Safety	Beta	Estimated Range of 3-5 yr. average prices 1998-2000		Current P/E Ratio	Est'd Yield next 12 mos.	Est'd Earns. 12 mos. to 9-30-95	(f) Est'd Div'd next 12 mos.	Industry Rank	Qtr. Ended	Earns. Per sh.	Year Ago	Qtr. Ended	Latest Div'd	Year Ago	Technical Rank	Where Options Trade
★★	209	Bio-Rad Labs. 'A'	(ASE)	BIOA	29	1	3	.85	40- 60	(40-105%)	13.2	NIL	2.19	NIL	8	3/31	◆.99	.58	3/31	NIL	NIL	1	
		Bird Corp.							SEE FINAL SUPPLEMENT - PAGE 839														
	605	Birmingham Steel		BIR	20	3	3	1.15	30- 45	(50-125%)	10.9	2.0%	1.83	.40	45	3/31	.45	.20	6/30	.10	.10	4	NYS
	130	Black & Decker		BDK	30	1	4	1.65	40- 65	(35-115%)	18.2	1.4%	1.65	.42	19	3/31	.27	.14	6/30	◆.10	.10	2	CBO
	1683	Blair Corp.	(ASE)	BL	34	5	3	.80	45- 70	(30-105%)	8.3	6.9%	4.10	2.35	91	3/31	◆.77	.88	6/30	.35	.35	3	
	2[illegible]1	[illegible]ock (H&R)		HRB	41	4	2	.95	60- 80	(45- 95%)	20.9	3.0%	1.96	1.24	26	1/31	.08	07	6/30	.312	.28	3	ASE
	1[illegible]4	[illegible]lount, Inc. 'A'	(ASE)	BLTA	46	2	3	1.05	75-110	(65-140%)	13.5	1.2%	3.40	.57	36	2/28	.70	.49	6/30	.142	.125	2	
	[illegible]	[illegible]oatmen's Bancshs.	(NDQ)	BOAT	33	3	3	1.00	40- 65	(20- 95%)	10.0	4.3%	3.30	1.42	77	3/31	.67	.82	6/30	.34	.31	4	CBO
	[illegible]	[illegible]ob Evans Farms	(NDQ)	BOBE	20	3	3	1.00	30- 40	(50-100%)	14.6	1.5%	1.37	.29	62	1/31	.33	.29	3/31	072	.068	3	
	[illegible]	Boeing		BA	56	4	1	1.00	70- 85	(25- 50%)	46.3	1.8%	1.21	1.00	46	3/31	◆.53	.86	6/30	◆.25	.25	3	CBO
	9[illegible]	Boise Cascade		BCC	32	1	3	1.05	55- 80	(70-150%)	10.4	1.9%	3.07	.62	20	3/31	.85	d1.35	9/30	◆.15	.15	2	CBO
	22[illegible]	Bolt Beranek & Newman		BBN	19	3	5	1.25	10- 19	(N- 0%)	NMF	NIL	d.21	NIL	6	3/31	◆d.27	d.14	3/31	NIL	NIL	1	CBO
	5[illegible]	Bombardier Inc. 'B'	(TSE)	BBDB.TO	30 (b)	1	3	1.00	35- 55	(15- 85%)	17.5	1.0%	1.71	.30	46	1/31	.46(b)	.37(b)	3/31	.075(b)	.053(b)	2	TCO
	16[illegible]	Bombay Co.		BBA	7⅝	4	3	1.55	18- 25	(135-230%)	11.5	[illegible]	.66	NIL	91	12/31	.41	.40	3/31	NIL	NIL	5	PHL
	22[illegible]	Borland Int'l	(NDQ)	BORL	9½	4	5	1.40	10- 15	(5- 60%)	[illegible]	[illegible]	1.99	NIL	6	12/31	d1.15	d.11	3/31	NIL	NIL	5	CBO
	11[illegible]	Boston Bancorp	(NDQ)	SBOS	35	4	3	.90	[illegible]	[illegible]	[illegible]	[illegible]	[illegible]	.80	79	1/31	1.06	1.35	3/31	.19	.19	4	
	1[illegible]	Boston Edison		BSE	24	4	3	[illegible]	[illegible]	[illegible]	[illegible]	[illegible]	[illegible]	1.84	85	3/31	◆.36	.35	3/31	▲.455	.44	4	
	2[illegible]	Boston Scientific		BSX	26	[illegible]	[illegible]	[illegible]	[illegible]	[illegible]	[illegible]	[illegible]	[illegible]	NIL	8	12/31	.24	.21	3/31	NIL	NIL	2	CBO
	9[illegible]	Bowater Inc.		BOW	[illegible]	[illegible]	[illegible]	[illegible]	[illegible]	[illegible]	[illegible]	[illegible]	[illegible]	.63	20	3/31	1.02	d.67	6/30	.15	.15	2	PAC
	18[illegible]	Bowne & Co.	(ASE)	[illegible]	[illegible]	[illegible]	[illegible]	[illegible]	[illegible]	[illegible]	[illegible]	[illegible]	[illegible]	.36	81	1/31	.12	.38	3/31	.18	.15	5	
238	16[illegible]	Bradlees, Inc.		[illegible]	[illegible]	[illegible]	[illegible]	[illegible]	[illegible]	[illegible]	[illegible]	[illegible]	[illegible]	60-.20	65	1/31	1.15	2.44	6/30	.15	.15	4	ASE
	12[illegible]	Brascan Ltd.		[illegible]	[illegible]	[illegible]	[illegible]	[illegible]	[illegible]	[illegible]	[illegible]	[illegible]	[illegible]	.76	37	12/31	.25	.01	6/30	.19	.19	3	
	3[illegible]	Brazil Fund		[illegible]	[illegible]	[illegible]	[illegible]	[illegible]	[illegible]	[illegible]	[illegible]	[illegible]	NMF	NIL	78	9/30	37.44(q)	21.06(q)	3/31	NIL	.08	2	
2240	1306	Briggs & Stratt[illegible]		[illegible]	[illegible]	[illegible]	[illegible]	[illegible]	[illegible]	[illegible]	[illegible]	2.9%	3.60	1.00	34	3/31	1.64	1.24	9/30	.25	NIL	3	PHL
	[illegible]	Brinker Int'l		[illegible]	[illegible]	[illegible]	[illegible]	[illegible]	[illegible]	[illegible]	16.3	NIL	1.04	NIL	62	3/31	.25	.22	3/31	NIL	NIL	4	PAC
	1255	Bristol-Myers Squibb		[illegible]	[illegible]	[illegible]	[illegible]	[illegible]	[illegible]-105	(30- 60%)	13.1	4.6%	4.96	3.00	24	3/31	1.29	1.14	6/30	.74	.73	3	CBO
	[illegible]	British Airways ADR(g)		[illegible]	[illegible]	[illegible]	[illegible]	[illegible]	60- 90	(N- 40%)	12.4	3.8%	5.23	2.50	49	12/31	.80	.44	3/31	695	595	3	PHL
	834	British Gas PLC ADR(g)		[illegible]	[illegible]	3	1	.60	40- 50	(N- 0%)	43.0	6.0%	1.14	2.95-2.85	16	12/31	.39	d2.52	3/31	NIL	NIL	2	
	407	British Petroleum PLC		[illegible]	88	3	3	.70	75-110	(N- 25%)	15.4	3.2%	5.72	2.85	76	12/31	1.47	d.37	6/30	.704	.46	2	PAC
	835	British Steel ADR(g)		BST	27	2	3	.80	35- 50	(30- 85%)	6.9	4.6%	3.94	1.25	16	9/30	.75(p)	.15(p)	3/31	.396	.093	2	NYS
	786	British Telecom ADR(g)		BTY	64	4	1	.85	70- 90	(10- 40%)	16.5	5.6%	3.89	3.58	87	12/31	1.28	1.18	3/31	1.401	1.217	3	NYS
	2216	Broderbund Software	(NDQ)	BROD	52	1	4	1.70	60- 95	(15- 85%)	34.7	NIL	1.50	NIL	6	2/28	.50	.22	3/31	NIL	NIL	1	PAC
	1229	Broken Hill ADR(•)		BHP	51	4	2	.70	▲65- 90	(25- 75%)	17.4	2.9%	2.93	1.50(h)	37	2/28	.64	.59	3/31	NIL	NIL	3	
	477	Brooklyn Union Gas		BU	25	▼5	1	.45	25- 30	(0- 20%)	13.2	5.6%	1.90	1.41	97	3/31	◆1.53	1.57	6/30	.347	.337	3	
	1537	Brown-Forman 'B'		BFB	32	3	1	.80	45- 55	(40- 70%)	14.2	3.1%	2.25	1.00	54	1/31	.54	.48	6/30	.248	.237	3	
	1669	Brown Group		BG	28	3	3	.90	45- 65	(60-130%)	13.0	6.4%	2.15	1.80	95	1/31	.21	d.06	6/30	.40	.40	4	
	344	Browning-Ferris Inds.		BFI	33	3	3	1.25	40- 60	(20- 80%)	17.8	2.1%	1.85	.68	40	12/31	.45	.34	6/30	.17	.17	3	ASE
1142	1507	Bruno's, Inc.	(NDQ)	BRNO	12	–	3	.95	14- 20	(15- 65%)	17.9	2.3%	.67	.28	25	12/31	.18	.12	3/31	.065	.06	–	CBO
	1762	Brunswick Corp.		BC	21	3	3	1.45	30- 45	(45-115%)	12.1	2.4%	1.73	.50	51	3/31	◆.42	.27	6/30	◆.125	.11	4	CBO
	1230	Brush Wellman		BW	19	2	3	1.05	30- 45	(60-135%)	13.6	1.7%	1.40	.32	37	3/31	◆.42	.35	3/31	.16	.05	3	
	321	Buckeye Partners L.P.		BPL	35	5	3	.60	40- 55	(15- 55%)	8.9	8.4%	3.95	2.95	35	3/31	.94	.97	3/31	.70	.70	3	
	266	Builders Transport	(NDQ)	TRUK	12	2	4	.90	25- 40	(110-235%)	11.3	NIL	1.06	NIL	33	3/31	◆.15	.11	3/31	NIL	NIL	4	
	1685	Burlington Coat		BCF	11	5	3	1.00	25- 40	(125-265%)	13.3	NIL	.83	NIL	91	12/31	1.06	1.38	3/31	NIL	NIL	5	PHL
	1627	Burlington Inds.		BUR	11	3	3	1.25	18- 25	(65-125%)	9.2	NIL	1.20	NIL	69	12/31	.19	.28	3/31	NIL	NIL	5	ASE
1602	284	Burlington Northern		BNI	60	2	3	1.20	80-120	(35-100%)	12.2	2.0%	4.93	1.20	13	3/31	1.10	.90	6/30	.30	.30	3	CBO
	451	Burlington Resources		BR	39	3	2	.95	55- 70	(40- 80%)	NMF	1.4%	.37	.55	84	3/31	d.04	.37	9/30	.137	.137	4	PHL
	855	Butler Mfg.	(NDQ)	BTLR	40	1	3	.50	75-115	(90-190%)	8.8	1.0%	4.54	.40	52	3/31	.72	d.29	6/30	.10	NIL	1	
	556	CAE Inc.	(TSE)	CAE.TO	8⅜(b)	1	4	.55	13- 20	(55-140%)	17.1	1.9%	.49	.16	46	12/31	.13(b)	.10(b)	3/31	.04(b)	.04(b)	3	TCO
1596	1307	CBI Inds.		CBI	25	3	3	.95	40- 55	(60-120%)	16.0	2.2%	1.56	.54	34	12/31	.46	.23	6/30	.12	.12	4	PHL
986	378	CBS Inc.		CBS	61	4	2	1.00	90-105	(50- 70%)	17.9	0.7%	3.41	.40	73	3/31	.32	.85	3/31	.10	.10	3	CBO
	1801	CCH Inc.	(NDQ)	CCHIA	17	3	3	1.00	25- 40	(45-135%)	20.2	4.1%	.84	.70	81	3/31	.31	.33	6/30	.175	.175	3	
1917	322	CDI Corp.		CDI	26	1	3	.80	25- 40	(N- 55%)	19.0	NIL	1.37	NIL	35	3/31	◆.36	.20	3/31	NIL	NIL	1	
1751	2181	CIGNA Corp.		CI	73	3	3	1.25	85-115	(15- 60%)	9.5	4.2%	7.72	3.04	17	12/31	2.42	2.70	6/30	.76	.76	4	CBO
	702	CIPSCO Inc.		CIP	29	4	1	.65	30- 40	(5- 40%)	11.9	7.0%	2.44	2.04	83	3/31	◆.37	.40	6/30	▲.51	.50	3	
	300	CKE Restaurants		CKR	7	4	3	1.05	17- 25	(145-255%)	35.0	1.1%	.20	.08	62	1/31	d.03	d.02	6/30	.04	.04	4	CBO
988	1686	CML Group		CML	7¼	4	3	1.50	25- 40	(240-450%)	6.2	1.4%	1.18	.10	91	1/31	.78	.72	6/30	▲.025	.02	4	PHL
	703	CMS Energy Corp.		CMS	23	3	4	.80	25- 40	(10- 75%)	10.3	4.2%	2.23	.96	83	3/31	◆.99	.92	3/31	.21	.18	3	NYS
	2182	CNA Fin'l		CNA	76	3	3	1.15	70-100	(N- 30%)	15.4	NIL	4.93	NIL	17	12/31	1.53	1.40	3/31	NIL	NIL	3	ASE
	1465	CPC Int'l		CPC	59	3	2	1.00	70- 95	(20- 60%)	17.3	2.5%	3.42	1.47	63	3/31	.73	.63	6/30	.36	.34	3	PAC
239	1763	CPI Corp.		CPY	16	3	3	.90	30- 40	(90-150%)	12.8	3.5%	1.25	.56	51	1/31	.86	.56	3/31	.14	.14	3	
★★	285	CSX Corp.		CSX	82	2	3	1.25	110-165	(35-100%)	11.9	2.1%	6.90	1.76	13	3/31	1.15	.71	6/30	◆.44	.44	3	PAC
	237	C-TEC Corp.							SEE FINAL SUPPLEMENT - PAGE 237														
	1028	CTS Corp.		CTS	33	2	3	.65	40- 60	(20- 80%)	10.6	1.8%	3.10	.60	10	3/31	.63	.48	6/30	.15	.10	2	
	2152	CUC Int'l		CU	40	2	3	1.30	35- 70	(N- 75%)	34.2	NIL	1.17	NIL	26	1/31	.28	.22	3/31	NIL	NIL	2	PHL
	787	Cable & Wireless ADR(g)		CWP	20	3	3	1.05	35- 50	(75-150%)	23.3	2.3%	.86	.45	87	9/30	.49(p)	.41(p)	3/31	.167	.145	3	CBO
	1082	Cabletron Sys.		CS	48	2	3	1.60	95-145	(100-200%)	18.5	NIL	2.60	NIL	22	2/28	.64	.47	3/31	NIL	NIL	2	ASE
	379	Cablevision Sys. 'A'	(ASE)	CVC	56	5	4	1.55	45- 75	(N- 35%)	NMF	NIL	d15.16	NIL	73	12/31	d5.91	d3.78	3/31	NIL	NIL	3	CBO
	1887	Cabot Corp.		CBT	39	1	3	.85	40- 60	(5- 55%)	11.4	1.4%	3.42	.56	14	3/31	◆1.17	.56	3/31	.14	.13	2	
1844	452	Cabot Oil & Gas 'A'		COG	16	5	3	.80	25- 35	(55-120%)	NMF	1.0%	d.54	.16	84	12/31	d.15	.04	3/31	.04	.04	5	
	1544	Cadbury Schweppes(g)	(NDQ)	CADBY	28	3	3	.85	30- 50	(5- 80%)	15.6	4.0%	1.79	1.12	32	6/30	.68(p)	.60(p)	3/31	.897	NIL	3	
237	1785	Caesars World							SEE FINAL SUPPLEMENT - PAGE 237														
	1641	Caldor Corp.		CLD	19	5	3	1.30	30- 50	(60-165%)	8.8	NIL	2.15	NIL	65	1/31	2.33	2.29	3/31	NIL	NIL	4	NYS
	504	Calgon Carbon		CCC	12	3	3	1.30	20- 30	(65-150%)	24.5	2.5%	.49	.30	61	3/31	.10	.06	9/30	.075	.04	4	PHL
	1882	California Energy		CE	17	3	4	1.15	35- 65	(105-280%)	15.7	NIL	1.08	NIL	55	3/31	◆.21	.20	3/31	NIL	NIL	3	PAC
	1154	California Fed. Bank		CAL	12	3	5	2.35	15- 25	(25-110%)	17.1	NIL	▼.70	NIL	79	3/31	◆.17	d11.53	3/31	NIL	NIL	4	CBO
	1029	California Microwave	(NDQ)	CMIC	30	3	4	1.25	40- 70	(35-135%)	20.3	NIL	1.48	NIL	10	3/31	.32	.30	3/31	NIL	NIL	1	CBO
	1420	California Water		CWT	32	5	1	.50	35- 45	(10- 40%)	13.3	6.4%	2.40	2.04	89	3/31	.16	.24	6/30	◆.51	.495	4	
	893	CalMat Co.		CZM	20	▼4	3	.95	20- 35	(0- 75%)	22.0	2.0%	.91	.40	28	3/31	◆d.16	.07	6/30	.10	.10	3	
	1173	Cambridge Shopping Ctr.	(TSE)	CBG.TO	12	4	3	.60	20- 35	(65-190%)	48.0	2.7%	▼.25	.32	67	12/31	.04	.08	3/31	.08	.08	4	
	1466	Campbell Soup		CPB	51	1	2	.95	55- 75	(10- 45%)	17.8	2.4%	2.86	1.24	63	1/31	.93	.81	6/30	.31	.28	2	NYS
	1577	Canadian Imperial Bk	(TSE)	CM.TO	34 (b)	3	3	.90	30- 45	(N- 30%)	8.4	4.4%	4.05	1.48	60	1/31	1.03(b)	.86(b)	6/30	.37(b)	.33(b)	3	TCO
	1030	Canadian Marconi	(ASE)	CMW	8⅞	4	2	.70	9- 12	(0- 35%)	68.5	1.7%	.13	.15	10	12/31	.03	.14	3/31	NIL	NIL	4	

(•) All data adjusted for announced stock split or stock dividend. See back page of Ratings & Reports.
◆ New figure this week.
(b) Canadian Funds.
d Deficit.
(f) The estimate may reflect a probable increase or decrease if a dividend boost or cut is possible but not probable. If two figures are shown, the first is the more likely.
(g) Dividends subject to foreign withholding tax for U.S. residents.
(h) Est'd Earnings & Est'd Dividends after conversion to U.S. dollars at Value Line estimated translation rate.
(j) All Index data expressed in hundreds.
(p) 6 months (q) Asset Value
N=Negative figure NA=Not available NMF=No meaningful figure

Source: Copyright 1995 by Value Line Publishing, Inc. Reprinted by permission; all rights reserved.

FIGURE 14.3   *Value Line* Company Listing

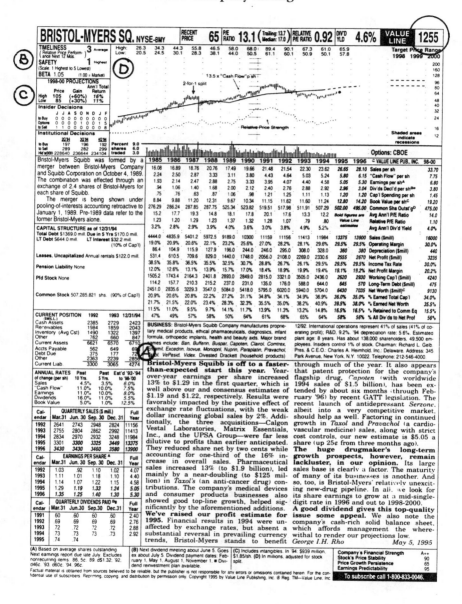

Source: Copyright 1995 by Value Line Publishing, Inc.
Reprinted by permission; all rights reserved.

Read it with questions like these in mind:

- Are serious problems mentioned?
- Is management changing?
- Is the product in demand?
- Is competition encroaching on market share?
- What's the overall future outlook for the company and its competitors?
- Is a summary opinion offered?

Was the report understandable? It's a nice surprise to see that it *is* written in everyday language. You can follow what's said without knowing in-house jargon. Now, if you are still satisfied that the company sounds good, go on to the next step.

3. Still looking at the full-page report:

At the top left corner, you'll notice a square enclosing the words *Timeliness* and *Safety* as shown below.

The page I'm looking at reports, "Timeliness: 3—average"; and "Safety: 1—highest."

Since we are searching for a stock with safety in mind, this *1* is right on the mark. Now we've gotten an opinion on safety from two reliable sources: the *Value Line Investment Survey* and the *Standard & Poor's Stock Guide.* We're in good company.

And timeliness? Think of timeliness as a barometer for the likelihood of near-term upward movement in the stock value. It's a research-based best guess aimed at helping to answer that painful question: Should I act now or wait until . . . Until what? Until the price is lower? Until the economy changes? Until the election is over? Until year end? Until the kids graduate?

Unless you become a charting devotee or want to analyze all the economic and market forces at work, take the advice of *Value Line.* They've done that work for you. Remember, however, the future is never guaranteed. There is always the risk of the unknown.

By the way, have you found a stock you like? Has it passed the requirements? Good. So, now do you write the check?

Not yet; we still need that *future* input.

4. Look again at *Value Line's* full-page stock report. At the top left corner, there is a second square titled Projections, as shown below. That's what we're looking for. It will give us an *educated guess* about the future.

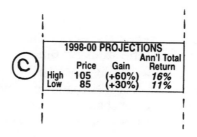

This projection is not carved in stone. It's a *Value Line* best *guess,* based on facts and analysis. Nothing in the future is certain; we know that. But look how easy they've made it for us to understand their projections.

Now, notice the chart spread across the top of the page. This is a quick glance at the historical direction of the stock price—and its hills and valleys along the way. I'm looking at Bristol-Myers Squibb on the *Value Line* dated May 5, 1995. Whatever issue you have in front of you, this chart is positioned in the same location on the page.

At the right border of the chart are three columns titled Target, Price, and Range. My issue lists the subtitles 1998, 1999, 2000. Notice that these columns are intersected by two lines broken into dashes. These lines give us a picture of the information given in the

Projections box. The upper dashes show the *high* price projection; the lower dashes show the *low* price projection. Do you see the numeric valuations noted at the right border in the item shown below?

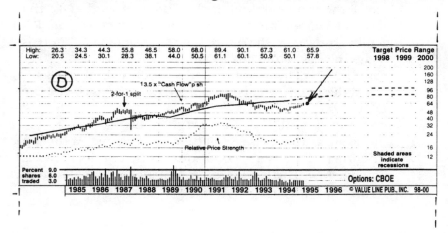

Next, see the dot entered at the tail of the price history chart? That's the *current* price of the stock (at time of printing).

Compare the current price of the stock to the future projections. Is the current price higher or lower than the projections? My issue shows the projections higher than the current price. Good! We wouldn't want to invest in a company on its way down.

Now, go back to the Projections box. My issue tells me, if the stock price reaches the *high* projection of 105, that would mean a 60 percent gain and an annual total return of 16 percent. It tells me that if the stock price moves up to only 85 (the *low* projection), it would mean a 30 percent gain with an annual return of 11 percent. The box also tells me their projection covers a three-year time period (1998–2000). What does your issue tell you?

Do you like the looks of the projections? Wouldn't it be nice to own a stock that could increase 30 percent to 60 percent? Remember, I said *could* increase. Okay, let's say you're satisfied with the projection, the safety, the business, and the dividend. Is it time to buy? Almost.

Tool C: Real-Time Input

It's time for the pièce de résistance: information that's hot off the wire. Call your stockbroker. She'll have her firm's recently printed research opinion, but more importantly, she has computer access to up-to-the-minute wire stories. Ask her to read to you the latest news release about your company and the outlook for its type of business.

Is the news bad or good? Does it confirm your other findings?

The Facts Are In

Okay, you've gotten input from three *reliable* sources. You have the stock's history, an educated projection about its future, and a report that's hot off the wire. Do you still like the company as an investment? Get this minute's price from your broker.

Go for it!

About Follow-Up after the Sale

The minute you invest, get ready for paperwork, reports, and statements. Here's where I really encourage you to work with a major firm. Investing is their area of specialization and their systems are in place to make your life easier.

Gradually, you may want to master all the ins and outs of *Value Line*. Who knows? You may be the next Wall Street guru. Take advantage of the expertise of your stockbroker. Ask her to explain the other sections on the *Value Line* report. Maybe one of these days you'll be comparing industry sectors and capital structure! Or not.

At any rate, whether you own one stock or build a portfolio of 20 issues, avoid unwanted surprises. Ask your stockbroker to send you reports periodically. There should be no charge. The reports will help you stay on top of your investments and to build a working relationship with your broker. And you'll be amazed at how interesting it is to follow new innovations in business.

Was This Research Necessary?

It was about here that a woman in one of my workshops began flipping through the *Value Line Investment Survey* and threw her hands up.

"There's a page in here that lists conservative stocks," she said to me. "Phooey. If I'd seen this, I wouldn't have bothered to make my own *A* list. All that work was for nothing."

For nothing? I don't think so. Too many investors have told me, if they hadn't sifted through the 5,100 stocks in the S&P's guide for themselves, they wouldn't have known to avoid that other 93 percent. It's a huge market, and a very mixed bag, with something for everyone. Including speculators.

Take off the rose-colored specs. The lower the ranking, the higher the risk. And, even the highest ranked stocks are not guaranteed.

I hope you've spotted a company you like. Start with 100 shares. Don't feel worried. Cautious, yes—but not worried. In a year, tell me what you bought and how you did. You'll do just fine.

Chapter 22 will help you keep score.

Chapter 15

*A*re Mutual Funds the Choice for You?

*Y*ou can't hide from mutual funds—their numbers are explosive. Even if a woman does not actively seek them out, she may still find mutual funds playing a role in her financial future. She need only sign up for a life insurance policy that includes internal investments or contribute to her employer's 401(k) retirement plan. (Like the individual retirement plan (IRA), a 401(k) allows employees to set aside monies pretax.) However, just because mutual funds are popular and familiar doesn't mean they are replacements for savings accounts or money markets.

What Is a Mutual Fund?

A fund—no matter if it's made up of stocks, bonds, mortgages, etc.—is a group investment based on the appealing (or appalling) idea that you don't have to know anything. The marketing message is "Join the crowd and let the experts do the thinking for you."

Put together a group of stocks and you have a stock fund. Put together a group of bonds and you have a bond fund. There are others, but we'll limit our talk to these. And if you think that investing in a mutual fund frees you from the terrible burden imposed by trying to choose individual stocks or bonds, think again. There are hundreds and hundreds of mutual funds. The August 26, 1996, issue of *Forbes* magazine rates 1,878 funds. The magazine also said the Investment Company Institute tracks 6,007 funds! Phew!

Mutual funds have been around a long time, rising and falling in popularity as their successes, failures, and the mood of the economy shifts. I don't have to tell you that today, in the 1990s, they pop up everywhere. If you have some lazy cash sitting in your savings, you'll surely be introduced to a *family* of mutual funds at your neighborhood bank. We'll talk more about families later.

If it ever was simple to know what made up a mutual fund, it is no longer. There are stock funds of every conceivable risk level, makeup, and purpose. There are too many to name, but here are a bare few: small companies, medium companies, large companies; funds for income, funds for growth, funds that combine growth and income; funds that specialize in a single foreign country or several foreign countries; funds of environmentally kind corporations. Funds can even vary in their tax consequences. Now, add the bond fund varieties and the landscape is mind-boggling. But behind all the varietal fund names are those same basic investments and activities we've already discussed. No matter how differently dressed, those individual investments come from the same marketplace and carry the same potential for risk and reward. The difference is, when you invest in a mutual fund, you are hiring a third party to take over your decision making.

Mutual Funds Have Expenses, Too

Ads tell us that funds are an easy way to diversify with smaller amounts of money. True enough. And diversification is safer than owning one or two stocks, but a fund's diversification and expertise come at a price.

Your mutual fund was no-load, you say? You paid no commission or costs? No matter. Low-load, deferred-load, or no-load, you can't escape the fees that nibble at your investment dollar. It is not a cost-free investment.

The mutual fund ads have to be paid for—they are a cost of marketing. Nibble nibble. Then there are the built-in costs of management: tax experts; attorneys; experts who choose, buy, sell, and monitor the investments; support staff, etc. Nibble nibble. Then, there is a pool of money left uninvested. Even though the mutual fund is a long-term investment, there are always investors who jump in and out for one reason or another. The fund must be able to provide that liquidity every day. This uninvested pool is similar to your own cushion fund. It's available cash set aside for anticipated expenditures. Can you see what's coming? If too many investors want out and the cash isn't available, the fund manager experiences a cash squeeze, same as you or I might.

Suppose you own shares in Fund X. For whatever reason, a number of investors have liquidated their shares and the reserve monies are used up. At the same time, there is a marked drop in the stock market. This loss in value does not escape the notice of other fund owners. They get nervous and want out. But since the cushion has been used up, now the fund manager has a choice to make. Should he borrow the necessary cash? We know there is a cost to borrow. Nibble nibble.

If the value of the fund's shares go lower, another layer of investors gets nervous and decides to sell. This accelerates the fund's cash squeeze. Maybe this time, instead of borrowing, the manager decides to sell fund positions. Because it is not the best time to sell, the sale eats into principal. Gobble gobble. The shares go lower, triggering another wave of selling by nervous investors. If the cycle continues, it can become a downhill sled ride.

There's no mystique about Wall Street. Illiquidity affects a mutual fund in the same way it affects you. If you don't allow yourself an adequate cushion, you may have to borrow or sell an investment. What happens if your mutual funds are down when you are forced to sell? You got it: Cr-unch. A big bite of principal disappears—forever.

It is not smart to invest cushion money in a mutual fund. A mutual fund is not a short-term parking place. It is a long-term investment. You cannot know what your funds will be worth on the day you need cash for that unpredictable emergency.

But what if the value of your mutual fund is up when you have to sell? Lucky you. You'll have the needed cash at little or no loss. But if that investment is doing so well, why penalize yourself by selling? Holding onto losses too long—hoping to recoup—and selling profitable investments too soon—fearing profits will evaporate—are two of the average investor's most common errors.

Wall Street thrives on predictions. You may, too. Just don't let your *cushion* money get caught up in the game. Keep cushion money liquid and whole. That way, you not only will get a return *on* your money, but a return *of* your money as well.

Recognize Investable Money

An attorney once asked me what *investment* I would recommend for monies he was holding for a client. He said he wouldn't need the money back for six to nine months. Even though he had a limited time and wanted no losses, the return on a safe, fixed, investment sounded too tame for him. He believed he could buy a few options and make a nice profit. Since I couldn't make such guarantees, we did not do business. You'd be surprised how few people understand that not all money is *investable*. And how much less of it can be used to *speculate*. But then, it's the results we're talking about, not the thrill of the moment.

Tools for Mutual Fund Information

The *Standard & Poor's Stock Guide*.   It's easy, and imperative, to investigate the track record of mutual funds on your own. Start with the *Standard & Poor's Stock Guide*. Find the section titled "Standard & Poor's Mutual Fund Summary." This is a great place to get an overall look at what the fund world is all about. The listings, which include hundreds of funds, are expansive enough for our needs and exclusive enough to keep us focused.

The introductory page of the mutual fund section explains each easily understood column but there are a few points we should discuss. First, go to the column titled Prin. Obj. (principal objective). No matter which fund you investigate, always identify its purpose. Do you want income? Find funds identified as *I* for income. Now go to the next column, titled Type, to find out what types of investments are in the fund. For instance, *BD* means bonds, *B* means balanced, *C* means common stocks. (Refer again to the introductory page.)

Now that you have found like-purpose funds, go to the column titled $10,000 invested 12-31-87 Now Worth. This tells you today's value of the $10,000 you invested ten years ago. Typically, a ten-year span will include both the up and down markets. It is at least a long enough period to be more fair in reporting results. If a fund has existed only three years and those years were all during a bull market, their numbers might look great, but how will they do when a down market compromises those returns? Long track records are important to study. If you ever begin to think a mutual fund can be used for cushion funds, refer to the five-year price comparison. This gives you an idea of a fund's price fluctuation. You can see it's anybody's *guess* what a fund will be worth on a specific day in the future.

Use the $10,000 . . . Now Worth results to see which fund has performed the best. You must compare apples to apples, such as income to income or growth to growth. If a fund is attempting to provide investors with income *and* growth, its results cannot be fairly compared to one looking for income only.

A few of the other interesting details you can find on this page include the year the fund originated, its size, cash equivalents, net asset value per share, costs to invest, highs and lows over the year, and income yields. Look over the facts that interest you. By the way, notice how many funds *originated* in the 1980s.

Morningstar Mutual Funds.   Now that you have your feet wet, take a look at Morningstar. You can subscribe directly, or locate this specialized publication at your public library. (See details in Appendix B.) As Value Line covers stocks, so does Morningstar cover mutual funds, offering a deeper look, rating, and commentary on each mutual fund. It's a fine source.

The mutual fund prospectus.   Choose a fund with a philosophy and objectives that match the requirements for your lifestyle and objectives. Then call up the fund or your stockbroker and request a current prospectus. This free pamphlet is required disclosure issued by the fund. Among lots of other information, it lists the *investments* owned by the fund (on the date the prospectus was published). Read through them. Would you be comfortable owning their selections? Do their choices reflect the quality and risk levels you prefer? What's the turnover rate? (This tells how often they buy and sell the portfolio.) Does the fund hold long term? If it's a bond fund, are the maturities mixed? What percentage of bonds are long term? Short term? Are the ratings of a quality you would buy? If you spend a few minutes with their list of holdings you'll have a good feel for the real character of the fund. If you see too many questionable holdings, look elsewhere.

What's a Fund Family?

Mutual funds may be grouped into a family. This is one company's offering of several types of funds, usually including a money market fund, under a recognizable banner. Look through the mutual fund listings in your newspaper to see family examples.

The family benefit for the investor is the convenience of exchanging from a fund with goal A, to a fund with goal B, without incurring fees. For instance, suppose you held shares of a growth stock fund while the market was rising and switched to a bond income fund when interest rates were high. The fund family offers several choices like this and the exchange is simple. Be aware, though, if you show a profit when you exchange out of a fund, it is a taxable event. The term *exchange* is used by the mutual fund, but the IRS still calls it buying and *selling*.

Why not choose stocks and bonds and create your own mutual fund. Remember, KISS. With an emphasis on quality instead of quantity, you'll know it's a fund for *you*.

Chapter 16

*Y*our Will: Can It Protect You?

A True Story

"Sell everything. It's what she wants."

His ashen-faced mother said nothing. She sat at his side, her eyes unfocused, staring ahead, past me, through me, to some other place. She hadn't moved or murmured since they'd come into my office and her son had led her to the chair that faced my desk.

He put his arm around her as an act of love. This frightened, protective son, fortyish I guessed, had come to rescue his suddenly widowed mother.

I tried to reassure him. "Your mother and father spent the past six months setting up their investments. They made safe choices. Combined with his pension and Social Security, your mother has enough income for the rest of her life."

He glared back as if he hadn't heard. "I have to support her now. I need money to do that."

"But suppose her investments are sold," I pleaded, holding out my cupped hands, "and now you have the cash in your hands. What will you do with it?"

"Put it in the bank."

"And each month, will you take out what's needed for your mother's expenses?"

"Of course!" He was defensive. He knew nothing about investing.

"But that's already arranged." I tried again, speaking quietly, pointing at the copy of the account in my hand, "These bonds and stocks are top quality. They produce income. See? Your mother receives this check every month."

I could almost hear his teeth grind. "I've put their house with a real estate agent and I want this stuff sold. I'm taking Momma home, to Pennsylvania, to live with me. I'll take care of her. I don't need your advice. Sell the investments."

"But your mother can transfer her account to Pennsylvania at no cost," I explained. "If she sells everything instead, she'll lose principal. And after selling, the cash will only have to be invested all over again to generate this income." Couldn't he understand? I pointed again at the account page before I leaned in toward his mother, "Mrs. H, are you sure this is what you want to do? Do you want to sell?"

She didn't even blink. She was like a zombie.

"I can't take instructions from you," I said to her son. "The account is in your mother's name. She has to tell me to sell." I hoped he would go away and think about what he was doing. "I have to know it's what your mother wants."

The last time I'd seen Mr. and Mrs. H together was less than a month earlier. They were thrilled. Their new retirement home was safe, paid in full, and their income was assured. They were happy to be in Florida. It was the fulfillment of their lifetime dream. Sunshine and palm trees. No more snow. And, if either were left alone, there would be no worries about security. It was their gift to one another.

Then Mr. H had the heart attack and died. And now, still reeling from shock, this new widow was being whisked away from her life by their well-intentioned son. Away from her safe, paid-for home. Back to ice and snow. To a room in her son's house.

If he succeeded, she would be dependent on him.

There was little I could do but follow the rules. "I'm sorry," I said again. "Your mother has to give me the instructions."

I waited. Mrs. H only stared.

It wasn't long until our firm received instructions to liquidate her account. Mrs. H's son had had himself appointed as her legal guardian. He was in full control of her life. Forever.

I don't know where she is today. But I do know, the day she woke up from the shock of her husband's death, she had another shock waiting. One that could have been avoided.

There's Nothing Simple about a Simple Will

"Wow, you never think you'll go nuts like that," a woman said to me. "Imagine my being stuck in my oldest's place—five grandkids and rock music? Yikes. Could my son do that to me?"

"Ask your attorney that question before you agree to a 'simple will,'" I said.

"Why?"

"Because there are choices. The attorney has an obligation to offer them. In an unbiased way. Did yours?"

"I dunno, Chuck called the attorney and said we needed wills. The attorney said he'd fix us up. Cheap, too. Seventy bucks each. Lucky, huh?"

Lucky? "Only if you know what you got for your money, compared to what you might have had. You've used comparisons to choose a house, mortgage, insurances, cars, bonds, certificates of deposit, prescriptions, toasters—"

"Okay, I hear you," she said. "You're right, that's exactly how I make decisions."

"So why accept a will without comparing it to alternatives?"

"Dumb, huh?"

Not dumb. "It's that old tape, the one that tells you to accept what you get, no questions asked. Erase it. When a bad cold takes you to the doctor," I asked, "does she simply hand over the medicine you ask for?"

"Never, she's got a string of questions. I've got a string of questions. Then I get thumped and scrutinized and—"

I interrupted, "The doctor mulls and hmms?"

"Yep. And *then,* I get whatever she thinks will cure me."

"Okay," I said, "demand that same, thoughtful diagnosis from your attorney."

A "simple will" is not "simple" for you; it's simple for the attorney. Your financial situation is the result of a lifetime of your efforts. And, your situation isn't like mine, or your neighbors'; it has unique aspects. It's special, so take a specialist's advice. You find a heart specialist for heart trouble. The heart specialist offers answers that are unique to you. He knows that just because everybody has a heart, that doesn't mean treatment is commonplace and "simple."

Size Up the Attorney

Ask your attorney questions. Find out who he is and how he works. Here are some questions to get you started:

What segment of law is the attorney's specialty? Estate planning, we hope. Take a minute and scan the Yellow Pages for "Attorneys." Just for fun, count how many areas are listed under "*we* (or *I*) specialize in . . ." Could you specialize in so many areas at once? If that is specializing, we should wonder what makes up a "generalist's" practice.

What percentage of the attorney's practice is devoted to this specialty? Twenty percent or three cases does not a specialist make. The attorney's interest will show up in this answer if you chat about it for a few minutes. What does he like best about law? What sorts of cases does he prefer? Before you know it, a picture of his practice and attitudes will emerge.

Does the attorney *believe* in living trusts? If the attorney does not believe, how can you get unbiased answers? If he's pro–will, he's anti–living trust (also called a revocable, amendable trust). I don't know what choice you will make, but you need a fair explanation and comparison to make that choice. Find someone else. An expert is a professional; he should be willing to answer questions and discuss your concerns and the impact of each decision, without prejudice.

A client told me about a recent visit her husband had with their attorney, who, by the way, had a long history with the family. The husband, eager to explore the idea, took in a newspaper article about living trusts.

"And?" I asked her.

"The attorney asked, 'If they're so great why doesn't everybody have them?'"

A living trust *protects* your control while you're alive. A will can't do that. A will is a *dead* document. Your eyes have closed for the final time before anyone reads it. Which is more important to you—health insurance or a prepaid burial plot? I know the answer, of course, is health insurance. We don't see bodies hanging around because they didn't have a space reservation. Someone will bury the dead.

But during life, we have concerns about our health and our lifestyle. We want to protect both. We do that by maintaining *control.* Be certain your attorney understands that you care about your *life.* Tell him that you love your family, the kids, the grandkids, and all, but death dispositions, taxes, and attorney expenses, which are the purposes served by a will, are secondary. That should introduce the subject of choices: pros and cons of wills and trusts for your special situation. If it doesn't introduce choices? End the interview.

Does the attorney prepare a *set* of estate-planning documents?   My own set includes the following:

- Living trust agreement
- "Pourover" will
- Certificate of trust
- General powers of attorney
- Durable powers of attorney for health care
- Marital property agreement
- Burial instructions

This list will give you an idea of what to expect. Don't let the titles scare you off—they serve basic purposes. Here's a layperson's explanation:

- The trust agreement is the *constitution* of your financial kingdom—it tells who you are, sets out your purpose, rules, powers, succession, and dispositions.
- The pourover will transfers any forgotten assets or surprise monies like lottery winnings received after your death into the trust so they will fall under the rules of your constitution.
- The certificate of trust is like a *Reader's Digest* condensed version of your constitution. It gives the story but leaves out

the juiciest passages. It's useful to give to third parties, so they have essential information, but not your personal details.

- The powers of attorney and of attorney for health care allow specific someones to sign for you if you aren't able. You say who the someones are to be.

Will you still have a separate will?

Yes, the pourover will is a *separate* document, and that's important to know. But since we're talking life *and* death, these two documents are coordinated to work together.

Will the attorney explain the purpose of each document?   Yes, expect it. In addition, my own attorney set up an index and an explanation for each section of the trust agreement, all punched and held in a three-ring binder. The trust document reads like a story and is written in English rather than legalese. (Make certain of this ahead of time.) With the help of the explanations, you shouldn't have any trouble walking through the trust. Educate yourself and then educate your family about what you've done. Because a living trust eliminates the need for probate and courts, your financial situation remains a private family matter. (See Appendix B for further reading.)

As part of his service, will the attorney help you transfer your assets to the trust?   To transfer is to sign instructions that change the way you hold title to something. You've changed or transferred accounts this way many times—for home ownership, car ownership, bank accounts, brokerage accounts, and so on. It's standard procedure to put assets you own under a title. Now those assets are being put under the trust title.

Your attorney can help with this paperwork. He has form letters, but don't rely on him entirely. You are the expert on your own assets. Titling your assets to the trust *now* avoids the time and cost of having someone else hunt for them if you become incompetent or die. Do it immediately.

Give every account (bank, brokerage, mortgage, etc.) a copy of your certificate of trust. If you neglect to title everything, you're going to be stuck with a probate treasure hunt—and the cost that goes with it.

Once you've retitled everything, relax. When the time comes, your account holders will refer to your certificate of trust and know just who (your named successor) to contact. It's a no-brainer.

What does a living trust cost? How long does it take to set it up?   The specialist attorney will be definite about answering these questions because preparing trust agreements is part of his normal routine. If he's vague, that's a red flag.

Watch for advertised free seminars on living trusts. You'll have an opportunity to hear lots of audience questions asked and answered, including discussions on costs. I haven't even touched on the many other benefits you should know about. Once you know more about this important alternative to simple wills, you can make an informed decision.

Too Little, Too Late

A living trust could have saved Mrs. H from her son's frantic maneuverings. Her simple will was useless. If Mr. and Mrs. H had had a living trust, the trust agreement would have named a successor to step in and take over when Mrs. H was unable to make decisions or care for herself. It would have preempted any attempts to place her under a guardianship. Like many others, you may think guardianships help people, but it's a last-resort answer. And, although there may be situations where a guardianship is a preferred answer, more often it can be a frightening trap.

You see, a guardian is a legal parent. You, the ward, are the child. You are treated as that child. You lose all rights forever. You cannot vote, drive, decide where or how to live, choose what you eat, decide who you see—and there's more.

The guardian decides *everything*. Including how to spend your money, with no guidelines about what you (now the legal "child") prefer. What's worse, the court can name who it pleases to become your guardian, even that dreaded sister-in-law or the nosy neighbor down the street. In at least one state, the guardian must be *qualified* by having taken classes. Can you imagine an out-of-state daughter asking to be appointed as guardian for her mother but, since she has not taken the appropriate classes, the court appoints a "qualified" neighbor instead?

"That's horrible," you might say.

Then protect yourself, I say. Name a successor trustee to stand in your shoes, if and when you aren't able. The trustee you name has no rights in your life and does absolutely nothing unless called on by you or by your inability to act in your own behalf.

Had Mrs. H had a living trust, she could have regained control again when she recovered. The living trust isn't a *perfect* answer— How could anything be?—but at least you name your replacement and set the rules for behavior in all matters.

You can name anyone you please as your *successor* trustee. If Mr. and Mrs. H had named their son, they would have talked with him and prepared him for his responsibilities. Or they might have named a qualified adviser to assist him. Or they could have chosen a specialist, such as a corporate trustee, to serve instead.

See Figure 16.1 for an idea of the confidential services a nonbank corporate trustee provides. When selecting your successor trustee, consider whether the person you have in mind could provide these services. Would you be more comfortable if your successor trustee were audited? Experienced in managing investments or business?

As a check-and-balance system, once your successor trustee steps up, he, she, or it should send out regular reports to you or potential beneficiaries. This is especially important when there is more than one potential heir. Siblings like to be informed on an equal basis. Today, even the individual trustee could accomplish this with little effort. The mainstream brokerage firm provides a monthly consolidated statement and, with proper authorization, will send duplicate statements to *interested* parties at no cost.

To consolidate your assets, the trustee could transfer liquid monies into the money market of a mainstream brokerage firm and use the check-writing privileges. With investments, CDs, and liquid monies held in one centralized account, all holdings and activities are reported monthly in the consolidated statement. Interested parties would see every expense and deposit. If we assume that the *investments* are held in this same account, the statement would also document all investment activity and values. The brokerage firm would not provide income tax service, of course, but the year-end statement does an impressive job of giving you details needed for your tax form. Having the consolidated statement is like having a private business manager. And the firm *is* audited.

FIGURE 16.1   Typical Duties and Responsibilities of Your
Professional Trustee

As your estate grows more complex, so too will the tasks you require from your trustee. Here is a general list of the services you can expect. I have italicized those often missing when individuals serve.

- Accepts responsibility for and takes control of trust assets (when requested or needed)
- Reviews terms of trust document
- Inventories assets and records tax cost basis
- Transfers assets to trust ownership and sets up accounting records
- Evaluates quality of assets/decides whether to hold or sell each security
- *Manages assets*
- Collects dividends and interest/reinvests cash
- Records all income and principal receipts and disbursements
- Pays bills, etc.
- Establishes investment strategy
- Regularly reviews trust assets for quality and diversification
- Distributes income to beneficiaries according to trust requirements
- Exercises discretion over additional distributions to beneficiaries
- Tracks taxable transactions and tracks income and changes in cost basis
- Files fiduciary income tax returns
- Regularly provides necessary tax documentation to beneficiaries
- *Submits actions to independent audit*
- Seeks legal counsel when needed
- Makes timely distributions as trust directs (partial and full)
- Divides shares among heirs
- *Provides accounting and tax data to each beneficiary*

When Trouble Comes

Wouldn't it be a relief to know you won't be up for grabs? You'd *know* someone would be there—and you'd know exactly who it would be. You could make certain they were smart about money and knew your plans. Couples usually name each other, but when the one left to stand alone can't cope, then what? Even that's not a problem if you've named a *backup* successor to assist or step in. And another backup, if you want; name as many as you like. The idea of setting up a chain of succession really isn't new.

Having the living trust is the same as our government having the Constitution. If something happens to the President of the United States, there is a named successor standing by. No catastrophe. Without delay, the President is cared for and things go on as planned. That's a godsend, isn't it?

I rest my case.

Chapter *17*

*F*inding the Right "Expert"

It's All in the Language

When my husband and I were recently preparing for a trip to Italy, we decided to learn the language. We never intended to master Italian, but to know enough to get by. Well, it didn't work out. When we asked a question, we were buried by an avalanche of gesticulations and rapid sounds strung together that left us gasping.

Ours was the same feeling some women have described about having asked an expert one innocent question. The answers flatten them.

There's a solution. Instead of trying to master the experts' lingo, the trick is to get them to speak your language. You needn't resort to hand signals as we did in Italy. Just try speaking to them this way: "This is what I want to do. How can you help me do it?" It's a far cry from the "What-shall-I-do-with-my-money?" question that the expert most often hears. And stating *your* goal first immediately sets the expert on the right path. Instead of immediately jumping ahead to conjure up *her* plan for your life, the expert can explain what skills and services she offers that will assist you in your quest.

Is that all there is to it? Not quite.

Find the Right Ear

Have you ever gone into a business office, and finding the manager out to lunch, asked the receptionist for assistance? Usually the receptionist would stop everything, listen, search for papers, and make 100 suggestions. That's very nice, but no matter how much time she took going through the motions—being nice, efficient, and wanting to be helpful—she just couldn't help you. Then the manager returned. In ten seconds, you learned that the person you needed was in the office next door.

You've got to be in the right *place* in order to find the right *person*. Otherwise the best questions in the world are a waste of breath. How are we supposed to know we're in the right financial place? It takes knowing a bit about what goes on behind the scenes.

Walking into the proper office is not the simple move it once was, when we were met with recognizable sounds and signs. Today, our old familiar institutions act like decorator crabs. Instead of pieces of shell, they adorn themselves with fragments taken from one another's businesses, hoping to appear more attractive to us—and thereby ensure their pocket profits—without inflicting the real *pain* of *change* on themselves. If we look closer, we can see that underneath the homogenized surfaces, each institution has preserved its uniquely different mind-set. The tacked-on tidbits have not transformed their original agendas.

We don't need pig-in-a-poke situations in our financial lives. We want to find experienced specialists, whose business includes familiar checks and balances. These systems were built in long ago for our protection. Where are they now?

What Can You Expect from Banks?

Practically everyone has had dealings with the familiar neighborhood bank. The subject of money comes up and the word that pops into our minds is *bank*. Banks represent savings and safety. Even with the shoddy history of failures in the depression and the more recent savings-and-loan debacle, the idea of bank safety seems untarnished. We can thank FDIC for that.

The banking industry has never underestimated the powerful message sent by marble columns and wall-sized safes, with tellers ensconced behind barred cages. All this has stood as testament to a place where your money was safe. And talk about labels! The FDIC label is reassuringly displayed, placed to be seen as you touch your hand on the door to enter. The message is clear: Inside these walls, all is safe, secure, and insured.

In return for this sanctuary, the fee earned on your deposits is shared by you and the bank. Or pay a fee and you can borrow money to work toward your dreams. But you may no longer know what banks, savings and lending institutions, are all about. There are surprises.

In most banks, today, you face a teller who—after eyeing your cash deposit—politely invites you to step over and visit with the "bank investment counselor" or the "personal banking officer." What follows is not the expected advice on better ways to save, but a surprising discussion of the benefits of mutual funds or annuities or maybe other insurance products.

"That happened to Jack and me last Thursday at the grocery store," my neighbor told me. "We'd made a quick deposit."

"Your bank is in your grocery store?" I asked.

"Sure, it's really convenient. It's the modern way."

Okay, but I wondered about their quick deposit. Was it *investment* money? Did they go into the bank wanting to *invest or learn about investing?* Or had they stopped by only to make a deposit, intending to keep the money safe and *liquid,* as a *cushion?*

So I asked her.

"Well, it was cushion money," she explained. "We'd planned on a six-month CD. But, after talking with the personal banking officer, we thought maybe we should have mutual funds. Everyone else does. And the lady said we'd earn more. Anyway, it was nice to get special attention. You like to be noticed, you know?"

But not caught unaware.

Attention, Shoppers

Banks, like the other institutions, are looking for ways to increase their income. Stretching into investments seems to be one choice of action. That's okay, but where is the *sign* in the lobby announcing their change of attitude toward your life savings?

Where is the sign telling you that you just left the insured *safe zone,* and passed over to the unpredictable *risk side* of the bank?

I suspect too many customers think FDIC insurance comes with the territory. FDIC insurance was designed to back the familiar accounts—checking, savings, CDs, etc.—but it does not stretch to include the bank's new ventures—the tack-ons. FDIC does *not* cover investments. There ought to be a sign.

Can You Get Service after the Sale?

A typical bank transaction might be an exchange of cash. It's once and done. Later you examine your monthly statement for interest earned or deposits credited. That's all there is to it. The transaction is history. But, making an *investment* is like adopting a wiggly, brown-eyed pup. Once it's yours, it needs watching over and nurturing, for a very long time. So ask yourself: Has the bank's "investment side" duplicated the sophisticated systems of the mainstream brokerage and insurance industries that are so essential to you for an orderly financial life? Does the bank offer the checks and balances you deserve? Can the bank ensure that you have first-rate communication or follow-up on investments? Read the following sections in this chapter on brokerage and insurance firms. Then compare their specialized services to the bank's investment and insurance connections.

What will the bank's broker in the lobby do if a hundred frantic investors call at once? Is there a switchboard to handle such a crisis? Is there a backup staff to step in? What if the crisis occurs prior to banking hours? The incredible electronic systems that exist in the mainstream brokerage firms would not be in place if they were not proved necessary.

The bank's sophisticated banking services—its backbone—are unavailable elsewhere. This is, as they have told us for many years, banking's unique strength. Their first-rate systems are designed to support savings, checking, loans, mortgages, CDs, cashier's checks, traveler's checks, government savings bonds, interbank transfers, electronic transfers, safety deposit boxes, ATMs, and the like. Luckily for us, these systems proved crucial to us all for our *banking* needs are in place here. Do your banking at the bank.

What Can You Expect from Insurance Companies?

The giant headquarters of insurance companies have given us some of the most distinctive buildings in our cities' skylines. These rich, soaring, enduring sentinels are built to shout their promise: They'll always be here, and for a fee, they will *provide relief from catastrophic financial problems.* Insurance buildings make a statement of stability.

The industry is timeless as a rock.

The insurance industry has spent a fortune to develop unique systems for specialized communication, processing, education, money management, and risk analysis. All are marshaled for one purpose, to ensure that it can keep its promise of rescuing its customers from financial catastrophe.

Suppose you insure your life with a $100,000 policy. If you die after making only *one* premium payment, your beneficiary still receives the full $100,000. Think of it. Where else can you find a guarantee like that? No other institution makes this promise.

In the past, insurance company experts took your premium payments and put them to work, making smart investment decisions that successfully backed their insurance policies. Your only involvement was to pay premiums and hang onto the policy over the years. You may have stashed a life policy in a drawer where it collected dust. But dusty, yellowed, or faded, it paid off when the time came.

Change has affected the insurance industry. Among other changes, updated mortality tables have brought down the cost of life insurance. Good for us, a cut in profits for the industry. Interest rates fell. Good for us, a squeeze for the industry. Now, to increase their attractiveness—and pocket profits—innovations have been introduced.

Among these new approaches are policies that invite *you* to make the investment decisions on your accumulated premiums. This effectively shifts the responsibility for success from the insurance company's shoulders onto your own. It's an appealing idea. Even enticing. Who doesn't think they can do better than a stodgy insurance company?

Whether the allure of making your own investments inside an insurance policy will prove to enhance results, time will tell. It does change that no-brainer, forget-about-it freedom you once enjoyed. And it does enhance the comfort of the insurance company.

There is no impact on safety, but the "opportunity" to make your own choices brings added financial pressure. Investing inside an insurance policy adds a layer of internal costs. Before you select a variable, universal, or similarly named insurance product, ask about those nibbles.

For instance, suppose the market is down, interest rates are low, and your "internal investments" earn less than 3 or 4 percent *before* policy costs are deducted. Consider the following:

- How is the death benefit affected?
- How is cash value affected?
- How is your premium affected?

Suppose you borrow from the cash value:

- How much is available?
- How is the cash value affected? Does an ongoing interest charge impact the cash value?
- How is the death benefit affected?
- How are premiums affected?

On any printed *projections* supplied by the insurance agent to estimate the future performance of any life policy, notice and ask these sorts of questions:

- If you pay premiums for a certain number of years and then premiums stop, what can trigger the need to begin paying again?
- What return is necessary for the policy to carry itself?
- What interest rate is used for the printed illustration you have in hand? Is it a current rate?
- What happens to the policy if rates drop 2 percent or more?

Insurance is unique in its ability to create an instant estate or to solve a financial crisis caused by disaster. The industry still offers whole life policies and term insurance. Prices are lower. *Fixed* annuities are still offered. These products are straightforward. They do what they promise.

By the way, the S&P guide includes a "Variable Annuity/Life Investment Summary." This summary covers "you-choose-the-investments products" from many insurance companies. It tells you a lot about the vehicles, including administration costs and surcharges.

Should You Borrow on Your Policy?

You know that old familiar question: "Should I borrow against cash value and invest that money?"

I have a story. It was the 1980s. Insurance companies dipped their risk-averse toes into the investment waters. With this new opportunity available for customers, an experienced insurance agent, still green about investments, helped a trusting, elderly woman to juggle her life policies around. She asked him if she was okay. He decided she could do better. Here's what he advised her to do.

He suggested she take out a new mortgage on her paid-up home; take that money and invest it in a *high-yield* bond fund; and then use the bond fund income to make the new mortgage payments. (She would theoretically increase her assets without needing any cash outlay.)

Next, she should borrow against the cash value of her husband's life insurance; use that money to buy additional life insurance; and make one large payment only. The new policy would carry itself. No other premiums would be due. (She would theoretically expect a windfall at his death, again with no need for more cash outlay.)

Like FDIC at the bank, life insurance has always allayed our fears about financial catastrophe, never created them. But today, this new element in the insurance firm invites risk. Where is the sign that warns customers? No one wants to be caught unaware.

Here are a few of the questions the trusting lady needed to ask her insurance agent:

- Are there penalties to borrow cash value?
- Are taxes generated if I borrow cash value?
- Does the *loan* affect the death benefit?
- Do I have to repay the policy loan?
- Can the *interest* on the policy loan gradually eat up the death benefit?
- Can the *interest* on the policy loan gradually eat up the cash value?

- Does the insurance company *guarantee* that the new policy will carry itself for life, or is the future based only on a computer *projection?*
- Is the high-yield investment safe?
- Can the high-yield income fluctuate?
- What happens if the income drops? How would I make the new mortgage payments?
- Would this strategy work with a triple-A bond fund instead?

If the lady had followed the agent's house-of-cards scenario, her formerly secure home would now be lost to foreclosure. That high-yield bond fund, meant to pay the mortgage, went bust. High yield means *high risk,* but the insurance-turned-investment-agent didn't understand that.

After interest rates fell, some insurance policies no longer carried themselves. If the lady had gotten a request to begin paying premiums again, on either or both policies, she faced financial disaster. She and her husband lived on Social Security.

Keep insurance clean, simple, and *dependable.* Use it for its intended purpose—*rescue* from financial catastrophe—not as a cause.

So, can you trust insurance agents? Yes, as much as you can trust any expert to know what's good for you. This expert was out of his league, pressed by a desire to please his customer. Education is key, and the major insurance companies have excellent *insurance* training programs. I've gotten terrific insurance advice at major insurance companies. But I didn't walk in and say, "Do I need insurance?" That answer is always yes. Do you need *more* insurance? That answer is usually yes. Should you be earning more on your money? Who would say no? Asking experts questions like these, is asking for someone else to mind your business. (See Chapter 21 to find out how much insurance you need.)

Find the Quality Firm

Make certain you are in the right office. There is an independent rating source for insurance firms. Ask the agent for their A.M. Best rating. Do business with the *best.*

Find the right expert. Ask for an agent who has earned the CLU or ChFC designation. These agents are experts on things like business planning (buy/sell agreements, key employee compensation), estate planning and preservation, insurance trusts, annuities, varieties of life insurance, and overall risk management analysis. They are specialists. And they are career agents, committed enough to have devoted time and effort to further their education. Other ways life insurance can be put to work are listed in Figure 17.1.

What Can You Expect from Securities Firms?

Numbers, prices, quotes, ticker tapes, and a buzz of frantic activity used to set the brokerage firm apart from any other office. The minute you stepped in the door you knew where you were. Now, the brokerage firms have gone quiet. With thick carpets and silent sophisticated computer terminals, they've dressed themselves in a new homogenized tone. Financial planning has entered the arena and cast its aura of uptown solidity for the customer. But, don't be misled. Beneath it all is the crusty, risky, whirling marketplace; the race for money.

The mainstream brokerage firm's systems that make possible the instant exchange of information and money, reach all over the world. They tap into every action that affects finances—from government, education, disasters, personality, currency, economics, uprising—and almost any other event you can name. And all of this, established over many years and at tremendous cost, enables the brokerage industry to keep its promise: *to provide opportunities for you to make your money grow.*

Just as banking and insurance have gleaned brokerage-like services, mainstream brokerage firms have mimicked banking and insurance. Do you have a checking account with your stockbroker? The brokerage firm's charge card and check-writing privileges are tied to a liquid, interest-earning money market fund. This money market at the mainstream brokerage firm may be insured for several million dollars. The good news is the emphasis on earning a return on your monies. It's a pleasant surprise to find the interest rate on this money market fund is credited sooner on deposited funds, and is higher than the rate paid by a savings institution. Even a tax-free money market is available. But the similarity to the bank stops there. The bad news (the inconvenience) is that no cash is available or accepted at the mainstream brokerage firm. Business is done by check. The check you write on your brokerage firm money market fund can be cashed at the *bank*.

FIGURE 17.1   General Purposes of Life Insurance

Life insurance is a unique vehicle that can be used to solve some of life's perplexing financial problems. Here are a few ideas:

1. **Create an Estate.** Where time or other circumstances have kept the estate owner from accumulating sufficient assets to care for his or her loved ones, life insurance can create an instant estate.
2. **Pay Off the Home Mortgage.** Many people would like to pass the family residence to their spouse or children free of any mortgage.
3. **Pay Death Taxes** and Other Estate Settlement Costs. Those costs can vary from a low percentage of 3 to 4 percent to over 50 percent of the estate. Federal estate taxes are due nine months after death.
4. **Protect the Business from the Loss of a Key Employee.** Key employees are difficult to attract and retain. Their untimely death may cause a severe financial strain on a business.
5. **Fund a Business Transfer.** Business owners often agree to buy a deceased owner's share from his or her estate after death. Life insurance provides the ready cash to finance the transaction.
6. **Replace a Charitable Gift.** Charitable remainder trusts provide tax benefits. For the benefit of heirs, life insurance can replace the value of the donated asset.

Can you find insurance at the brokerage firm? A familiar product of the insurance industry, the fixed annuity, has been marketed through the mainstream brokerage firms for years. Annuities have been well received by teachers as funding for their retirement incomes. Today, as the number of *stockbroker–financial planners* grows, their awareness of life insurance applications in estate planning is growing also. Review Figure 17.1 to see some of these uses.

Is the insurance product a tack-on or a reliable, properly serviced source? This may be the exception to the specialist-source rule. Since the systems are in place to support life and annuity products, you should be well served. The reason is that, behind the frontline stockbroker, the insurance representative is also available to help you. Also, since the brokerage firm represents several insurance companies, your choice is widened. On the other hand, the scope of insurance is narrowed: You have little chance of finding expert advice on sophisticated life insurance problems from the average stockbroker. And no health, homeowner's, renter's, business, medical, or casualty insurance is offered. For comprehensive insurance help, see the insurance specialist.

Would a smart investor acquire life insurance through her stockbroker? Yes, if she knows what she needs, how it fits into her overall financial situation, and she has checked out the A.M. Best rating on the product. Please note that, although insurance products are offered at the mainstream investment firm, don't think of them as *investments.* Insurance products fulfill the promise to pay a *predictable* lump sum or income. It is unlikely that they can compete with a *growth* investment. Mixing up the purposes of insurance and investments creates an oil-and-water marriage.

The *core* business of the mainstream brokerage firm is to offer investments and market access for everyone. Their services are designed to help you stay informed. Monthly statements report on every aspect of your financial holdings. Accounts are insured by SIPC. Firms are regulated and *audited.* Many reports are readily available. Educational seminars and publications are offered.

These giants have extensive training programs, but one stockbroker cannot possibly know everything or monitor every change in the marketplace. So, behind the broker are systems and an impressive array of support people. This broker is a pipeline. She has real-time information and specialists at her beck and call.

The Right Expert

Stockbrokers often specialize. Find one in tune with your interests. If you walk in and ask at the receptionist's desk for a stockbroker, you will be paired with the broker-of-the-day. This is the person whose turn it is to take incoming calls and walk-ins.

If you ask to see the manager, he can match you up. But, wait! If the manager offers to handle your account, ask what he specializes in. If he is a *producing* manager, he is in competition with the brokers in his office. Truth is, he may be too busy and preoccupied with office matters to serve you as you deserve. Tell him you prefer to interview one or two other brokers as well. How can he refuse? See Figure 17.2 for tips on how to interview and get off on the right foot.

A woman once told me she and her husband had had an accountant who invited them to invest their income tax refund in a limited partnership he "knew about." It happens. When experts slip in questions that have nothing to do with their specialty, it can catch anyone off-guard.

"Did you invest with the accountant?" I asked.

"No," she answered. "My husband won't invest with anyone who wears shoelaces."

Too often, experts reach beyond their expertise. Ironically it's probably from their lack of expertise. They don't realize the underlying pitfalls of casual advice.

Don't you hate to be caught off-guard? I do. I once presented an investment-estate planning seminar with an attorney, who later tried to sell insurance to my clients.

Overreaching is an onerous "service" women rarely talk about but often experience. Each of us probably knows an attorney who manages money for a friend of a friend—or of mother or aunt Billie. The closeness of it all makes you think that maybe you should talk to him. Attorneys seem to know about everything. But, wait a minute. What you should be asking is: Is the attorney a money expert? Does he have the training or experience? Does he have the necessary systems in place for real-time information or monitoring or reporting? Is the attorney *audited?*

The attorney may be expert at *earning* money, but managing it for others? That raises questions that any client has a legitimate right to have answered. Be on guard: Any specialist, any expert, might slide over into *other* areas of our lives if we're sloppy about our business. It's an invitation. But thankfully, the regulations, supervision, and laws put in place by many industries are meant to protect us when we find ourselves embroiled in problem-fraught situations.

A Special Note to Widows, Divorcees, and Singles

If you are alone and your stockbroker adjusts your monies without your written permission, she's subject to punishment. If you are alone and an insurance agent invests without your permission or holds your money in his account, he's held accountable. If you are alone and an attorney slides over to control your personal and financial affairs, who is there to intercede? Mind your own business—or someone else will.

FIGURE 17.2   The Starter Checklist

Collecting Your Thoughts Ahead of Time

I'd like to see a stockbroker who is: __ male   __ female

__ younger   __ mature

__ aggressive __ conservative

I'd like a specialist in: __ mutual   __ financial
                                     funds   planning

__ stocks   __ estate
                     planning
__ bonds

__ trading/   __ insurance/
options   annuities

__ is a generalist

Suggested Questions for the Get-Acquainted Chat

Background (training). How does one enter this field? Did you like the training program?

Experience (longevity in business). My neighbor speaks highly of this company; have you been with them long?

Special focus (types of investments). What sorts of stocks do you watch? Do you like bonds? My son trades stocks—do you do much of that? Do you follow dividend-paying stocks? Do you conduct seminars? Do you send out updates on stocks your clients hold?

Availability (in office, by phone). Are you here when the market opens? If I want to place an order, how early can I phone you? Are you in the office late? Can I call you anytime?

Personality. I'm new at investing—do you mind lots of questions? I am so conservative I squeak—does a customer like that bore you? I won't be trading—once I buy a stock, I'll hold it until the cows come home. Do you prefer clients who are active? Do you mind working with a client with a small account? What's your favorite type of client?

Suggestions of Things to Tell Your Stockbroker

What I have in mind. My goal is to achieve reliable blue-chip income. I am a beginner. I've done my homework, but I'd like to take it slow. I want only the best quality, no matter what else seems to be the exciting idea of the day. If my experience is good, as time goes on, I'll be interested in building a portfolio.

FIGURE 17.2 The Starter Checklist (Continued)

What I expect. I expect confidentiality. I want to know my questions are welcome and that I will get understandable answers. I won't take advantage of your time, but I'll need proper understanding. For instance, on every investment, I want to know all costs to buy and sell, the details of the investment, and both the worst and best possible results. I welcome your input, but I'll make my own decisions. I won't give you the right to make any transactions independent of me. (Do not sign papers establishing a discretionary account. It gives the broker authority to buy and sell without your authority.) Are my guidelines agreeable to you?

After Your Conversation, Ask Yourself the Following:

Is the broker knowledgeable? Personable and easy to understand? Is the broker willing to work *with* me instead of steamroll over me? Will the broker respect my attitude about risk? What personal service does the broker offer clients? Do I know my risk tolerance? What sort of investor am I?

Take this test. Discuss it with your broker. It's important that you two see eye-to-eye.

The Personal Profile Test for the Starter Checklist

Rank each answer according to its importance to you (1 = most important).

1. Why do I want to invest?

    ❏ To provide secure current income
    ❏ To grow a nest egg for a future event
    ❏ To protect my standard of living against inflation
    ❏ To cut my tax liability
    ❏ To provide income for retirement in ____ years
    ❏ For the challenge and fun
    ❏ Other (specify): _____

2. What do I want to improve about my present situation?

    ❏ I don't know where or how to start investing.
    ❏ I don't have a plan to tell me why I need certain investments.
    ❏ I think I'm scattered rather than diversified.
    ❏ I'm disappointed with the returns on my investments.
    ❏ I want to reduce the worry about risk.
    ❏ I need to build in more flexibility.
    ❏ It's presently okay, but I need advice to go further.
    ❏ Other (specify): _____

FIGURE 17.2   The Starter Checklist (Continued)

3. How much time do I have right now to devote to investing?

    ❑ I have enough time for only a quick review each month.
    ❑ I can make time to evaluate a new choice.
    ❑ I do not have time for ongoing study and daily monitoring.
    ❑ Other (specify): _____

4. What's my emotional temperature?

    ❑ I'm confident once I understand; then I like to make my own decisions.
    ❑ From time to time, I need expert backup for reassurance.
    ❑ I tend to worry about bad news.
    ❑ Sometimes I do things on the spur of the moment and suffer later.
    ❑ I'd like a professional to manage my investments.
    ❑ Other (specify): _____

5. Stocks fluctuate, but what if one of mine dropped a major amount?

    ❑ I would be on the phone to the broker to investigate.
    ❑ I'd make a hold or sell decision based on the company's situation.
    ❑ I'd get out of the market and never buy another stock.
    ❑ One stock's failure would not affect my opinion of other holdings.
    ❑ Other (specify): _____

6. In tune with my stage in life and current situation, these are my priorities for the next five years:

    _____% Safety
    _____% Growth
    _____% Income
    _____% Taxes
    = 100%

Note: If you currently have investments in place, do they reflect your priorities?

FIGURE 17.2   The Starter Checklist   (Continued)

Things to Ask about the Investment before I Invest

Always, but *always* ask:

- **When does it mature?** (There are only two answers: "never," or "on this maturity date.")
- **What will I get back?** (Again, there are only two answers: "I don't know," or "this sum."
- **When can I sell?** (Is the money tied up? Or is it liquid? Is there a penalty to sell? Does the price fluctuate?)
- **What's the worst that can happen? The best?**

Not urgent, but important to know:

- **How soon will I receive a confirmation of this transaction?** (The confirmation ["confirm"] should be mailed to you next day.)
- **Can I have a receipt for my check?** (Write checks to the *firm* with your account number noted on them.)
- **How will I keep track of my investment's status?** (Will you receive monthly statements? Can you follow it in the newspaper? Will you receive special reports?)
- **Will you let me know if something unexpected happens?** (This is a difficult request, unless a broker has devised a special system to monitor customer accounts. Some have.)

Chapter *18*

*S*potting Seductive Scams

A grey-haired couple popped into my office one afternoon. "He just retired," the wife said, jabbing a thumb at her grinning husband, "and we need investment advice for our future."

Their eyes twinkled with excitement. "Tell me about your intentions," I said.

"Oh, he just got his pension. $150,000 in one lump sum. How much income can you get for us?"

"Absolutely no stocks," they added. "No *risk*. This is all we've got and we can't replace it."

We talked for awhile about possible choices. They wanted nothing to do with insurance products, so securing a lifetime income from annuities was excluded. After considering their inexperience and fears, I suggested U.S. government-guaranteed bonds, paying 6 percent. That would produce an annual income of $9,000. ($150,000 × .06 = $9,000.) We would adjust for liquidity and flexibility, but 6 percent was a starting place.

They shook their heads, "No, no. We can't live on $750 a month. We have to get more."

It was clear that, despite their lack of understanding of the marketplace, they had already made up their minds. They were in no mood to be confused by facts. They listened tight-lipped as I explained the connection of risk levels to real current, competitive interest rates. But, no proof was enough to convince them that my major brokerage firm information was accurate, or that the choices we discussed reflected the entire mainstream marketplace. Disgusted, they scooped up their papers and rushed out, determined to find *someone* with answers they liked. Unfortunately, that's who they found.

A month later, I picked up the evening newspaper and there they were, pictured on the front page. Their smiles were gone. The headline read, "Couple Swindled out of Life Savings."

Here's what happened: Through an advertisement, they'd met a certain "financial representative" who had promised them a 12 percent return on "U.S. government-guaranteed bonds" *if* they would invest the entire $150,000. They had to act quickly because it would not be available long. What luck! What timing! They jumped at it.

The news article reported that, because the "representative" was confined to a wheelchair, his office was not always open. To accommodate him, the couple made out their check, *in the "representative's" name,* and slipped it under the locked door.

"How could anyone be so dumb?" you might ask. But once this couple felt sorry for the man, it became easy to overlook his irregular office hours, and easier to interpret his eagerness as sincerity and a desire to help. Until finally, nothing could dampen their willingness to accommodate him in any way necessary, to make his work less of a burden, if it meant they could capture that 12 percent! $18,000 a year.

Do I detect sympathy?

This won't happen to you if you recognize the signs. I'll point out the signs that this couple overlooked or ignored. Remember, avoiding trouble is all about *reliable* sources, *reasonable* returns, and *you.*

Reasonable Returns

There is *one* U.S. government market and it's in the world spotlight. Today's rates are quoted on television, radio, newspapers, and by major brokerage firms. There are no secret, forgotten, or overlooked bargains. When you know, from a *reliable* source, what current rates are, trust what you know. That's truth. Anyone promising you significantly more on the same investment has you targeted. If the going rate is 6 percent, it's 6 percent. Oh certainly, maybe a firm will shave a price to get the sale. But if a quote is 2 percent higher than what you know is the going rate, hide your money.

How do you know the *going rate?* Call any two major brokerage firms and ask for a quote on the same product. Apples to apples, remember. If there were a super exciting rate available, they'd be the first to know.

Beware the sound of legitimacy. When a crook works a scam, he goes all out. He promises outrageous, sure-fire results. He wants you to drool. He knows your tendency to *believe* newspaper ads, radio ads, or dramatic speeches at public gatherings. He's well-dressed, bright, and confident. Even though it's fictitious, he'll tell you he's got an *in* with the marketplace that the big firms don't know about. Just ask him.

He may win you over completely when he mentions the words *U.S. government guaranteed.* He knows what you want to hear. He speaks with comforting authority, promising you the moon. Even though it's smoke and mirrors, he'll join you at the kitchen table and explain away your doubts, with winning sincerity, while you write your check.

Talk investing at a reliable firm. You may not *like* the rates, but at least you can *believe* them.

A Loss Is a Loss

Is that little voice reminding you that you've lost money at the so-called reliable firm? Pay attention to that inner voice. A reliable firm can be counted on to give you reliable information, but, reliable *information* does not a safe investment make. It simply means that the information, the description, is *factual.* You can still lose money because of the choices you make.

At a reliable source, you can trust that the investment *exists.* So your only risk is in the *performance* of the investment. And the ratings and rankings we discussed help you decide *how much* risk exists. A mainstream brokerage firm doesn't guarantee that their investments are safe. It's just a reliable place to do business. It's a department store, with something for everyone. Some investors love risks, and some won't budge without guarantees. But the structure, the systems of the firms, have those nice built-in checks and balances for your protection, such as receipts, confirmations, insured accounts, monthly statements, widespread communications, in-house supervision, and so on. These firms aren't perfect, but they are audited and they are accountable. It's the best reliability we've got.

And you won't ever have to slip checks under a locked door.

And, please, don't *ever* write investment checks to *individuals*.

How to Detect a Scam

Which of these ads is a scam and which is a *reliable* risk?

> SICK OF CDS? Earn 18%–20% on
> guaranteed, secure mortgages.
> CALL NOW! 123-1234.

> If you are not earning 14%–16% on your investments,
> call XX SERVICES.
> Secured real estate investments. 345-4567.

After reading these newspaper ads you might be tempted to call up both. Is that smart? It's dangerous. Don't touch that phone.

Do an armchair analysis. Take another look at the ads. Are the advertised rates *reasonable?* Here's how to test for reasonable or, in other words, *believable* rates.

1. Check your reliable source. Ask any major bank in your community.   Today I made a phone call, asking for the loan officer for new real estate loans. "What are today's rates on first mortgages?" I asked.

He said, "*First* mortgage rates, 30-year fixed, are 8.7 percent. To a *creditworthy* borrower, the bank will lend with only 5 percent down."

I jotted that down, thanked him, and asked for a transfer to the *consumer* loan department.

"What are today's rates on *second* mortgages?" I asked.

He said, "That rate is 9.5 percent–10 percent for ten years. The borrower *must have good credit* and retain 20 percent equity in the real estate."

"In other words," I asked, taking notes, "if I owe $70,000 on a $100,000 house, the bank would lend me $10,000 on a second mortgage?"

"Yes," the loan officer replied. He gave me additional examples.

These quotes I've been given tell us what rates are today in the *mainstream* marketplace. Creditworthy borrowers pay 8.7 percent on a first mortgage and 10 percent on a second. This is a benchmark to judge other information because we know the information from the bank is true.

2. Compare these reliable rates to the advertised rates. The advertised rates are higher, but we need more information to determine if the ad is a scam. Remember, apples to apples. We know that a bank or anyone else who has to charge 14 percent to 20 percent in today's market, is scraping borrowers from the bottom of the barrel. You have to ask yourself how bad your own credit would have to be to be charged such exorbitant rates.

So even if the ads are for *real,* these investments are risky: The rule in the legitimate investment world is the higher the rate, the riskier the investment. That's because the weaker the situation, the harder it is to attract money. The rate has to be higher to make the risk worthwhile. What would it take for you to lend $10,000 to your partying neighbor who has declared bankruptcy twice in his life and can't keep a steady job? If at all, I bet you wouldn't lend him money at only 8 percent. Even credit card issuers charge 15 percent or higher. This tells you what their risk is, doesn't it?

So, don't bother calling up either of those wonderful-sounding ads. It's asking for trouble. Without leaving your chair, you already know their rates don't make sense for your life. That's the value of the reliable source. And it's only one phone call away.

Reliable Risk

I did phone the 14 percent to 16 percent ad. Here's how it went: "I read your ad. Do you *sell* existing mortgages?" I asked.

"No. Lenders come to us looking for an investment. Borrowers come to us looking for money. We put them together for a fee, paid by the borrower." In other words, these people are match-makers. Once the parties get together, this company is paid and *gone.*

"What do your investors typically earn?" I asked.

"Most often, 14 percent to 15 percent."

"Are these second mortgages?" Often second mortgages carry high rates.

"No. We create only first mortgages." Wow! first mortgages at 15 percent?

"Why don't your borrowers go to a bank?"

"Either they or the property cannot qualify for a bank loan," he said. In other words, lousy credit, doubtful property.

"How much can they borrow?" Were loans made with no money down?

"They can borrow no more than 60 percent of property value. The borrower must have 40 percent equity." So that's why the ad read "secured" real estate.

"Can the lender investigate the property and the borrower before she agrees to lend?" Are these real people with real properties who want to borrow?

"Yes. We offer a bound book of information about both property and borrower. It includes a fee appraisal, county assessments, title insurance, and credit report. If you like the deal, we open a loan escrow at the title company." These people package a shaky deal to give it a substantial look.

"Are the properties local?" I hoped I could take a look.

"In this half of the state." Oops. Beware of out-of-town real estate.

"Who holds my money?"

"We never hold money. The lender's money (mine) is deposited into the loan escrow at the title company. Our fees are deducted, and the borrower receives the net amount. The title company issues the paperwork." This is thorough documentation, checks and balances, for transfer of monies on a risky investment.

"How do I collect my monthly loan payment?" I asked.

"The title company sets up a collection escrow account," he answered. "They disperse the checks and keep an accounting." Bookkeeping by a third, neutral party is good. But accurate bookkeeping does not imply regularity of payments. If the borrower makes only a few payments, it's your problem.

Because the "matchmaker" company has an established, local address, and the Better Business Bureau has no negative reports, this appears to be a legitimate investment. A very high-risk investment—which requires further study—but it's being handled through a reliable source.

As for the other ad, it's too blatant. No call is necessary. It's fictitious. You're smart enough to know better than to call.

But, what if *they* call *you?*

Well, Hello, Mrs. Target . . .

The timing couldn't be better. Just this week, while working on this chapter, someone did call. I guessed that the young woman on the other end of the line was smiling, her voice was that friendly. She was taking a poll about customer satisfaction, and asked if I would mind taking a minute to answer questions.

"Okay," I said, and she swung into her pitch. "How many people live in your home?" Nothing wrong there. After that, came questions about our ages and then, income. I balked. "Who did you say you represent?" I asked. Click.

When an innocuous-sounding caller eases her way into questions about details, you are being set up for a scam. She (or he) will finally ask you to confirm your bank account number for their files. Then she will ask your street address, credit card number, if your neighbor is on vacation, and even if you are employed.

Whether it's a way to strip your accounts or stop by the house and relieve you of a few possessions (while you or that neighbor are at work or on vacation), it happens in seconds. You've said it and it's too late.

So, even if you think the caller sounds legit, tell her you're on your way out and ask if she will send a letter. Call them back at a number you know is legitimate. Once involved in a conversation, you can give away information and not realize it. Don't pit yourself against the guy who practices all day every day. He's got a cheat-sheet in front of him with responses to your every word.

And Then There's *You*

A stockbroker shared this story about a wealthy widow. Even though she had developed a trusting relationship with her female stockbroker, the widow was surprised one evening by a call from her stockbroker's husband. The husband had a terrible problem. It seemed that money he was expecting from a real estate settlement would be delayed. The money would arrive one week too late to settle on a new property. "I'm really in a jam," he said.

"How much do you need?" the widow asked.

"$100,000, but it's only for five days. If you help me, I'll pay $5,000 for the use of your money," he pleaded.

"How did you know to ask me for the money?" she asked.

"I've gone over your account," he said, "and I see you've got more than enough in the money market. And my wife always speaks so highly of you."

Was it his flattery that caused her to consider it? Perhaps she thought that they were such a nice couple. Or that anyone might get caught in a squeeze. Or that five days was nothing—and $5,000 profit was generous . . . very generous. Whatever she considered, ultimately, she agreed. The next day, she took her personal check, made out to the husband, and delivered it him at lunch.

She didn't!

She did.

Seven days later, the widow tried to phone the stockbroker. "Oh, sorry," the operator said, "that number has been disconnected."

Those Precious Checks and Balances

Reliable firms have been around for a very long time. They have a system of safeguards for their customers' protection. For instance, your investment account is held in strict confidence. Why wasn't the widow outraged when she learned that her stockbroker's *husband* had access to her account information? It was a flagrant violation of privacy.

A reliable firm does not permit their stockbrokers to invest with customers, to participate in customers' financial affairs, or to invite customers' participation in theirs. The request for a loan was a screaming violation.

Then, the widow made out her check to the husband, no questions asked, no collateral, and no written promissory note. An unbelievable act of foolishness for a "sophisticated" investor. Enacted in a totally unbusinesslike location.

She must have been lonely, or flattered, or too flustered to think straight—or maybe she had her eye on that $5,000. Greed—the *G* word. It's a necessary ingredient for the swindle.

The Enemy Is Us

A divorcee, who had a small money market account, dashed into my office one day. I knew her as a fear-filled woman who, despite our many lengthy educational sessions, refused to venture into even the safest investments. Now, she cried about losing money in penny stocks. "What?" I couldn't believe it. "You put money into penny stocks when you wouldn't consider a U.S. Treasury bill?" I asked. Penny stocks are notoriously speculative, the true pig-in-a-poke. "Where? When?" I asked.

"Over the phone. The man was so insistent I sent him only $5,000 at first. He kept calling me every few days. The stock went right up, but when I wanted to sell, he said to buy more!"

"You sent a second check?" I asked. "After he ignored your sell instruction?"

"Yes—so then," she sobbed, "when he said I had more profit," she sniffed and dabbed her eyes, "oh, the stock more than doubled! I wanted to sell again, but he said I should add money and buy this other company that was about to shoot up and, well, it's been a few weeks, and I just added it up. I've sent him $55,000!"

"Who is he? Do you have statements? Receipts?"

"Not yet, their computer has been down. But I'm worried. And I want my money back."

It was her battle. Instead of seeking legal help she left, determined to call him and demand that he sell her stocks and send her the proceeds immediately. It would force his hand. A week later she came back in, to put $500 into her money market account. "Well?" I asked. "How did it go?"

"I c-couldn't sell. He said my money is okay and I should stop being a baby. He asked if I didn't trust him . . . well . . ."

"You didn't send him *another* check?"

"Just $2,000. But he promised to send everything back at the end of the month."

Smart investing takes the three *R*s:

- Reliable source
- Reasonable returns
- Rational you

Enuf said.

Chapter 19

*J*ust Beginning? How to Plan, Persist, and Prosper

*Y*ou come to this section organized, expert, properly peppered with warnings, and prepared as anyone to carry on management of the family's *existing* finances and investments. With time and more experience, you'll likely venture beyond the straight-A approach. That act of confidence comes from having a solid understanding of what you're about. But if you are satisfied and choose not to expand, that's okay, too. You can maintain a secure financial picture by following the rules we've covered.

Ironically, everything I have said about investments can be held against me. No rule is foolproof. Just pick up the evening news and there will be an exception. However, be confident. You have reliable keys to guide you, help you spot weaknesses, and head off problems—without running to the sidelines. That's as good as it gets.

As for me, knowing you've reached a knowledgeable level of financial control and confidence, I thought my job was done. That is, until an anxious career woman—who had just finished reading these very same chapters—burst my bubble. "What about *me?*" she asked. "I'm single, 40, have an IRA, and I'm scared to death I'll never be able to retire. Is it true what all the articles tell us? Do we need a million dollars?"

Good question. I told her I would include some Q&A for younger women.

"Questions and answers?" she asked incredulously. "Do a whole section!"

So here it is. If you are a woman starting from scratch, these next chapters are especially for you.

What Should You Be Doing with Your Money Right Now?

First, if you are a woman who has not yet set aside funds for her future, there are some urgent facts to know before it's too late. Don't plunge into this section unless you've read the earlier chapters, however. This new information is to be added to the solid grounding you've already acquired. This section is the fine tuning.

Then, once you've completed the entire book, *act*. Run to the financial institution of your choice to set aside the first monies for your future. Here's why.

Time Is Precious

There are mysterious forces at work that you cannot escape. Whether you are a city dweller with sophisticated carefree leanings or a Bible-belt stoic burdened with fears of the aftereffects of your every move, there is one great leveler in your life—*time*. Each of us has an equal number of minutes in our days. Time is so much of an ordinary concept that we fail to see the powerful role it plays. Yet, the good news is, with *time* on your side, you can achieve startling financial success with almost no skills or effort. And the bad news is, once it begins to pass away, the power of time is irrevocably lost to us, and we must work harder and become more and more clever, disciplined, and lucky to make up for its loss.

Bernard Baruch said he would willingly stand at street corners, hat in hand, begging passersby to drop their unused minutes into it.

Time Builds Wealth

Let me demonstrate with dollars and cents what time does for working money. Suppose your retirement date is age 65. You have no savings and cannot free up more than $167 a month to invest. Let's say you can earn 8 percent on that monthly deposit and reinvest the earnings at the same rate. Should you begin investing now? Let's find out.

		Investing $167 per Month		
Beginning Age	*Years to 65*	*Total Saved*	*Total Earned @ 8%*	*Total You Have!*
25	40	$79,680	$503,690	$583,370
35	30	59,760	189,289	249,049
45	20	39,840	58,589	98,429
55	10	19,920	10,561	30,571

See the impact of *time?* Look at those totals in the last column. The long and short of it is, in the example presented, time or the lack of it makes a mighty difference. At retirement, if the 25-year-old earned 5 percent on her $583,370 total, she'd have an annual income of $29,169. On the other hand, if that 55-year-old earned 5 percent on her $30,571 total, she'd have an annual income of $1,528. Pretty scary. That's a high price to pay for procrastination. Surely the 50-year-old could have found $167 a month to set aside when she was younger—especially when today's statistics predict a retirement spanning 25 years.

The Three Seasons

	25 Years of Parental Support	*40 Years of Self-Support*	*25+ Years of Support from Pension/Social Security/Investments*
Ages:	1–25	25–65	65–85+
	Learn	Save	Enjoy

Time is powerful, but it isn't the whole secret. Setting aside a monthly sum by sticking it in a shoe will not bring financial growth no matter how long the money is stashed. By itself, time is not enough.

Money must be put to *work.* The sooner you begin saving, the less savings it takes and the easier it is to find a reliable place for money to work. That's because of another powerful force: compounding.

"Money is of a prolific, generating nature," Benjamin Franklin told us in 1748. "Money can beget money—and its offspring can beget more."

That's his way of explaining the magic of compounding. Let's see how that prolific nature looks in action.

How Money Begets Money

On the following page is a year-by-year example of what happens internally in both a compounding CD and a simple-interest CD.

Each delivers what it promises. The informed investor reads the fine print. And you can see that she gets *paid* for doing so. Money earns money 24 hours a day for someone. It is never static. Are the earnings coming to you? The important thing is to attract that flow *to* you, not *away* from you.

Invest $10,000 in a five-year CD at 5 percent. The savings institution offers either simple or compound interest. Take a look at the example in Figure 19.1. Then decide which CD you would choose?

By the way, you can *convert* a simple-interest investment into a compound return. When interest is credited, transfer it to a money market account. Money market accounts do compound. Ask your broker for a prospectus. It will explain how often the funds compound. The more frequently they are compounded, the higher the return; that is, as long as the rate remains the same. Ask for a dollars-and-cents example.

If your simple-interest investment is held at a mainstream brokerage firm, the interest payment will automatically flow into the money market, creating the opportunity to compound. Remember, money at work is earning money for *somebody* 24 hours of every day. If you aren't getting the additional earnings, someone else is. Of course, if you take the earned interest and spend it, you make the return simple on any investment.

Suppose you accepted a 30-day job. How would you like to be paid: a flat $2,000 for the 30 days? Or would you accept a penny paid the first day and allow it to double for each of the remaining 29 days? See the second example in Figure 19.1.

FIGURE 19.1   Comparing Compound and Simple Interest*

Compound Interest				Simple Interest		
Principal+	Earn @ 5% =	Yr End Total	year	Principal+	Earn @ 5% =	Yr End Total
$10,000 +	$500 =	$10,500	1	$10,000 +	$500 =	$10,500
10,500 +	525 =	11,025	2	10,000 +	500 =	11,000
11,025 +	551 =	11,576	3	10,000 +	500 =	11,500
11,576 +	579 =	12,155	4	10,000 +	500 =	12,000
12,155 +	608 =	12,763	5	10,000 +	500 =	12,500
12,763 +	638 =	13,401	6	10,000 +	500 =	13,000
13,401 +	670 =	14,071	7	10,000 +	500 =	13,500
14,071 +	704 =	14,775	8	10,000 +	500 =	14,000
14,775 +	739 =	15,514	9	10,000 +	500 =	14,500
15,514 +	776 =	16,290	10	10,000 +	500 =	15,000

TEN-YEAR TOTAL: $16,290 versus $15,000
Which pocket profit would *you* rather have?
Lend money for a compound return. Borrow money at simple interest.

*Figures are rounded.

In workshops, this demonstration never fails to surprise the volunteer who runs the calculation on a simple calculator. For fun, try it yourself. This is what it looks like:

Day	Income	Day	Income
1	$ .01	16	$ 327.68
2	.02	17	655.36
3	.04	18	1,310.72
4	.08	19	2,621.44
5	.16	20	5,242.88
6	.32	21	10,485.76
7	.64	22	20,971.52
8	1.28	23	41,943.04
9	2.56	24	83,886.08
10	5.12	25	167,772.16
11	10.24	26	335,544.32
12	20.48	27	671,088.64
13	40.96	28	1,342,177.20
14	81.92	29	2,684,354.40
15	$163.84	30	$5,368,708.80

Never forget the power of compounding. Burn it into your memory. Watch for opportunities to use it. With reasonable returns and adequate time, you can trust molehill amounts to build mountains.

The Million-Dollar Retirement

But can you save enough to retire? First of all, let's see if those scary articles are true. Do you need $1 million dollars to retire? The answer, your cost of living, is found by comparing your Cushioned Cash Flow Worksheet, Income Monitor, and Living Expenses form. If you haven't completed those forms, you are at the mercy of someone else's opinion.

Update your keys to come up with a reasonably realistic figure. Maybe 70 percent of your current expenses? You are the expert. What expenses would you eliminate at retirement? If you retired today, would you sell the house? Sell the car? Okay, you have a good estimate of the cost of retiree living.

Now, what about inflation? Experts warn about our loss of buying power because of ever-present inflation. They will scream at this advice, but let's *forget* inflation for now. KISS—keep it superbly simple. We don't need talk about what tomorrow's dollars will be worth in today's terms or vice versa. Because if you maintain control of your lifestyle and schedule investment *flexibility,* which maintains choices in your investments, whatever happens to the economy and interest rates (review the time line for liquidity in Chapter 13), you'll be right on target. You won't be caught in a corner. If CDs and bonds shoot up to 13 percent in the midst of a roaring inflation, you'll be earning those rates on your investments.

Is there an expert who *really* knows the precise steps to take for perfect financial success? Do people at the top have special answers? I don't think so. President Harry S. Truman, after hearing an "on the one hand . . . and on the other hand . . ." analysis by one of his top money advisers, groaned, "Can't someone bring me a one-handed economist?"

Using what we know, we can estimate a future scenario based on today. Truth, is, your income stream and the lifestyle it provides can be parallel to your future situation—*if* you put some familiar guidelines into that vague idea of *future*. Let's build a scenario.

Let's say at age 65 you *need*
   an income of $50,000. $50,000
Let's also say you'll *have* a
   $15,000 pension   −15,000
You still *need* $35,000 to make up the difference
Suppose you *have* Social
   Security of $10,000   −10,000
You still *need* $25,000 to make up the difference

Where's that $25,000 income going to come from? Assuming you have no knight in shining armor coming to your rescue, you'll have to accumulate savings to produce it. How much? Savings of $500,000 earning 5 percent will generate $25,000. We have a target.

Can you reach that goal with little sums? Let's use time and compounding to find out. Suppose you do not have a large lump sum from savings or inheritance. Can you accomplish much with little sums, such as monthly savings from your *investable* cash flow? Refer to your Cushioned Cash Flow worksheet. Estimate how much excess cushion money you have at year-end. Refer to your Living Expenses form. Is there a way to tighten the ship? To be successful, the sums set aside must come from investable dollars. This isn't going to be a diet that you give up at summer's end. The sums must be set aside for the rest of your employed life. But, that small sacrifice will be more than worth it. Wonderful things come in small packages, as you can see in the following illustration. Notice how the required monthly savings drops with each one percent increase in earnings.

Monthly Savings Needed to Accumulate $500,000 by Age 65

Age	Years to 65	Monthly Savings Needed When Earning*			
		5%	6%	7%	8%
30	35	$ 451	$ 364	$ 292	$ 233
40	25	854	739	639	550
50	15	1,888	1,743	1,607	1,481

*Earnings compound annually.

About Social Security

Are you scared that Social Security will go away? Okay, let's play *what if*—What if you don't receive the $10,000 Social Security income we plugged into the example? Well, you'd have to shrink up your retirement lifestyle or find a way to make up the annual $10,000 shortfall. That means you'll have to look to your own assets to produce $35,000 income instead of $25,000.

Ouch. At 5 percent, you'd have to accumulate $700,000 to produce $35,000 a year. But, is the $35,000 income impossible to achieve? Who knows? Rates fluctuate. If rates are 7 percent when you retire, you'd earn $35,000 on $500,000. So, when you plan for that vague, faraway future, remember it will come with good surprises, too. If rates are 8 percent when you retire, you'd make the $35,000 on a sum of $440,000.

And even if you play what-if all day long, that's about as close as you can get to nailing down your retirement. But you know what? It looks like retirement may be possible with *half* of that scary million.

Take heart. If you are 40 years old, you have a great chance to make that $500,000 deadline with monthly savings. Our estimates use very conservative returns. You'll do better.

Who knows what you'll earn on those monthly savings over the years? *No one.* What if by the year 2000 you earned 10 percent? And besides, do you really believe Washington will pull the Social Security rug out from under the fastest-growing age group in the United States? It's doubtful the entire population is suddenly going to become instant self-sufficient financial wizards and millionaires.

Worry about things you *can* change. And remember, any change as fundamental as eliminating or modifying Social Security would be put in place gradually, over many years. Older workers will be grandfathered, not tricked. When something is grandfathered, it means a new law will not affect it. Younger working people will have *time* to prepare under the new system. In the meantime, are you aware of the status quo?

If 100 people started even on their careers, what would their financial status be on retirement in 1992?

- 93 of them would receive Social Security benefits, representing a mean income of $6,634.
  - For 63 of those, the $6,634 would equal one-half their total income.
  - For 26 of them, the $6,634 would equal 90 percent or more of their income.
  - For the remaining few, the $6,634 would be their *only* income.
- Assuming 3½ of the retirees who did not receive benefits would be flat broke, that leaves a scant 3½ retirees who would be financially independent.

Source: Frank B. Hobbs with Bonnie L. Damon, *65+ in the United States,* (Washington, DC: U.S. Dept. of Commerce/U.S. Dept. of Health and Human Services, April 1996), 4–14, 4–15.

Surprisingly these statistics have not changed much over the past 30 years, despite the media urging us to build a nest egg for our retirement. The saddest note of all is that, as of 1992, although women represented 58.4 percent of the elderly population, they represented 71.3 percent of the elderly poor.

Too many women feel that if they ignore their daily financial maintenance, it will take care of itself. They set themselves up to be victims. Take control now. There is power in *small* savings. You have the *keys* to put them to work.

If you have $500,000 set aside for your retirement, you will have life choices and smiles. (See Figure 21.1.) Even if you live past 90, you will indeed have provided for that older woman you will one day become.

Chapter 20

*M*atching Your Investments to Your Goals

*I*f you had to study all horse breeds first, you might never have an animal hitched to your wagon. If you had to understand all computers before buying, you'd probably stick to a pen and paper. And if you have to understand all investments first, you'll probably end up in a savings account. Life isn't long enough to learn all the ins and outs of everything. I've never dismantled a gasoline engine, but I surely had a driver's license when I hit 16.

Put your attention and your money where it does the most good for your own purposes. We don't have to drive an 18-wheeler to use the highways and find the proper destinations when a small family automobile does the job. When a financial expert says she can double that return, if you'll only move your money to these new "whatevers," keep your eyes on your goal, and arrive there in the vehicle of your choice. I once heard a broker tell a client his zero coupon bonds were old fashioned and should be sold. It was outrageous. But, because we are going to go about investing wearing blinders, those ego threats and distractions will be as futile as crocodile tears from a lawyer.

Tame the Dreaded Financial Plan

It's easy to talk a good story, but have you tried putting money plans on paper? Ouch. That's cringe time. There are all these *things* in our futures: things we *need* to have, things it's *nice* to have, and—cluttering up the picture even more—things we *don't need* to have. So we cry for help, and here come the professionals. Financial planners have sprouted up all across the country, hoping to serve as psychiatrists for our money problems.

Do you really need someone else to plan your life? No, don't answer that yet, it's an unfair question. Maybe your financial future does seem like a hopeless maze. Well, don't give up, there's a light at the end of the tunnel. And, actually, because you have already set up the keys, you have little left to do. So let's knock off that planning phobia.

You might be nagging yourself with questions like: Can I set aside monthly sums? Will they be large enough? How do I diversify my inheritance? Jot down your questions and park them here until later. Letting those concerns creep in now is like hemming and hawing over vacation clothes before you've decided on the trip. You wouldn't pack clothes for every climate and all activities, would you? Of course not. What-to-wear outfits come *after* you've decided where you'll wear them. It's the same with your plan. Forget the money for now. We're not ready to choose. First, we need a financial destination. Let's look at what we know and what we can expect about our destination.

This Is Your Life

Your expected life span.   How many years will it be until you are 85?

Example A, "Planning for Life Events Sample," in Figure 20.1 shows a 40-year-old with an expected life span to age 85.

1. Photocopy the blank form in Appendix A, "Planning for Life Events."
2. Label the *first* slash/line with your current age (above the line). This is *you* in your life.
3. Label the *final* year/slash line at age 85 or whatever age you expect to reach (above the line). This is your *life*.

FIGURE 20.1   Planning for Life Events Sample

Example A Life Span

age 40
1996

$15,000 pension ann income........
$10,000 Social Security ann income........
retire
2023 * age 65
age 85+
2041

* $500,000 @ 5%=$25,000 income........

(#)

Example B Expected events

Above the line: events and/or dollar amounts due you
Below the line: dollar amounts needed to pay for events

- college Don/Ted
2000 '01 '02 '03 '04 '05
  *   *   *   *   *   *

+inheritance
$50,000
2011 * age 55

-buy
business
2016* age 60

+$15,000 pension ann income........
+ $10,000 Social Security ann income........
retire
2023 * age 65

rd the world trip
2028* age 70

age 85+
2041

age
40
'96

* $10,000

* $500,000   * $25000

@ 5%=$25,000 income........

(#)

Don$8000-8000-8000-8000

Ted$8000-8000-8000-8000

(Total$8000-8000-16000-16000-8000-8000)

Your expected retirement year.   Above the line representing the year you will retire, enter the year and the word *retire*. Refer to Example A in Figure 20.1.

Other expected major financial events.   Will you: Buy a house? Pay for college educations? Receive an inheritance? Buy or sell a business? Take a long trip?

1. Enter each event and year above the appropriate year/ slash line.
2. If the expense, as in a college education, repeats over several years, repeat the entries above each year it will occur.

The Total Picture

Example B in Figure 20.1 reflects our 40-year-old's expected life span—let's call her Maggie—with all her predictable major events plugged in. Whew! Her future is crowded with events—mind-boggling, but no worse than the library without the card catalog. Event confusion is more of the same. Let's clear the air.

What does each event cost?   The events are entered, but we must know their cost. After all, the event will only *happen* if we have the money there at the right time. Translate each entry into dollars as shown in Example B of Figure 20.1.

1. For monies coming in, enter the expected amount *above* the line.
2. For expenses, enter the estimated cost *below* the line:
    *   For the retirement date, break your hoped-for income into two portions. Enter the income from outside sources, Social Security, pensions, etc., *above* the line.
    *   *Below* the line, enter the lump sum needed from your own assets to produce the required cash flow (note the interest rate used).

Picture Your Life Events

This lifeline illustration is a worksheet and a tool. Maggie can see all the events of major importance in her future and what they'll cost. That might be the entire picture, but it's too busy. Where does she look first? What does she do first? The dilemma of too many choices is like a mother's first day at home alone when the last child goes off to school. She jumps in the car and drives down the nearest highway eyeing the clock, her windows open, air-conditioning on, radio blasting, and windshield wipers going, while she sings a nursery song, chews a fingernail, and realizes she has no idea where she's headed.

Understand Your Goal

Blinders come in handy when you want to go one way at a time. The form in Figure 20.2, Understanding the Goal, is going to help establish boundaries, our blinders. We'll use this form to build a *profile* of each goal. That profile will guide us to investment choices.

About any financial goal, you'll need to know:

1. Will the event occur at an unknown time? On a specific date?
2. Does the event require a specific sum of money? An income stream?
3. What are the consequences if the required monies are not available?
   - Can the event be postponed?
   - Are you willing to forego the event?
   - What are you willing to do to ensure financial readiness for this event?

Notice we still have not talked about dollars and cents.

Understand Your Investment

Okay, set aside the Understanding the Goal form for a minute and turn to Figure 20.3, to the form called, Understanding the Investment. We're putting together a puzzle: Once you see the shape of the piece in your hand, you know what puzzle shape to search for next. That's what the goal profile does—it gives the event shape. And just as the eye scans all the puzzle pieces—continually excluding and excluding until only those pieces that are a possible match are considered—that's how we'll exclude inappropriate investments.

Understanding the Investment is the tool that makes the search for a match quick and easy. The match will have the right *shape* or profile. You won't have to take Investment 101 or listen to a litany of choices before you make a smart choice.

Certain questions must be asked about any investment:

- Will the investment mature on the specific *date* as needed?
- Are there penalties for accessing the monies on a specific date? On other dates?
- Do you require a specific *sum* from the investment?
- If the investment does not perform as hoped, is there an alternative source of funds for the event?
- Will the investment produce the ongoing income stream desired for the needed period of time?
- Will the income remain constant or vary? Is that a hindrance or benefit?
- Does the investment require constant monitoring? Do you have the time and tools to accomplish that? Does anyone?
- Will the investment increase or save taxes?

The Main Event

Okay, but what are we trying to match up? Go back to your Understanding the Goal form. I hope you were dead honest answering the last question: "What am I willing to do if this goal is not reached?"

On Maggie's Example A in Figure 20.1, it's obvious that her retirement ranks as a do-or-die event. That's her number-one goal. Her main focus. And even though the college educations are important, she does have alternative sources to make them possible. The remaining events appear to be nice-to-haves but not need-to-haves. They can be modified.

Using your answer to that last question, select your do-or-die event. Write it down as number one on your lifeline. Then assign the remaining events a number on the importance scale, using a one-to-ten scale—with one being the most important. Event number one is *your* main event. You have your destination.

FIGURE 20.2   Understanding the Goal

Questions/Events	College Costs	Buy Business	Retirement	Trip Round the World
Is the money needed on specific date?	Yes/ each year for 6 years	No-within 10-15 years	Yes	Yes
Is a specific sum required?	Yes	Yes- minimum $10,000	Yes	Yes-minimum $20,000
If investment fails is there an alternative source of funds?	Borrow on house student loans part time work co-op schools	No	No	No
Is an on-going income stream required?	No	No	Yes for rest of my life	No
On what date should income begin?	n/a	n/a	Jan 2025	n/a
*What am I willing to do if this goal is not reached?	use alternative source of funds	Forget it	Must be reached I'll see to it..pay off house..save	Take car trips/ cruises

* Your answer to this question establishes the real importance of each goal.

Review the chart once again. Using a scale from one to ten, number each goal for its importance.

Now complete a <u>new</u> timeline for your life. Insert only your #1 ranked event.

FIGURE 20.3   Understanding the Investment

Questions for Investments	Money Market/Savings	Cert of Deposit	Deferred Annuity Fixed	Bonds: Tax-free/Taxable	Stocks: w/div or w/o div	Mutual Funds: Stocks	Mutual Funds: Bonds	Real Estate
Specific maturity date?	n/a always available	yes	see below: Income	yes	no	no	no	no
Specific sum at maturity?	n/a	yes	see below: Income	yes	n/a	n/a	n/a	n/a
Specific sum guarantee?	no	yes FDIC	min guar see Income	yes	no	no	no	no
Early access penalty?	no	yes	yes	yes/ market risk	market risk/ commissions	market risk/ maybe commissions	market risk/ maybe commissions	market risk/ commissions/ cost of sale
Risk of principal?	insurance backed account	until maturity	no	until maturity	yes	yes	yes	yes
Income stream?	if use interest	ask	yes/you say when	yes except zero bonds	yes with dividends	yes w/ div or withdrawal	yes w/div or withdrawal	if income property
Convert to income w/o cost?	yes	n/a	yes	yes except zero bonds	yes with dividends	yes with dividends	yes with dividends	don't know
Income stream guarantee?	interest rate fluctuates	yes	yes/once set in motion	with insured bonds	no	no	no	no
Tax impact?	your choice	taxable	deferred 'til payout	your choice	taxable	taxable	your choice	ask CPA
Investment easy to manage?	none required	none required	none required	use keys to monitor	use keys to monitor	use keys to monitor	use keys to monitor	hands-on management

Shift to the second time line on your page. Enter only your beginning age, expected life span, your number-one goal—*one* only—and the year in which it occurs. Just as Maggie did in Figure 20.1, you are setting priorities. Prioritizing does not rule out other events, it simply puts them in perspective. Now we can focus.

Link the Information

Now, look at your Understanding the Goal form. Notice the requirements of your number-one event. Compare those requirements to the investment *features* listed in Figure 20.3.

Here's an example for Maggie's "retirement" goal:

- Is retirement money needed on a specific date? Yes.
- Go back to your Understanding the Investment from. If you include investments with either guaranteed income or a specific maturity date, how many match? Only three.

The likely matches are the fixed vehicles: CDs, deferred annuities, or bonds. (Although money market accounts and savings accounts are included on that chart, we won't use them as investment choices. They are temporary parking places for money.)

Three Possibilities

Let's work with the three choices. If you want no financial surprises, any of the three fixed investments, or a combination of them, might accomplish your goal. Just as each food in a meal has a purpose, so does each investment vehicle in a plan. Served together, the items create a balance, a complementary whole. Diners use a fork, knife, and spoon to get at the foods. Investors might use small sums or have to accumulate large sums to access different investment vehicles. So let's look closer at these three matches.

1. The Fixed Deferred Annuity

Strengths.   You can choose time-tested insurance companies that are top-ranked by A.M. Best. An annuity accepts either small periodic payments or a large sum. The annuity defers taxes on your savings until you decide to spend them. You decide when the income begins. The insurance company ensures that once begun, the income will continue for life. It requires no management on your part. At death, taxable proceeds go to a beneficiary without probate.

Limitations. The interest rate fluctuates throughout the years of saving (this may be good or disappointing); however, the insurance company guarantees a minimum rate. Once you request income, the payout is fixed. (If inflation occurs, the annuity income will not increase to keep up, nor will it reduce if recession comes.)

So? There is great appeal to the fixed deferred annuity to build a strong foundation to a retirement plan. Your savings are insured and managed for you, tax-deferred. Income is reliable and lifelong. Annuities have been around for a long, long time. Fixed annuity income is probably best used as a *portion* of the overall retirement income, because the payout, which may stretch over a 25-year retirement span, cannot be increased. It will be ready to pay income when you retire.

2. The Certificate of Deposit

Strengths. It is available in small and large sums. If the total held at any one institution does not exceed the $100,000 FDIC limit, it is an insured vehicle. To maintain flexibility and be ready to take advantage of rate increases, the maturities can be staggered. No management is needed other than keeping an eye on rates.

Limitations. The interest earned is subject to tax. Unless the certificate compounds internally, you must transfer the earnings, as paid, into another vehicle. You are responsible to monitor the total of principal and interest held in one institution so that it does not exceed the FDIC limitation.

So? Certificates of deposit can serve as a portion of overall savings if you can arrange compounding. Maturities can be staggered for flexibility. If the certificates of deposit are held in a pension plan, taxes are deferred. If your retirement savings include an IRA, Keogh, or corporate plan held at a major brokerage house, you will have a broad choice of investments, including the money market, CDs, annuities, bonds, stocks, and mutual funds.

Continuing to roll over CDs during retirement, as rates fluctuate, provides inflation protection to your fixed annuity income. CDs give you a chance to change your mind at each maturity.

3. Bonds

Strengths.   Little management is required: you'll confirm receipt of interest payments and transfer them to compound in the money market. You know what you'll have at maturity. Maturity dates can be scheduled to coincide with a future event. Bonds are available tax-free or taxable. Bonds can be bought with insured backing. Zero bonds, so named because they pay zero interest, are available in small dollar amounts. They are sold at deep discounts and mature on a given date at $1,000 per bond.

Because U.S. government zeros and corporate zeros are taxed annually—even though no interest is paid out—they are best held in a retirement account, sheltered from taxes. Tax-free municipal zeros are available, but since the term is long and you receive nothing along the way, look for insured muni zeros.

Limitations.   Bond interest does not compound unless you so arrange it. Bonds cannot be purchased at "so much" per month, larger sums are required. Hold bonds until maturity to avoid loss of principal from market risk.

So?   Zero or corporate bonds in a retirement account, and tax-free bonds held outside retirement accounts, are good for fine-tuning a retirement investment plan. They can be used to schedule definite maturities and reduce taxes. Stagger maturities for flexibility and increased return. They fit nicely into a retirement plan.

Is This Enough?

Maggie stated that she absolutely had to reach her retirement goal by that "definite" date. By selecting matching "definite" investments, she can sleep at night without worrying. As long as she continues to set money aside and earn at least 5 percent, she'll be able to retire as planned, on schedule.

It might appear that Maggie's financial security is settled, but she is much too young to rely only on a fixed return. Taking even a small dollar amount for stocks will add another layer to her program, and this layer just might bring unexpected growth to her assets. She might exceed her goals. And it's that possibility, proven by history, that leads even the most conservative investors into the stock market.

Are Small Sums Enough for Wall Street?

You can invest only small sums? Don't let that stop you from selecting dividend-paying stocks for reinvestment. For a reasonably priced subscription to *Better Investing* magazine, you can educate yourself on another entry to the stock market. The magazine may also be available at the public library. Here's an excerpt showing how NAIC (National Association of Investors' Corporation) presents their low-cost investment plan:

A one-time set-up charge of $7.00 plus the cost of one share of stock in any of the more than 150 companies listed (listed on the magazine page) will get you started with a new holding in your personal . . . portfolio. Then add to it regularly in the future at little or no additional charge. . . .

You'll recognize many of the stocks on their list, which keeps growing, by the way. And for the investor who can purchase only a share or two at a time, this method will protect those sums from being eroded by brokerage commissions. Look into it. (See Appendix B for more information.)

Hidden Helpers

Contribute to your corporate-based retirement plans. Since those dollars are pretax, you invest 100 percent of each dollar. And, since earnings on that money are also sheltered from taxes, they will reinvest at 100 percent. You are way ahead of the individual whose savings are bitten by taxes before they reach the investment, and the earnings on the investment are bitten again.

Does your company offer a matching contribution to your plan? If the company contributes a dollar for every two you contribute, you are speeding ahead. Don't overlook these benefits. Make the maximum contribution if you can manage it. Trim your living expenses to make that contribution possible.

In addition to pension plans, which have set ceilings on contributions, you can invest as much as you like outside your retirement plans. Annuities outside the plan are invested with after-tax dollars, but once in the annuity the earnings are not taxed—until you take money out as income.

Suppose you contribute the maximum allowed to your 401(k) but you cannot find any fixed investments offered in the plan. Ask your employee benefits person to include a fixed investment in the 401(k) plan. Meanwhile, ask for prospectuses on the funds offered. Study their holdings. Decide which fund buys the quality of companies you want to own by looking them up in the S&P guide. Review Morningstar at your library for another opinion. Don't try to make a 25-year decision. Choose a balance that will best defend you over the coming two to five years.

Thinking in percentages, suppose you diversify your 401(k) monies by thirds. Allocate 1/3 to a blue chip stock mutual fund, 1/3 in a short- to intermediate-term bond fund, and leave 1/3 in the money market fund. If stock funds go up, your assets increase. If interest rates drop, your bond funds increase. If rates on bonds are too low and stock prices are too high, the money market will give you a return on your money while you wait safely to see what's going to happen. If you think that's keeping one foot on land, one in the boat, and a hand on the rope, you're right. The secret is balance and knowing when to jump, and nobody can give you the perfect combination.

The percentages you choose will depend on your acceptance of risk and your age (see Figures 20.4 and 20.5).

Figure 20.4 represents the classic layering of investments according to risk:

- The *lowest* layer of the pyramid (3) represents *foundation* investments. The outcome is known. There is little risk if the investment is held until maturity.
- The *middle* layer (2) represents *growth* investments. The outcome is not known and there is no maturity date. You

FIGURE 20.4   The Investment Risk Pyramid (Although not every vehicle is included and not every situation is alike, you can use this pyramid as a general guide to risk.)

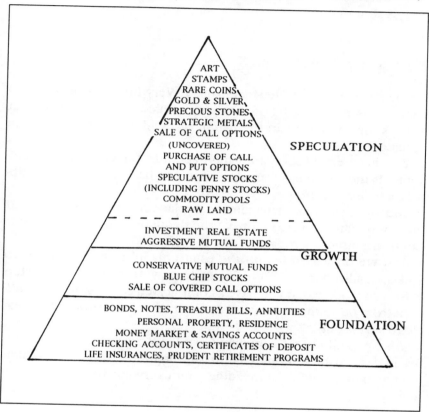

would assume this risk because of the opportunity for growth. If the dividend-paying growth investments are depressed when retirement arrives, dividends are still available to pay the expected income.

If dividend-paying stocks are not selected, the retiree is faced with selling depressed stocks to reinvest in an income-producing vehicle. This layer is the inflation protection to the foundation investments.

- The *peak* of the pyramid (1) represents *speculation*. High risk is assumed with these vehicles because there is hope of dramatic success. The percentage assigned to this level should not exceed 5 to 10 percent of your overall investments. Even that small percentage reduces as you approach retirement, when the time remaining to recover from losses is slim to none.

You're on Your Own

You've been *planning* since page 1. Very little has been left to chance. Your daily cash flow has been spelled out. You know what it takes for you to live in the manner to which you have become accustomed.

You have established a cushion account for unexpected incidents. If the car needs four tires, you can handle it without skipping a week's dinners.

You have put risk management in place through insurances. If the house catches fire, you have the deductible at the ready. You can begin directing repairs.

And we discussed *beginning* estate planning and the need to seek specialized input. With a living trust, you know who will step in for you if needed. If you have a complicated estate situation, children from other marriages, and so forth, get to the proper legal eagle to sort it out.

You worked out a Cushioned Cash Flow worksheet that identifies excess cushion monies as *investable* funds. You know which money to invest without invading your everyday life.

Match Your Life to Financial Events

Make yourself a lifeline for investments to match your events. (See the Dream Fulfillment worksheet in Appendix A.) Draw whatever pictures it takes for you to see your financial picture. Draw a new one each year as you progress toward your main goals. For now, set up a file folder labeled Financial Guides. Insert all your financial pictures and guides so they'll be at your fingertips.

Use the Rule of 72 (refer to Figure 8.4 or to Appendix A) to estimate what you'll have in the future. That's as close as anyone can get. Trust your estimates.

FIGURE 20.5   How Your Life Stage Affects the Investment Pyramid

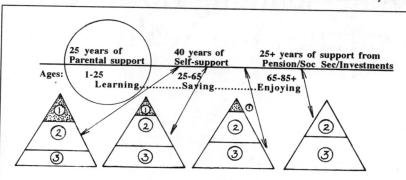

1. High Risk–Speculation

   This is the high-roller taken with the hope of a bonanza. Restrict your plunge into this category to 5 to 10 percent of your overall assets. Decrease that percentage as you grow older, as time and opportunity needed to recoup losses is diminished.

2. Growth–Deferred Results

   These are long-term investments intended to grow the needed nest egg for future income and maintain financial defense against inflation throughout life. Representing a major portion of your investments in the early years, growth will give dominance to foundation investments in later years when more guarantees are desired.

3. Foundation–Serious, Safe

   This is the anchor in any investment program for predictable and/or guaranteed results and income. Foundation vehicles can be used at any stage of life. The percentage in this category increases with your age in life.

Reminder: Any investment program must be made up of *investable* dollars only.

Now, consider your secondary goals. Review your answers to the last question on Understanding the Goal. Once you know your fundamental situation is in place, once you know you can retire, then work on the secondary goals. You have your financial picture in focus. The limitations are whatever your situation imposes. Would it be worth moving to a smaller town? Living in a more modest house? A lower taxed state? Giving up the country club membership? Only you can answer those questions.

Do it.

Now.

Chapter 21

*U*nderstanding How Much Insurance You Really Need

*N*o one wants to think about dying too soon. It may never happen. But if it does, your dependent children or parents or spouse, could be left unable to care for themselves. How do you ensure they'll have food, clothing, shelter, and personal care as long as needed? With money, but money alone is not enough.

There are two steps involved in protecting those you care for:

1. Arranging for the monies to be there (we're using insurance).
2. Arranging for *separate* management for the monies and the dependents.
   - For instance, in a living trust, you might name a professional nonbank corporate trustee to manage the monies.
   - Then, in that same document, name an individual or individuals to serve as guardian and protector of your dependents.

This calls on two specialists, each doing what he or she does best, without conflict of interest; each using the other as a check and balance, and each positioned to make the best decisions for the welfare of those dependents.

How Much Money for How Long?

It's tough to estimate insurance needs by unpeeling the complexities of your life. You probably have savings and own all manner of valuable *things*. Forget all that. We can get an answer quicker and easier by building from the ground up.

Pretend you are alone and have nothing. The first assignment is to create solutions entirely by insurance. Then, we'll construct real life. Okay?

The picture starts with you.

1. Draw that familiar horizontal line across the page to represent your life.
2. Place yourself in your life.

Is that you midway in the "30s" section? It appears you have small children and the youngest is due any minute. Well, if you died *today*, they'd have years of dependency ahead of them. Yes, and what about college? Stop right there. Don't clutter the picture. Focus on the basics: food, clothing, shelter, and care. If you know that's all arranged, you won't have poor little match girl dreams.

We need to build a framework. How long will your dependents need support?

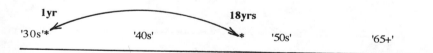

The life insurance income must continue until the youngest child becomes 18 (see asterisks). We have the *term*. Okay, but how much is that support going to cost?

Assuming today's income supports your current lifestyle, let's aim for that same income after your death. If you currently earn $50,000, you'll need life insurance proceeds that can be invested to produce that same $50,000 a year. Okay, there's our second detail, the required *payout*. Can insurance produce a $50,000 a year cash flow?

The Goal Determines the Lump Sum Needed

Upon your sudden demise, a lump sum is immediately supplied by the insurance company. It will be put in the hands of the financial manager you named. He or she will follow your instructions. Is it your intention to provide $50,000 a year for a term of 18 years? Or do you intend to provide that income *plus* pass on an inheritance for your heirs? You will select entirely different insurance coverage depending on your intentions.

Here's why.

Income Plus Inheritance

Suppose a lump sum is invested to earn 6 percent. Now you withdraw the 6 percent earnings. What happens? Not much.

The lump sum is *not* diminished. Your dependents have the annual income. Plus, at the end of the 18 years, the target date, they would have choices. Since the lump sum would remain intact, they could continue to receive the income ad infinitum. Or, at certain ages, the financial manager could disperse the sum to them as an inheritance. (In the real world, there may be fees to a professional manager and/or income taxes to heirs.)

This arrangement would look like this (Example A):

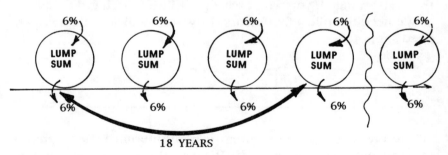

18 YEARS

Income for a Term

When you buy a house, the mortgage is *amortized*. That allows you to repay the loan with equal monthly payments for a certain number of years. We'll use 30. Since each payment is part *interest* and part *principal*, at the end of the 30 years, the mortgage is paid off. The bank's income is gone.

Suppose you amortize an insurance lump sum the same way. Invest the sum at 6 percent, but now you take equal withdrawals of 9 percent each month. What happens?

Since each withdrawal *exceeds* the investment earnings, each withdrawal takes the 6 percent interest plus a part of principal. At the end of 18 years, when the goal is reached, the lump sum is used up and the income ends. The dependents do not have an inheritance.

It would look like this (Example B):

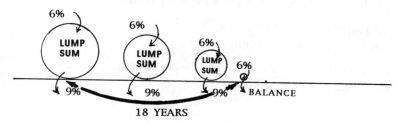

18 YEARS

We'll put these two approaches to work a little later. But the framework is not complete. We still don't have a lump sum target. Let's nail that down.

Reasonable Returns

We need an 18-year income of $50,000. How large a sum will it take to produce $50,000 a year? That depends on what that sum could reasonably earn. What's reasonable? Who knows? The only way to be certain of what rates will be—*if* and *when* you die unexpectedly—is to find out at the time. And you won't be here. So, we'll use what is reasonable today, let's say 6 percent. Get your calculator. This is a fun experiment.

How to Find the Lump Sum

And the formula is simple—divide desired income by expected interest rate to determine lump sum:

$50,000 (Annual income desired)
÷ 6% (Reasonable return expected)
= $834,000 (Lump sum needed from insurance)

Is that right? Yes. ($834,000 × .06 = $50,040)

That's a major purchase, but just go along for now, okay? We're only exploring numbers.

Oh, and don't put your calculator away yet.

Let's see what that $834,000 would do using Example A (the sum earns 6 percent; we withdraw 6 percent):

1. It would produce $50,000 a year income for 18 years.
2. Then it would remain intact and give the heirs continuing income until dispersed as a hefty *inheritance*.

And using the $834,000 as in Example B (the sum earns 6 percent; we withdraw 9 percent):

1. It could produce $75,0000 a year income for 18 years.
2. Then it would be *used up*.

You Can Become Insurance-Poor

It would be nice to wave a magic wand and give the dependents everything, but . . . let's see if we can pare down that insurance cost. Still have your calculator handy? Okay, try this: $50,000 ÷ 9% = $556,000 (rounded).

By using Example B, we can achieve the goal of $50,000 a year income for 18 years using 35 percent less insurance. That's not too shabby. At this point, call your stockbroker and ask for a quote on *term* life insurance. She has the answer at her fingertips. Ask about a 15-year (or more) *fixed* premium. That way you won't have financial surprises. Stop here if the insurance coverage is affordable and it reaches your goal. You are ready to act on your information.

If you are the sole bread winner, with no assets, you can provide 18 years of $50,000 income for your dependents with a life insurance death benefit of $556,000, invested to earn 6 percent. Instruct your financial manager to use Example B for your beneficiaries, withdrawing 3 percent *more* than the sum earns.

Sure, that sounds fine, you say. But what's the mystery method that tells you the lump sum really will last 18 years? That's a pretty important piece of the puzzle, and so far it's missing! You're exactly right. We can fix that easily, with no math involved.

FIGURE 21.1   How Long Will Your Money Last?

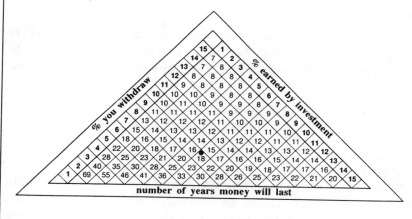

How Long Will Your Money Last?

or "Amortizing a Lump Sum"
% out >% in = lump sum diminishes
at end of selected term, sum is used up.

Our example:
Locate the % earned—right side (6%).
Locate the % you withdraw—left side (9%).
Follow to the intersecting block to discover years the money
will last (18).

The banking industry's financial charts are available at your public library, if you prefer firsthand research. But guess what? There's a ten-second shortcut. Take a look at the pyramid in Figure 21.1. I've circled the meeting point of 6 percent *earned* and 9 percent *withdrawn*. That intersection tells us that the money will last 18 years. It matches our goal. So, that means if a sum earns 6 percent, you can withdraw 9 percent (3 percent excess), and the money will still last 18 years.

The rules are:

% out < in = lump sum grows, income continues ad finitum
% out = % in = lump sum remains same, income continues ad infinitum

% out > in = lump sum diminishes, income ends when sum is used up
< means "less than"
> means "greater than"

Experiment with varied returns and withdrawals. Try different ways to produce income for college expenses or long-term withdrawals from a *retirement account.* It's a quick what-if reference for any kind of lump sum and situation.

Note: In the real world, withdrawals from retirement accounts are subject to income taxes.

Bring on the Savings

You just solved your problems with insurance alone. You will insure your life for $556,000. But, suppose you have savings. You do! You have $156,000 in savings and investments. Okay, let's include those dollars:

$556,000 (Insurance required) – $156,000 (Savings)
= $400,000 (Insurance still required)

Using Example B, the insurance is cut again and you still reach your goal.

If, when we started our journey, you were disappointed at the $834,000 estimate (using Example A), now you have other choices. First, by switching to Example B, the insurance needs dropped to $556,000. Now, adding your $156,000 savings (still using Example B), the insurance needs drop to $400,000.

You have cut the insurance estimate in half. It is affordable. Your goal is reached.

Bring On the Partner

Okay, now let's include your employed spouse or partner. He's a big part of this picture. The goal is the same: $50,000 annual income for 18 years.

Switch back to those income dollars for a minute.

The goal is to provide $50,000 annual income (Partner's income –$30,000). You still need $20,000 in income.

Now the goal is $20,000 annual income.

Desired income ($20,000) ÷ Percent earned (6%)
= Lump sum required ($334,000)

Check that answer: $334,000 × .06 = $20,040. Close enough.

Using Example A, the insurance need drops to $334,000. At 6 percent, it will provide $20,000 income. Since the withdrawals equal the earnings, the heirs will have the lump sum as an inheritance at the end of the 18 years.

Using Example B, the lump sum drops again:

Desired income ($20,000) ÷ 9% = lump sum required ($223,000)

Check that answer: $223,000 × .09 = $20,040.

Now check the pyramid in Figure 21.1 to see if the money will last 18 years. (The lump sum earns 6 percent and withdrawals are 9 percent.)

How much insurance do you need? You now have an answer that fits your life.

Another Viewpoint

If your partner wants to know how much insurance he needs, use the same process. Build from the ground up. However, if he died suddenly, would you quit your job to stay home with your children? Death creates many waves; not all are financial.

Once you know the amount of life insurance needed, the next question is which type? Debating between term insurance or whole life (with its many variations) is beyond the scope of this book. Cost, term of need, purpose, and other situations in your life all play a role in that decision. Have your facts lined up before you see your insurance expert. Do business with a top-ranked company. You have analyzed your life. You know what you need. KISS. You'll make the right choice.

The heart-wrenching thing about life insurance is wanting to provide our loved ones with everything. Always. The sky's the limit. Then financial reality steps in. Give yourself a break. You are already supporting today's financial life and tomorrow's retirement—and both of those are realities. To *sacrifice* today for the sake of a disaster that may not occur—well, you get my point. When it comes to insurance, do the best you can to put your mind at ease, but don't take food off the table.

Chapter 22

*K*eeping Score: Monitoring Your Financial Fitness

*A*dd together Your Income Monitors and Living Expenses forms for five years and what have you got? A jolting picture of how much money has gone through your fingers. It's a real eye-opener on the here-and-now lifestyle.

So, about that future you've planned so carefully: How do you know if you're making progress toward your dream? Totalling *put-aside* retirement contributions and savings tells only the beginning of the story. And if you've already arrived at that *future*, are you staying the course?

First Comes Financial Reconnaissance

Just totalling up money put aside for retirement is like a fleet admiral tallying the seaworthy vessels assembled for Operation Z. It's a necessary step, but it doesn't produce results.

What counts is what happens once the admiral's ships—and your *put-aside* dollars—are deployed. No admiral worth her salt would orphan the fleet out at sea. Instead, she shifts into command mode to monitor its progress. She's at the ready to take evasive action, defensive action, or seize opportunity—all with a mind to speed ahead to the objective. Nothing is more important than the day she shouts, "Mission accomplished!"

Put on your admiral brass. You've completed the tally of your put-aside dollars. Now it's time to set up a minute-a-month command sheet for your deployed dollars, so you can take evasive action, defensive action, or seize opportunity. Nothing is more important than the future day when you shout, "Mission accomplished!"

Next Comes Score Keeping

If the details get lost in the shuffle, the entire financial operation can be lost. We need a score-keeping form. Can you spare three hours of your time over the next year? That's 15 minutes a month—less time than it takes to water the lawn. And keeping score will bring a new zest to your life. It provides a monthly moment to cheer and pat yourself on the back. You know we can all use more of those moments.

Would we crowd into the bleachers at basketball games if those tricky shots weren't scored against a tough opponent? Of course not. We love the challenge. Exhibitions are fine, but there's a thrill to competition. Well, investing is a game of competition, too, and it's thrilling to watch the points add up.

The Game Rules

Each player (that's you) must deploy *investable* monies through reliable sources, for reasonable returns, in quality investment vehicles, using flexibility and diversification, while continuously monitoring results and progress.

- The aim. To reach a stated goal in a given period of time despite constantly changing circumstances.
- The time limit. However long it is from *today* to the date of your event. _____ yrs
- The score needed to win: The dollar amount of your financial goal: $_____
- The prize. Financial independence (describe) _____
- Who may enter. Entry is compulsory. Penalties are meted out for failure.

The Score Sheet

Figure 22.1 is a sample Keeping Score form. (Photocopy the blank form in Appendix A.)

We'll first collect the facts on your far-flung money. Then, using this single sheet of paper, you'll be able to scan for answers to those pregnant questions you try not to ask, like these:

- Are you closer to your retirement goal today than you were a year ago? By how much?
- Are your investments worth more today than they were six months ago?
- Did one of your stocks lose half its value before you noticed? Did you call your broker in a panic, only to have her tell you it was *good* news?
- Interest rates have fallen. Have your bonds appreciated?
- Do you have too much money in growth?
- When did you sell the shares of Waste Management?
- What does your investment pyramid look like?
- Of your total investment value, how much exceeds your cash contributions?
- One account dropped $3,000 in January. Why?
- When did you buy that speculative stock?

Once a year (probably in January, but don't wait—begin now):
1. List all your investments:
    - Include all accounts: brokerage, bank, etc.
      Since we are looking at *values,* include every investment listed on your monthly statements, ignoring whether or not it produces income.
2. Assign each investment to a risk level from the pyramid in Figure 20.4:
      1. Speculation
      2. Growth
      3. Foundation

Okay, the form is set up.

FIGURE 22.1   Keeping Score Form

KEEPING SCORE 1991

Sample showing January investments of Mary & Paul Smith. Includes all accounts:
Living Trust, which replaced their joint acct (TR); Paul's 401K (P-401K); Paul's IRA (P-IRA); Mary's IRA (M-IRA)

Investments	Risk	Jan	Feb	Mar	Apr	May	Jun	Jly	Aug	Sept	Oct	Nov	Dec
Amr Exprs-TR	2	5280											
DfAnnty7%-TR	3	7210											
Mny Fnd-TR	3	36716											
MgdAcct-TR	2	116932											
MnyFnd P-401K	3	8036											
MnyFnd P-IRA	3	6860											
AMRCorp P-IRA	2	5287											
WsteMgt P-IRA	2	3837											
Mny Fnd-M IRA	3	2083											
PacGEPfd-M IRA	3	10450											
ZroTreas-M IRA	3	10950											
ZroTreas-M IRA	3	7300											
GRAND TOTAL		220941											
SPEC VALUE	1	0											
GROWTH VALUE	2	131336											
FDTN VAL	3	89605											
% IN SPEC	1	0											
% IN GROWTH	2	59											
% IN FDTN	3	41											
DEPOSITS (+)													
WITHDWLS (–)													

Once a month (when you sit down to pay bills):

1. From the statements, jot down on the Keeping $core form the monthly value reported for each investment listed.
2. Enter any cash withdrawn or deposited from listed accounts.
3. Total the month's column. Use your calculator. Make it quick and easy.

If you wish to break down the totals as shown on the Keeping Score form—and you'll be glad you did—here's how:

4. Total each risk group individually.
5. Enter in blocks indicated: Spec Val   1
                                 Growth Val   2
                                 FDTN Val   3
6. Compute the percent held in each risk category. (Group Total ÷ Grand Total = Percentage)
7. Enter results in the blocks indicated:
                                 % In Spec   1
                                 % In Growth   2
                                 % In FDTN   3

Note: The score-keeping format can easily be set up on a computer. Use a spreadsheet to do the math for you. Toss out January's printout when you print February's. This is a cumulative record. One page equals one year. Ten pages equal ten years!

8. For reference, sketch a small pyramid under your beginning month. Indicate the percentage you hold in each of the three risk levels.
9. Repeat the pyramid at the end of the year. Compare them. Does the pyramid represent diversification suited to you and your situation? Have the percentages shifted since the year began? Why?

Investors spell out what they want and put it in place, but, without realizing it, as time goes by they gradually slip away from their goals. It happens one decision at a time, until one day the investments are out of whack. Use the pyramid as a reminder. It will act as a check on your decisions.

Six Months Later

Figure 22.2 is an example showing six months' score keeping of Mary and Paul Smith. Notice how their list has changed since January? They've bought new investments and have sold others. Change is the real world, and a score-keeping system has to handle that without creating a muddle. Does this form keep it simple?

Go to Figure 22.3 and we'll dissect the Keeping Score form.

1. What do Mary and Paul own at the end of June in all accounts?
   (See (1): each entry listed in the June column)
2. When was Waste Management sold in Paul's IRA?
   (See (2): final entry)
3. Why did the Money Fund-TR, suddenly drop in value?
   (See (3): funds went from money fund to pay for stock purchases)
4. Why did Money Fund-P 401(k) increase suddenly in March?
   (See (4): $4,000 deposit)
5. Why did the Money Fund–TR lose value in May?
   (See (5): withdrawal of $3,000 from the account)
6. Why didn't proceeds from the January sale of stocks (P IRA), show up in the Money Fund-P IRA?
   (See (6): Paul made a new purchase in that account)
7. Have the assets increased between January and June?
   (See (7): June total – January total = Increase;
   $265,285 – $220,941 = $44,344)

Try these on your own (experts have to work alone sometimes):

- In what month did the Smiths buy AG Edwards in the trust account?
- What stocks were sold in January in all accounts?
- Which stock peaked in value in March?
- What percentage of the investment plan is rated speculative?
- Which investment is rated speculative?
- When was the speculative stock purchased?

Didn't expect it to be so easy to answer those, did you? No fumbling needed.

FIGURE 22.2   Keeping Score Form: Six-Month Sample

KEEPING SCORE 1991

Sample showing six months' investment values of Mary & Paul Smith Includes all accounts: Living Trust, which replaced their joint acct (TR); Paul's 401K (P-401K); Paul's IRA (P-IRA); Mary's IRA (M-IRA)

Investments	Risk	Jan	Feb	Mar	Apr	May	Jun	Jly	Aug	Sept	Oct	Nov	Dec
AG Edwrds-TR	2					1316	1704						
Amr Exprs-TR	2	5280	7512	8362	7586	6660	7326						
DfAnnty7%-TR	3	7210	7251	7292	7333	7374	7415						
Mny Fnd-TR	3	36716	28529	28647	28754	25861	25987						
AbbottLbs-TR	2		4687	4800	5137	5137	5175						
SaraLee-TR	2		3500	3692	3912	4037	4037						
ZipComputr-TR	1						6724						
MgdAcct-TR	2	116932	137172	145934	148914	153771	147134						
MnyFnd P-401K	3	8036	8042	12062	12114	12164	12215						
MnyFnd P-IRA	3	6860	5884	1522	1529	1535	1542						
AMRCorp P-IRA	2	5287											
WsteMgt P-IRA	2	3837											
AmElPwr P-IRA	2			4368	4443	4312	4256						
FlPwrLtPfd P-IRA	3		10174	10624	9156	10262	10000						
Mny Fnd-M IRA	3	2083	2091	2114	2347	2357	2367						
PacGEPfd-M IRA	3	10450	10750	10550	10500	10700	10550						
ZroTreas-M IRA	3	10950	11091	11117	11189	11272	11312						
ZroTreas-M IRA	3	7300	7394	7397	7459	7514	7541						
GRAND TOTAL		220941	244077	258481	260373	264272	265285						
SPEC VALUE	1	0	0	0	0	0	6724						
GROWTH VALUE	2	131336	152871	167156	169992	175233	169632						
FDTN VAL	3	89605	91206	92325	90381	89039	88929						
% IN SPEC	1	0	0	0	0	0	3						
% IN GROWTH	2	59	63	65	65	66	64						
% IN FDTN	3	41	37	35	35	34	34						
DEPOSITS (+)				+4000									
WITHDWLS (-)						-3000							

FIGURE 22.3   Keeping Score Form 1991: Six-Month Sample

KEEPING SCORE 1991

Sample showing six months' investment values of Mary & Paul Smith Includes all accounts:
Living Trust, which replaced their joint acct (TR); Paul's 401K (P-401K); Paul's IRA (P-IRA); Mary's IRA (M-IRA)

Investments	Risk	Jan	Feb	Mar	Apr	May	Jun	Jly	Aug	Sept	Oct	Nov	Dec
AG Edwrds-TR	2												
Amr Exprs-TR	2	5280	7512	8362	7586	6660	7326						
DfAnnty7%-TR	2	7210	7251	7292	7333	7374	7415						
Mny Fnd-TR	3	36716	28529	28647	28754	25861	25987						
AbbottLbs-TR	2		4687	4800	5137	5137	5175						
SaraLee-TR	2		3500	3692	3912	4037	4037						
ZipComputr-TR	1						6724						
MgdAcct-TR	2	116932	137172	145934	148914	153771	147134						
MnyFnd P-401K	3	8036	8042	12062	12114	12164	12215						
MnyFnd P-IRA	3	6860	5884	1522	1529	1535	1542						
AMRCorp P-IRA	2	5287											
WsteMgt P-IRA	2	3837											
AmElPwr P-IRA	2			4368	4443	4312	4256						
FlPwrLtPfd P-IRA	3		10174	10624	9156	10262	10000						
Mny Fnd-M IRA	3	2083	2091	2114	2347	2357	2367						
PacGEPfd-M IRA	3	10450	10750	10550	10500	10700	10550						
ZroTreas-M IRA	3	10950	11091	11117	11189	11272	11312						
ZroTreas-M IRA	3	7300	7394	7397	7459	7514	7541						
GRAND TOTAL		220941	244077	258481	260373	264272	265285						
SPEC VALUE	1	0	0	0	0	0	6724						
GROWTH VALUE	2	131336	152871	167156	169992	175233	169632						
FDTN VAL	3	89605	91206	92325	90381	89039	88929						
% IN SPEC	1	0	0	0	0	0	3						
% IN GROWTH	2	59	63	65	65	66	64						
% IN FDTN	3	41	37	35	35	34	34						
DEPOSITS (+)				+4000									
WITHDWLS (-)						-3000							

The Transformation Is Complete

Do you see how essential it is to your financial health to have your rich information at your fingertips? What once was clutter has been transformed into a power base of information that builds confidence.

The Keeping Score form is a vital source of ongoing, up-to-date fingertip expertise on your *progress*. Look how quickly you became an expert on the activity and worth of the Smiths. The fun of the financial challenge begins with setting aside the monies. The feeling blossoms when you send those monies out into the world to compete for returns. It bursts into full flower when you stand back and actually see the progress. That's smelling the flowers along the way. And when you reach that goal? Sweet success.

Well, there you have it! The nuts and bolts of financial freedom. Take another look at that woman in the mirror. See how that well-deserved confidence puts a spark in her eye?

Chapter 23

*T*en Questions from Women Just Like You

*Y*ou've worked hard and have accomplished wonders. Now go for it. Build on your knowledge. Spread your financial wings. There's nothing new under the sun, and you know the underlying basics of all money schemes. I wish you joy in asking questions. I wish you confidence to doubt foggy answers. Remember, you *are* smart enough. If you don't understand, someone's explanation is unclear.

Just in case you still have some lingering concerns, here are ten questions sent to me that you may find helpful:

1. You refer to *major* securities firms or the *main-stream* firms. How do I recognize them? These are full-service brokerage companies. Ask if the firm is a member of the New York Stock Exchange and other principal exchanges. The Securities and Exchange Commission requires each member firm to maintain a specified amount of liquid capital to meet its obligations to customers. (There's that cushion again.)

2. You mention dividend-paying stocks. What's wrong with owning nondividend-paying stocks right up until we retire? Meet Mr. A and Mr. B, both 65-year-old investors. Mr. A owns $500,000 of dividend-paying common stocks. Mr. B owns $500,000 of nondividend paying stocks (growth stocks). To retire in 30 days, each needs an income of $25,000 from his investments (5% × $500,000).

As luck will have it, two weeks before the retirement date, the market drops. (This example is based on a real situation. Do you recall the day the market fell 500 points?)

Mr. A suffers a $100,000 drop in his stock value, but the dividends are unaffected. They continue as usual. He retires on schedule, his income untouched by the market fluctuation.

Mr. B, however, cannot retire as he hoped. He also lost $100,000 of his stock value. And, since he has no dividend income, he'll have to convert his investments. If he pays taxes on the sale, and commissions when he reinvests, his plans are further delayed. If he manages to reinvest $380,000 and earn 5 percent, his income would now be $19,000, a $6,000 shortfall. A harsh lesson from expecting illiquid investments to be worth a specific amount on a specific date.

3. There are hundreds of mutual funds. Which one is safe?   No investment is risk free.

4. I pay an annual fee on the IRA I bought. Is that common?   The IRA, individual retirement account, is not a product, but the name of an *account* sheltered from current taxes. You "bought" an investment that is held in the IRA account, probably a CD. A major brokerage firm does not limit your investment to a CD, but offers a variety of choices. Fees to administer the IRA account vary with the institution. Compare fees and choices between banks and brokerage firms.

5. I thought we had five days to pay for a stock or bond. When was the time shortened?   Trade date plus three, or T+3, effective in June 1995, allowed only three days until settlement for a securities transaction. The Securities and Exchange Commission planned to shorten the settlement cycle further by requiring settlement in same-day funds by early 1996. (As of this writing, the SEC requirements are not in effect.) The inconvenience to the customer will likely encourage investors to hold more funds at the brokerage firm. This way, purchases can be deducted automatically from the accounts. Allowing a firm to *capture* your investable monies makes it crucial for you to know you are dealing with an established, mainstream firm. Have your phone orders read back for accuracy. Unless the industry makes major changes, confirmations will no longer arrive prior to settlement date.

6. We had a living trust drawn up by our bank's trust department, naming them as our successor trustee. Can we change trustees in the future if we wish? Be careful that, in accepting free legal services, you are not obligating yourself unknowingly. Make certain your trust document specifically states that you can change successor trustees and that it sets out a simple procedure for doing so. Ask about penalties for transferring the account.

7. Is it possible to name more than one successor trustee, just in case? Yes. Name as many as you like (within reason). First, name M. If M were unavailable or unable to serve, B would step up, then J, then K. And finally, in the event all else fails, the backup nonbank corporate trustee you name would step up. The corporate trustee is not going to die, divorce, fall ill, or move away.

8. Is it true that if I own real estate in two different states, there will be two probates on my estate? Yes, if you have only a will. A living trust avoids probate.

9. My mother's attorney kept the original of her will. Do I have to stay with him for probate? No. Choose the attorney with whom you wish to work.

10. Do I have to provide my attorney with original documents? Use photocopies whenever possible. Ask for descriptive receipts for originals, and keep photocopies of the documents for your files.

Now It's Your Turn

The more experiences we share, the quicker women everywhere will be cured of the dreaded financial phobia. If you've benefited from the information in this book, please pass it on. If you have comments or questions, please write me in care of the publisher. I'd be delighted to hear from you—and to learn from you.

Thanks, and good luck, expert!

*P*ower Base Forms

Changing Look-At Forms into Working Forms

Don't let the size limitations of this book limit your financial progress. Think of these reduced power base forms as you would the hard grains of raw rice. In their tiny, untouched state they seem useless, but it is this very state that allows them to be easily transported and stored. And once received, it takes only one step to transform them into a source of reliable, satisfying stability.

Take a quick trip to the photocopier of your choice and have the powerbase forms enlarged to the right size for you. The standard 8½" by 11" works well and fits into the file folders. Store the extras in a file folder for next year.

FIGURE A.1 Living Expenses Form

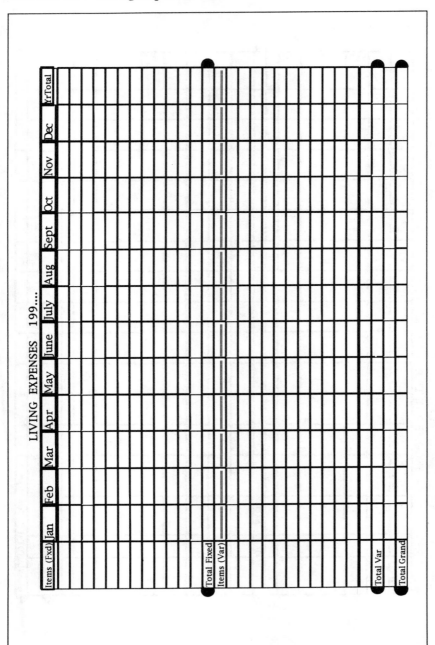

FIGURE A.2   Income Monitor

FIGURE A.3   Preretiree Income Monitor

Held SPEND-ABLE	Qty	Item	Peace of Mind	Jan $	Feb $	Mar $	Apr $	May $	Jun $	July $	Aug $	Sept $	Oct $	Nov $	Dec $	Year Total
TOTAL SPENDABLE INCOME---$																
INVESTMENT INCOME																
TOTAL *INVESTMENT* INCOME--$																
GRAND TOTAL ALL INCOME---$																

PRE-RETIREE INCOME MONITOR   199....

FIGURE A.4　Monies Put Aside from Payroll

MONIES PUT-ASIDE FROM PAYROLL (pre-retiree Income Monitor supplement)

Held	Qty	Item	Peace of Mind	Jan $	Feb $	Mar $	Apr $	May $	Jun $	July $	Aug $	Sept $	Oct $	Nov $	Dec $	Year Total

TOTAL PAYROLL MONIES PUT-ASIDE FOR INVESTMENT $ ---------

FIGURE A.5 Cash Flow Worksheet

CUSHIONED CASH FLOW   199...

MONTH	INCOME -	OUTGO=	NET CASH
			dip into or add $?
January	-	=	$
February	-	=	$
March	-	=	$
April	-	=	$
May	-	=	$
June	-	=	$
July	-	=	$
August	-	=	$
September	-	=	$
October	-	=	$
November	-	=	$
December	-	=	$

Carry frwrd	Jan +/-	Feb +/-	Mar +/-	Apr +/-	May +/-	Jun +/-	Jul +/-	Aug +/-	Sept +/-	Oct +/-	Nov +/-	Dec +/-
$	$	$	$	$	$	$	$	$	$	$	$	$
$	$	$	$	$	$	$	$	$	$	$	$	$

Cushion $_____

FIGURE A.6   Looking for Cash: Borrowing

Questions for borrowing	Passbk Savings	CD	Stocks	Bonds	Mutual Funds	Defer. Annuty	Whole Life Ins	Real Estate
Can I borrow against it?								
How much can I borrow?								
How soon can I get the money?								
Do I have to sign papers?								
Are there up-front costs?								
Are there other costs?								
Must I make payments during the loan period?								
Do I still earn (interest or dividends) during the loan period?								
What happens when the investment matures?								
Provide these figures: a. what I will have at maturity with loan? b. what I will have at maturity without the loan?								
Speak to:	Teller	Accts supv.	stockbrkr	stockbrkr	stockbrkr	insr agnt stkbrkr	insr agnt stkbrkr	real est loan officr

*************************LOOKING FOR CASH*********************************

FIGURE A.7 Looking for Cash: Selling

Questions for selling	Passbk Savings	CD	Stocks	Bonds	Mutual Funds	Defer. Annuty	Whole Life Ins	Real Estate
Can I cash out or sell a portion?								
How soon can I get the money?								
Are there selling costs?								
Are there penalties for selling?								
Will the proceeds be taxable?								
How much will I net?								
Do I have to sign papers?								
Speak to:	Teller	Accts supv.	stockbrkr	stockbrkr	stockbrkr	insr agnt stkbrkr	insr agnt stkbrkr	real est loan officr

*******************************LOOKING FOR CASH**

FIGURE A.8   Time Line: Planning for Life Events

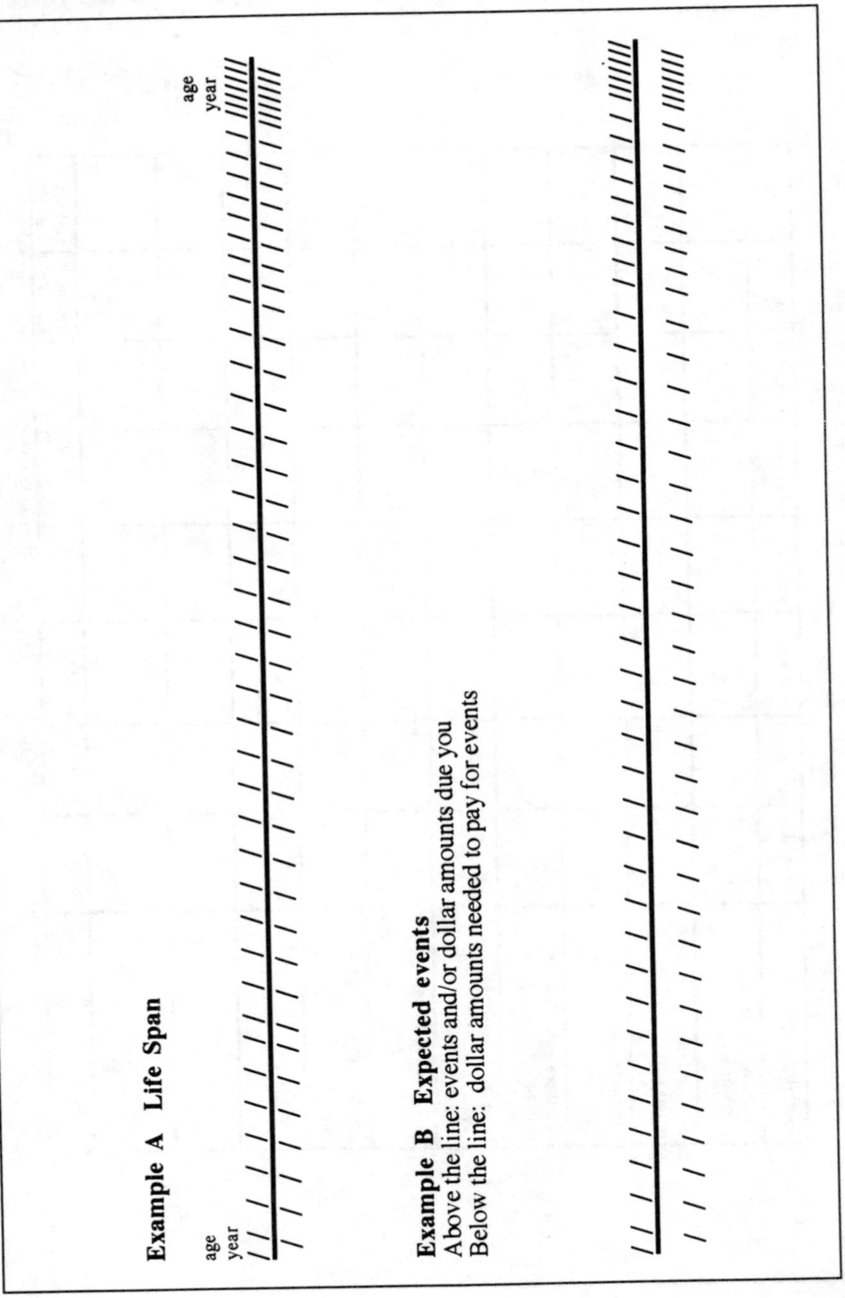

Example A   Life Span

age
year

Example B   Expected events
Above the line: events and/or dollar amounts due you
Below the line: dollar amounts needed to pay for events

age
year

FIGURE A.9   Understanding the Goal

Questions/Events			
Is the money needed on specific date?			
Is a specific sum required?			
If investment fails is there an alternative source of funds?			
Is an on-going income stream required?			
On what date should income begin?			
*What am I willing to do if this goal is not reached?			

* Your answer to this question establishes the real importance of each goal.

Review the chart once again. Using a scale from one to ten, number each goal for its importance.

Now complete a new timeline for your life. Insert only your #1 ranked event.

FIGURE A.10   Understanding the Investment

Questions for Investments	Money Market/ Savings	Cert of Deposit	Deferred Annuity Fixed	Bonds: Tax Free/ Taxable	Stocks: w/div or w/o div	Mutual Funds: Stocks	Mutual Funds: Bonds	Real Estate
Specific maturity date?								
Specific sum at maturity?								
Specific sum guarantee?								
Early access penalty?								
Risk of principal?								
Income stream?								
Convert to income w/o cost?								
Income stream guarantee?								
Tax impact?								
Investment easy to manage?								

FIGURE A.11   Time Line: Dream Fulfillment

Example A   Life Span with Financial Events Indicated
Above the line: enter years and name of event
Below the line: enter sums needed

age
year

age
year

Example B   Planned investment payoffs
Above the line: enter investment type in place
Below the line: enter dollar amounts available or maturing

FIGURE A.12 Keeping Score Form

KEEPING SCORE 199___

List each investment. Identify by account and risk level. Enter monthly values taken from statements.
Take a minute-a-month to scan your financial progress. One page = one year. What does your pyramid look like?

Investments	Risk	Jan	Feb	Mar	Apr	May	Jun	Jly	Aug	Sept	Oct	Nov	Dec
GRAND TOTAL													
SPEC VALUE	1												
GROWTH VALUE	2												
FDTN VAL	3												
% IN SPEC	1												
% IN GROWTH	2												
% IN FDTN	3												
DEPOSITS (+)													
WITHDWLS (-)													

FIGURE A.13   How Long Does It Take to Double Your Money?

How Long Does It Take to *Double* Your Money?

Use the rule of 72.
Divide any interest rate into 72.

$$\frac{12 \text{ years}}{6 \overline{)\,72}} \qquad \text{or} \qquad \frac{7.2 \text{ years}}{10 \overline{)\,72}}$$

Start with $10,000 earning 6%.   Start with $10,000 earning 10%.
In 12 years, you'll have $20,000.   In 7.2 years, you'll have $20,000.
In 24 years, you'll have $40,000.   In 14.4 years, you'll have $40,000.

How Long Does It Take to *Triple* Your Money?

Use the rule of 115.
Divide any interest rate into 115.

$$\frac{19 \text{ years}}{6 \overline{)\,115}} \qquad \text{or} \qquad \frac{11.5 \text{ years}}{10 \overline{)\,115}}$$

Start with $10,000 earning 6%.   Start with $10,000 earning 10%.
In 19 years, you'll have $30,000.   In 11.5 years, you'll have $30,000.
In 38 years, you'll have $90,000.   In 23 years, you'll have $90,000.

FIGURE A.14   How Long Will Your Money Last?

Here's an example showing withdrawals of a specified sum. A 65-year-old retiree withdraws $30,000 each year from a $350,000 nest egg earning 7 percent.

Age	Beginning Balance	Earnings	Withdrawals	Ending Balance
65	$350,000	$24,500	$30,000	$344,500
66	344,500	24,115	30,000	338,615
67	338,615	23,703	30,000	332,318
68	332,318	23,262	30,000	325,580
69	325,580	22,791	30,000	318,371
70	318,371	22,286	30,000	310,657
71	310,657	21,746	30,000	302,403
72	302,403	21,168	30,000	293,571
73	293,571	20,550	30,000	284,121
74	284,121	19,888	30,000	274,009
75	274,009	19,181	30,000	263,190
76	263,190	18,423	30,000	251,613
77	251,613	17,613	30,000	239,226
78	239,226	16,746	30,000	225,972
79	225,972	15,818	30,000	211,790
80	211,790	14,825	30,000	196,615
81	196,615	13,763	30,000	180,378
82	180,378	12,626	30,000	163,004
83	163,004	11,410	30,000	144,414
84	144,414	10,109	30,000	124,523
85	124,523	8,717	30,000	103,240
86	103,240	7,227	30,000	80,467
87	80,467	5,633	30,000	56,100
88	56,100	3,927	30,000	30,027
89	30,027	2,102	30,000	2,129
90	2,129	149	2,278	0

FIGURE A.15   How Long Will Your Money Last?

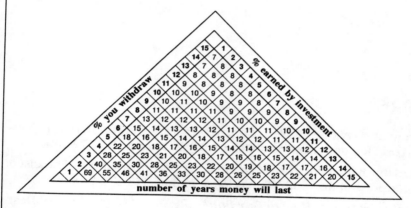

How long will your money last?
or "Amortizing a Lump Sum"
% out > % in = lump sum
at end of selected term, sum is used up.

Our example:
Locate the % earned—right side (6%).
Locate the % you withdraw—left side (9%).
Follow to the intersecting block to discover years the money will last (18).

*R*esources

Books

Dreman, David. *The New Contrarian Investment Strategy.* New York: Random House Publishers, 1982, phone: 212-572-2600.

Graham, Benjamin. *The Intelligent Investor,* 4th ed. San Francisco: Harper and Row Publishers, 1973, phone: 415-477-4400.

Littauer, Stephen. *How to Buy Bonds the Smart Way.* Chicago: Dearborn Financial Publishing, 1996, phone: 312-836-4400.

Pederson, Daniel J. *U.S. Savings Bonds.* Detroit: TSBI Publishing, 1995, phone: 313-843-1910.

Schumacher, Vickie and Jim Schumacher. *Understanding Living Trusts.* Los Angeles: Schumacher & Co., 1990, phone: 213-859-0800.

Magazines

Barron's, Dow Jones & Co., 200 Burnett Road, Chicopee, MA 01020; phone: 800-628-9320. (Business newspaper.)

Better Investing, National Association of Investors Corporation, 711 West 13 Mile Road, Madison Heights, MI 48071; phone: 810-583-6242. (Magazine with NAIC low-cost investment plan.)

Forbes, Forbes Subscriber Service, P.O. Box 37162, Boone, IA 50037; phone: 800-888-9896. (Business magazine.)

Morningstar Mutual Funds, Circulation Department, 225 West Wacker Drive, Chicago, IL 60606; phone: 800-735-0700. (Published every other week in two sections.)

Standard & Poor's Stock Guide, Standard & Poor's Publishers, 25 Broadway, New York, NY 10004; phone: 800-221-5277.

The Value Line Investment Survey, Value Line Publishing, Inc., P.O. Box 3988, Church Street Station, New York, NY 10008-3988; phone: 800-833-0046.

The Wall Street Journal, 200 Burnett Road, Chicopee, MA 01021; phone: 800-JOURNAL.

Pamphlets

About . . . Planning for College, Consumer Information Center, Dept. 55, Pueblo, CO 81009 (Free).

How to Buy Annuities, The Irrevocable Life Insurance Trust, and many other pamphlets on specific topics. Ask at your major brokerage firm. (Free.)

Social Security: What Every Woman Absolutely Needs to Know, (D14117), AARP Fulfillment (EE0589), P.O. Box 22796, Long Beach, CA 90801-5796. (Free: allow four to six weeks for delivery.)

What You Should Know about Buying Life Insurance. Washington, D.C.: U.S. Office of Consumer Affairs and the Consumer Information Center. Pamphlet prepared by the American Council of Life Insurance, U.S. Office of Consumer Affairs, and the Consumer Information Center; phone 800-338-4471. (Free.)

Resources

Bond information: Federal Reserve Bank, phone 202-874-4000.

Social Security: When you get Social Security retirement or survival benefits, phone national toll-free number: 800-772-1213 7 AM–7 PM.

Suppliers

Rolodex Corporation, office products: available at office supply stores.

Fellowes Corporation, 1789 Norwood Ave, Itasca, IL 60143; phone: 708-893-1600. (Manufactures the Bill Payment Center, which is available at office supply stores.)

$\mathcal{I}$ndex

About the Author

*S*he came, she saw, and she retired to write about it, freed from the restrictions of the profession. During her 20 years helping clients with their financial decisions, Joyce Ward wore the caps of real estate broker, insurance representative, stockbroker, Certified Financial Planner, teacher and lecturer, all with an eye to giving her clients the broadest view of an integrated financial life.

Struck by the commonality of financial threats faced by women in all circumstances and ages, she turned to writing to pass on to other women the protective insights gained from her personal observations and experiences.

Outside of speaking engagements, writing, and traveling, she shares life with her artist husband in the Pacific Northwest.

New
CD-ROM Money Maker Kits
from Dearborn Multimedia

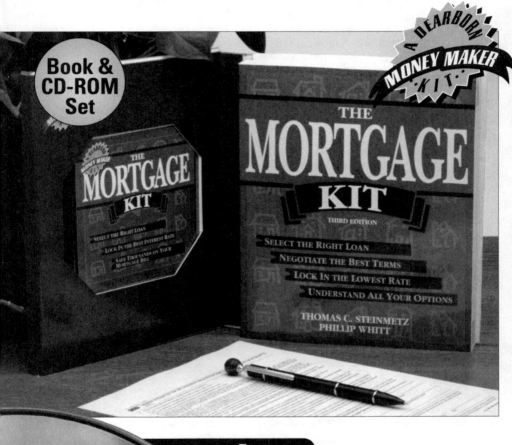

Book & CD-ROM Set

A DEARBORN MONEY MAKER KIT

THE MORTGAGE KIT

THE MORTGAGE KIT
THIRD EDITION

- SELECT THE RIGHT LOAN
- NEGOTIATE THE BEST TERMS
- LOCK IN THE LOWEST RATE
- UNDERSTAND ALL YOUR OPTIONS

THOMAS C. STEINMETZ
PHILLIP WHITT

SELECT THE RIGHT LOAN
LOCK IN THE BEST INTEREST RATE
SAVE THOUSANDS ON YOUR MORTGAGE BILL

Features:

- *25 minute video help with the author*
- *12-28 interactive printable forms per CD-ROM*
- *On-Line glossary of terms*
- *Quick-start video tutorial*
- *Interactive printable book on CD-ROM*
  (Print out sections you like for closer reading or writing notes.)

Start Enjoying Greater Financial Freedom
Triple Your Investment Portfolio

SAVE Thousands on Real Estate as a Buyer or Seller

Successfully Start & Manage a **<u>NEW</u>** Busine